CONSCIENCE
ACROSS BORDERS

*An Ethics of Global Rights
and Religious Pluralism*

Vernon Ruland, S.J.

with a Foreword by Rembert Weakland, O.S.B.
Archbishop Emeritus

D1067181

University of San Francisco
Association of Jesuit University Presses
2002

Library of Congress Cataloging-in-Publication Data

Ruland, Vernon.
  Conscience across borders : an ethics of global rights and religious pluralism / Vernon
Ruland ; with a foreword by Rembert Weakland.
      p. cm.
  Includes bibliographical references and index.
  ISBN 0-9664059-2-7 (pbk.)
  1. Religious ethics. 2. Environmental ethics. 3. Human rights--Religious aspects. I.
Title

BJ1188 .R85 2002
291.5--dc21

                                                                                    2002075011

Distributed by:
Fordham University Press
University Box L
Bronx, NY 10458

TABLE OF CONTENTS

FOREWORD

Rembert G. Weakland, O.S.B.,
Archbishop Emeritus

There is an urgency in the air these days that pushes us all to become better acquainted with global religious Ways other than our own. Even if one is not a professed member of any known world religion but accepts a label like that of secular humanist, it is still important to know where each tradition stands today on given issues. These Ways are far from dead. They influence what is happening in the world, especially politically, beyond what we may have ever imagined. We must also remember that most of them were not affected by the separation of church and state premise that has characterized our culture in Europe and especially America. For this reason, religion and politics are inextricably intertwined in many parts of the world. Thus, we sense a duty to be better informed if we want to understand what other people think and why they approach issues the way they do. Only then can we hope to live peacefully on this globe.

Most of us in Europe and the United States knew that one day the knowledge and discipline needed to relate sanely to many other religious traditions would come upon us, but we put off thinking seriously about it till now. Some might even think it is too late. After September 11, 2001, the world has not been the same. Whether or not we accept the theory that ultimately the great religious traditions will be the source—if not the immediate cause—of clashes that are without resolution, we still sense the need to know more about the similarities and the differences that characterize them.

Where can we turn for guidance? Most of us had taken courses in world religions when we were in college but have long forgotten even the terminology. Then we may have seen these various Ways as the products of fascinating cultures that we would have little contact with beyond the general interest of enlightened tourists. But now things have changed. We urgently need to see all world religions as attached to individual persons, groups, nations, and cultures different from our own, with their own histories, stories, symbols, and values. I am sure that many Americans thought that eventually all these other cultures with their religious beliefs would give way to the stronger American consumer-centered way of life and that these "other" religions would become mere historical remnants. Instead, we now see that many around the globe judge American culture and its religious substratum unworthy of imitation or emulation. Rather, there is an outright aversion to it and an effort to reject it. This factor alone may force us to take more seriously what our own culture is like and what other cultures fear in it. These contrasts are now at our doorsteps. Again the question must be asked: Where does one look for intelligent guidance in the maze of information needed to grasp what is happening?

At first Christian scholars in Europe and America attempted dialogue with these other Ways from their own religious point of view, one that put heavy emphasis on speculative theology and metaphysical categories. Soon it was seen that this form of dialogue was limited. The Euro-American categories at times proved distorting or inadequate, and did not respect the very nature of other traditions. The results were not very helpful. The categories were simply not shared in a way that permitted equal and authentic participation by everyone.

Then scholars talked of a spiritual sharing, a dialogue of spirituality. We Benedictines, in particular, were interested in this form of dialogue. It was beneficial and led to a deepened mutual understanding and empathy. Monks from other religious ways, especially those with an indigenous monastic tradition, began to share the life of Christian monks and vice versa. But this dialogue could only go so far, since the underlying anthropological premises were not openly treated. Thus, questions like the nature of the human person, the way the person relates to this physical world and to God, were always in the background. Although useful, this method of approach to mutual understanding was not complete.

A third way of approaching the question came about. One could call it the ethical approach. It began rather from a wider range of human experience and showed how similar if not identical problems are faced in each culture. "Solutions" are prompted by the religious-ethical traditions in which each culture is rooted. Vernon Ruland, S.J., is a pioneer in this approach and his work shows how fruitful it can be. With a command of all the religious Ways that is remarkable, he is able to weave a tapestry of ethical issues helpful for entering into the experience of a vast number of diversified religious views. This moral approach, together with the virtues that sustain such an approach, are the subject of this book.

The author was wise in selecting for his first ethical examination the question of ecology, how the human person relates to the world and where God stands in that equation. This question, fundamental to all religious Ways, highlights the contrasts and the similarities between Ways. It is a felicitous beginning. The concern for ecology is prominent today in almost all religious Ways, except perhaps in the Euro-American context, where some Ways have often neglected it. Nevertheless, it is a good beginning point. Only then does Ruland approach the more difficult area of human rights, ending with an examination of the document on ethics drawn up by the World Parliament of Religions in 1993. Although the material covered is voluminous, the reader will not get lost, since many signposts are available.

Not long ago I was asked to participate in a TV program that wished to treat of the ethical issues involved in human reproduction from the viewpoint of each major religious Way. I was asked to represent the Christian (not just the Catholic!) perspective. I smiled and said it was an impossible task and I was indeed the wrong person. But the approach is significant. In the public forum the question is no longer one of finding out what each religion might teach about a given subject but how these teachings compare, one to another. In this way, without perhaps realizing it, the more metaphysical and anthropological questions are being raised. Just as it would be impossible for one person to represent what the Christian denominations teach about human reproductive issues, so it would be impossible for someone to say what all of the Muslim world teaches on a given subject. One is immediately confronted with the pluralism within each religious Way—that Way lived out variously by each of its adherents. Ruland does not shy away from this conundrum. Who speaks, for example, for the Catholic Church? He does not fall into the trap of trying to isolate authority figures, but talks more about the diversity of religious experience among those people who profess a given religion. This approach is a significant and wise sociological solution to an otherwise intractable dilemma. He talks more about the experiences of the adherents than the official teachings of any group. In this way he is able to trace similarities that are remarkable.

The touchy question in any interfaith dialogue that always comes to the fore is how to avoid a postmodern relativism. It is easy if one only tries to give a descriptive account of what each group believes and values. But it is more difficult if one tries to arrive at some kind of consensus that bridges group differences. It is not easy to avoid the pitfall of relativism, on the one hand, and the strictures of an imposed uniform ethics for the whole world, on the other. The author does not try to avoid this issue but deals with it head on. The amazing amount of consensus on issues of ecology and human rights permits him to do so. He detects strands of affiliation reaching beyond individual religious groups and creating at times a kind of substratum of agreement that is surprising. Again, these strands are not necessarily what is said or written by the authority figures but rather what is practiced and believed by the adherents.

The final chapter is most important. Values are not only a matter of imposed legal measures but the inner conversion of people trying to adhere to these values. Values will survive in a culture only if they are sustained by virtuous individual lives. An examination of virtue-ethics is rudimentary among scholars at this time, but has become increasingly productive. The significance of the virtues can be tested, for example, by probing environmental questions to their fullest. Ruland's discussion of frugality will not resonate well with many who espouse the Christian way of life, especially if shaped excessively either by consumerist values or by the so-called Protestant work ethic.

But other virtues are just as important as frugality. In this context, as the author points out, one must examine in the United States what sociologists have called "civil religion." So often in interfaith dialogues one forgets that this civil religion can be stronger in the experience of people than the values of the Christian denomination they come from. Often we say that some Catholics are first Americans and then Catholics. Not all have assimilated both legacies into one coherent personality. Reactions to the destruction of the World Trade Towers brought forth many expressions of this civil religion. Americans of all denominations, for example, tend to prize the value of fair play. Terrorism hits directly at this virtue. Moreover, most abhor the taking of innocent human life, no matter how right the cause involved. Even if Americans do not reflect on all the religious underpinnings that support such values, they respond instinctively with moral conviction. The last chapter of this book becomes then a stimulating source for further examination of the relationship between rights and virtue, a crucial topic if interfaith dialogue is to be fruitful.

The approach, then, that is taken in this book, namely, the ethical one, ultimately opens up a whole array of other approaches that will follow: the theoretical or speculative, the spiritual or ascetical, and the very practical and experiential. There is no doubt that it is the best way to begin a fruitful analysis of what happens when adherents of differing religious Ways begin to learn about each other in this kind of open and respectful approach. It can then lead to mutual enrichment and, it is hoped, a deepening of each one's own tradition.

PROLOGUE

We experience ourselves, our thoughts and feelings,
as an entity separated from the rest,
somewhat an optical delusion of consciousness,...
restricting us to our personal desires
and to affection for only the few people nearest us.
Our task must be to free ourselves from this prison
by widening our circle of compassion
to embrace all living beings
and the whole of nature in its beauty.

—ALBERT EINSTEIN

The modern challenge is how to live with uncertainty.
The basic fault-lines today are
not between people of different beliefs,
but between those believing with some uncertainty
and those believing with a pretense of certitude.

—PETER BERGER

This book originated a decade ago in a two-hour discussion which I was asked to guide by a communication arts professor at the University of San Francisco. Convinced her undergraduate seminar needed to interject some civility into squabbles about ethics, she had searched for a Catholic theologian to demonstrate the necessary steps for making a sound moral choice. While preparing for that assignment I was intrigued to uncover new angles on overfamiliar material. Though I found the eventual session with students exhilarating, I recognized that my teaching approach disturbed some of them. In retrospect I can imagine a few reasons why.

First, I was drawing upon my background as a Catholic priest, of course, but also as a licensed family therapist and a professor of world religions. Viewed through the lens of depth psychology, a simple moral choice, like any mature decision embedded in a unique individual life, was beginning to look ever more complex. And instead of providing these students with moral convictions based on Christian premises I was encouraging them to study the moral teachings also of other religious traditions, and even humanist alternatives. Though explicitly opposed to moral relativism I seemed to offer no definitive answers but only new questions. Maybe people should have been forewarned about the motto posted on my office door: "I don't have any solutions but I surely admire the problem." I concede, however, that more than one student has quoted this caution back at me whenever I get too assertive.

The seminar members split mostly between dogmatic moral traditionalists and amoral skeptics. I discovered few willing to follow my middle path between exact logical deduction at one extreme, and a shallow relativism at the opposite, which treats moral choices as little more than preferred ice cream flavors. Somehow both groups expected me to act as a moral beacon of certainty. The strict deductionists could be typified by one young woman deploring the hippy permissiveness and New Age muddle of her parents. In sober reaction to their excesses she claimed her own generation now demanded clear undebatable commandments from the Church. From an opposite perspective, skeptics and rebels had their own reasons for distrusting my apparent reluctance to take the moral high ground. They seemed to need a straight-man stereotype with all the answers, a fixed star for measuring how far they might safely drift to explore their doubts. Alert to these two differing motives behind the ache for certainty I determined someday to write a book that would map out a middle course—between an ethics of legal deduction and an ethics of subjectivity or relativity.

Marx was correct to prod academic types like me. Inclined merely to reinterpret the world we must also try to change it. Midway between meditative analysis and militant activism, the present book offers an interpretation less of the present than the emerging future: a practical blueprint to direct the currents of moral, religious, and social change. My title and subtitle imply a comparative religious ethics rooted in the major world religious traditions, a moral vision embracing the Sacred, the natural environment, and the range of human conscience anywhere, all interconnected. The approach is crosscultural, polyreligious, and interdisciplinary in scope.

The issues I have selected for detailed scrutiny could not be more borderless or global—nonviolence, ecology, human rights, and cross-religious dialogue, topics introduced respectively in chapters 2, 3-4, 5-6, and 6-7. Though my focus is mostly social ethics and minimal legal rights, I will not slight the maximal range of aspiration within each moral individual. Throughout the book but especially in chapter 7, I explore a few virtues pivotal for a sound moral life—human self-worth, frugality, moral-religious scrutiny, and responsive listening.

As my central thesis I argue the need for a new comprehensive ethics. Its goal must be both negative and positive. As a negative preliminary, I want to dismantle all rationales for domineering—including one economic or ethnic group by another, colonized people by colonial powers, society by the nation-state, individuals by civil and religious bureaucracies, women by men, the young by their elders, or the natural world by human beings. Then as a positive aim I will try in each moral controversy to hear out all sides with empathy, yet still reach beyond barriers in search of a global moral consensus. These barriers include the customary walls between sovereign nations, between religious traditions, between humanity and the natural world, and especially between the moral and religious dimensions of experience. In particular I hope to bridge the subversive dichotomy between horizontal duties based on moral reason, and vertical duties based on a divine-command. From my perspective any religious maturity worthy of the name must express itself in moral action, and any genuine moral concern is virtually religious already.

My intended audience is first the literate college-educated public, and second, the questioning intelligent undergraduate or graduate student. At times I revisit concerns raised in two of my earlier books, *Sacred Lies and Silences* (Liturgical Press, 1994), and *Imagining the Sacred* (Orbis, 1998), where I implied an ethics without tracking down implications. Notes are located after the text, so that readers can investigate a preferred subject further, check the accuracy of my sources, or verify if a controversial interpretation is based on a wider consensus or just my own idiosyncratic viewpoint.

While brainstorming for the original seminar discussion mentioned above, I rummaged through stories from my own life where I hoped to detect some issues of conscience that really left their imprint. I had never forgotten the critique written by a college composition teacher beneath a story of mine about death by freezing in the Arctic: "Try to write about something you've really experienced." Thus, I proceeded to dredge up various memories from childhood. Among them I reconstructed one painful decision to inform on a gun-toting friend involved in a grocery store robbery. This narrative has now ended up as the central case-study in chapter 1, an illustration of guidelines for shaping a mature moral decision. In commentary on that case-study I examine ethical methods that do not depend on exact deductive reasoning.

Each chapter in the book circles around a few central stories from this well-spring of narrative—recounted either from my own expeience, or from modern classics of fiction, film, and cartoons that have touched me. I tend to seek what T.S. Eliot calls an objective correlative, an image or story to distill my major insights. For example, the ideas I introduce in chapter 2 about conscience, dissent, and sectarian dualism have their graphic correlative in the life-stories of draft dissenters I often interviewed during the Vietnam War. Described in chapters 3 and 4, my late-ripening concern about an ecological apocalypse can be traced to recent friendship with a local Apache environmentalist, treks through various polluted international countrysides, and notably my preadolescent remorse over cruelty to animals.

Somewhat insensitive to human rights abuses in my own nation I was not stirred to protest until witnessing blatant rights violations during a 1987 Singapore visit, recounted in chapter 5. Interviews with a few staff members at the Business for Social Responsibility offices in San Francisco taught me practical incentives that now spur some multinationals to implement the UN Bill of Rights. Vivid episodes from my own teaching and counseling experiences surface with more frequency in the last two chapters. Chapter 6, mulling over student value-surveys and my conversations with people of diverse religious backgrounds, recounts my attempts to fathom the current mind set of moral relativity and religious postmodernity. After extended debate with an African Muslim friend I realize that no religious dialogue is viable until each party owns up to major weaknesses and crimes within its own tradition.

A research trip of four months to Nepal and my year's pastoral assignments as a young priest in England offered the settings for a few extraordinary encounters highlighted in chapter 7. I listened to people's stories at a boisterous meeting of British labor delegates and also a hospital ward of elderly muscular dystrophy patients. I tried to read behind the tributes by grieving students of a beloved Katmandu story-teller. This final chapter, my apologia for an overlapping ethics of liberation, virtue, character, narrative, and empathic listening, should come as no surprise. For I have been telling countless moral stories and illustrating the ethical impact of story-telling, almost since my first page.

ACKNOWLEDGMENTS.   Darwin's memoirs describe his habit of jotting down not the acclaim by critics but the most damaging facts and arguments mobilized against each of his books. Painful and thus more likely to be discounted and forgotten, these objections often proved to be the most fruitful for his revised edition. I am grateful to the following for feedback, proofreading, and mostly for hard-hitting critiques of earlier drafts: Paul Bernadicou, S.J., Tom Cavanaugh, Chris Hayward, M.D., David McSpadden, Jonathan Miller, John W. O'Malley, S.J., Richard Ruland, Joseph Van de Mortel, and most of all, my editor Alan Ziajka, USF director of institutional research. I am indebted to Jim Muyo and his USF Publications staff, especially Eugene Vinluan-Pagal for his cover design and copyediting. Sarah Blackburn and Ken Yoshioka of USF Information Technology Services guided me through various computer roadblocks. A liberal endowment from the USF Arts and Sciences faculty research fund helped me cover publication costs.

I appreciate the openness of my students these last few semesters in comparative religious ethics, tackling successive versions of this book as an experimental text. Ecology and human rights issues are so timely that tomorrow's newspaper or TV documentary can introduce new data or angles that dismantle the tidy synthesis erected today. In each effort to revise and update I recognize again how provisional, fallible, and quixotic any study of this sort must be. The words seem dated even by the time they first reach the publisher. At some arbitrary moment I had to jump from the moving train of events and my endless attempts to comprehend them.

Within widening circles of gratitude I should include all my students of various nations and religious backgrounds, especially those raring to ignite my social conscience. And also my friends and family, helpful librarians and computer technicians and editors, and a providential line of teachers and mentors who have inspired the shaping of my personal religious-moral Way.

1

ANATOMY OF A SOUND MORAL CHOICE

A FEW CLASSICAL SCENES OF MORAL DECISIVENESS REMAIN unforgettable. Even two millennia after, many people still hear the dissenting voice of Socrates who preferred to die rather than give up his right to speak and teach freely under an oppressive Athenian regime. And Sophocles' Antigone is forced to choose between obeying the religious obligation to bury her brother or obeying Creon's death-sanction against breaking the curfew. "What laws of heaven have I transgressed?" she protests to Creon. "I never thought that by a breath a mortal man like you could annul or override heaven's laws, unwritten and immortal."

Huck Finn aboard his Mississippi raft proves as fearless as his Greek prototypes. At the midpoint of Twain's *Adventures of Huckleberry Finn* the boy must decide whether to restore Jim to slavery under Miss Watson or to help him escape further downstream. The yearning to liberate his black friend disturbs Huck, for he had always found Miss Watson kindhearted, and he cannot justify stealing her human property. "The more I studied about this," he says, "the more my conscience went to grinding me, and the more wicked and more low-down and ornery I got to feeling."[1]

The novel inserts a tricky irony into this interior debate. For Huck associates the label *conscience*, not with his deepest moral intuition, but with those faulty Sunday-school maxims, the folk wisdom of his pro-slavery community. Thus, regressing to the norms of his earlier training, he now determines to write Miss Watson a letter betraying Jim's hiding place, a gesture that at first makes Huck feel good and washed clean of sin. Yet soon he finds himself unable to pray, aware that somehow his "heart isn't right." Mulling over the good times Jim and he have lived together, and Jim's true human worth, he at last plunges into a momentous decision. He tears up the letter to Miss Watson and resolves to liberate Jim, no matter what the spiritual consequences: "All right, then, I'll go to hell." Rather than heaven and its inhumane values, he chooses the antithesis to such a heaven, his own authentic conscience.

The heroic choices by these three characters underline a feature common to almost any serious moral decision. To begin with, most people go about daily life reassured by an unexamined context of social convention and law. Imagine an ideal democratic society where citizens have the right to treat each law as a question, not an imperative. Viewing civil law as a social contract, they may choose to obey a specific ordinance, or try to reform it through legislative change, or to disobey it with respect and accept the penalty. Yet granted this right in theory, they will seldom in practice have the time or motivation to call laws into question. The range of people obeying laws as a gesture of dependent conformity, I suspect, outnumbers those obeying as a mature interdependent choice. The conventions in society function as a largely unexamined shield, a secure fortification against chaos. The average person tends to act on the premise that these silent commands are fair, perhaps even marked by an aura of sacred legitimacy. Even Socrates, though questioning almost everything else, never seems to challenge the right of his Athenian judges to sentence him to death, a decision he associates with divine fate and justice. And Huck Finn takes for granted that local Christian church leaders will uphold Miss Watson's right to repossess her own slave.

Conscience can be defined as a sense of accountability toward the moral center that gives underlying coherence to each individual life. Thus, conscience must be distinguished from what Freud calls the superego, that undifferentiated legacy of social and family values communicated to each individual. As conscience matures, each person will gradually test out, select or discard, and personalize this superego influence. Genuine guilt results from a deliberate violation of one's conscience, whereas irrational guilt feelings or counterfeit guilt arise from a conscious or even unconscious violation of the superego. A favorite cartoon satirizes this distinction between real guilt and its counterfeits. In a prison cell one convict advises another: "It's perfectly all right to *be* guilty but it's unhealthy to *feel* guilty."

Like most priest-confessors I have spent years hearing out anonymous voices in the confessional and helping them explore this crucial distinction. Granted that no single moral choice can be freed totally from its superego lineage. Yet I have been learning to discern the qualitative difference between the irrational guilt feelings Freud describes and a genuine mature guilt, between the unexamined superego heritage and one's own examined conscience, between rebellion against an external directive and against an authentic inner directive. It is my conviction that the mark of an integrated human being is to take responsibility for one's own unique appropriated values, for any conscious betrayal of these values, and for the possibility of genuine contrition and restitution. If we could each realize our own distinctive guilt, as Carl Jung observes, we would find an enrichment, a unique sense of honor and spiritual dignity.[2]

Perhaps most people, on the contrary, treat the values of family and society, imprinted on their superego, as the only horizon imaginable. A counseling client of mine, for instance, once recounted his childhood experience of vicious beatings from an alcoholic father, with his mother and uncle hovering nearby as impotent accomplices. Like a prisoner abandoned to darkness he felt an adult conspiracy around him, a despair at being unable to reach out for help beyond this dungeon. At the extreme it is possible to picture a family or community just this obedient, the population fully socialized, in which the interior disposition of every member exactly matches external behavior.

The so-called normal people in any society tend to be the majority, shaped more or less by the unchallenged values of that culture. The minority are often treated as deviant. Prone to discredit nonconformity under labels of disease or fraud, the majority tend to forget that a consensus in any society can be undermined, not just by defying it but by embodying it to an absurd extreme. I recall a cartoon about an Aztec pyramid, with a youth at its apex about to be butchered in sacrifice. At middle level two elders watch another young victim resistant to his guards straining nearby to drag him upstairs to the altar. "These self-centered young people!" says one observer to his companion. "Today they're no longer as religious as they used to be." The trickster figures of Native American folklore, the jester who holds up a mirror of ridicule at court, or the archetypal Holy Fool of Russia—the so-called irreverent and mad can spur us to reexamine our conventional gauge sifting genuine faith or sanity from their distortions.

Breaking through the inert consensus of normalcy, rumors may surface one day of a very different realm from this one. Suddenly the majority ethos begins to lose its veneer of permanent durability. Now an existential boundary-situation opens, exposing gross limitations. In retrospect the accepted verities look shallow, lopsided, or disgraceful. Antigone reaches her arms to the sky for help, a mythical space ruled by the "laws of heaven," Socrates commits himself at last to his compelling inner "voice," his daimon, and Huck finds his initial compliance overruled by an acute disquiet, the promptings of his "heart."

As Albert Camus explains in *The Rebel*, an authentic "No" can be an implicit affirmation of one's belief in a realm of unequivocal values. Having put up with the lash for years, a slave one day at last draws a line, the limits to his tolerance. That part of himself which he demands to be respected has to be placed above everything else, even life itself. As a last resort the slave is willing to accept the final defeat of death rather than be deprived of freedom, his "personal sacrament." For Camus, a mature act of rebellion implies a transition from facts to rights—a world of what-is, now transformed into what-ought-to-be. With the force of Descartes' inaugural premise, "I think, therefore I am," the act of dissent summons a person from individual isolation into solidarity with the entire human race. "I rebel—therefore *we* exist."[3]

The shift to a higher, deeper, better, or more comprehensive perspective is sparked most often by an unmistakable injustice, either against oneself or someone close, or even against a stranger. Though condoned by civil law, such an extraordinary crime, so people maintain, cries to heaven for vengeance. Once discounted as remote, the outrage itself now looms much nearer home, and an individual begins to feel solidarity with fellow victims anywhere. As Nazi violence closed in on him, Lutheran Pastor Martin Niemoeller reached this very insight, by now perhaps the most famous cry of protest in a century of political and racial persecution: "First they came for the Jews, and I did not speak out because I was not a Jew. Then they came for the Communists, and I did not speak out because I was not a Communist. And then they came for the trade unionists, and I did not speak out because I was not a trade unionist. And then they came for me, and there was no one left to speak out for me."

Case Study: The Gunman and the Informer

In my own childhood, probably about the age of ten, I recall struggling with a moral decision that seems representative enough to deserve retelling. It captures one of the first moments I stepped from the realm of conventional obedience into a realm of embryonic conscience. Whereas Huck Finn probed his conscience aboard a raft and alone, relatively isolated from the laws and customs of his society, I had to wrestle with my conscience while engaged actively with my family, ring of friends, civil and school authorities, and my faith community. The facts are few, but despite an evident fallibility of recall, they seem carved in memory. In our Catholic grade school class there was one boy physically taller and sturdier than the rest of us, an impetuous free spirit, widely admired and liked. Though prone to drift into a mist of private daydreams he cultivated a tough street-wise facade.

One morning I happened to take an unfamiliar alley shortcut on the walk to school. Here at the center of a crowd stood this same boy, shooting a loaded pistol at cans ranged along a garage roof, to the applause of a few classmates whom he was encouraging to experiment with the gun. At each pause to reload he strutted about, twirling his pistol like a film cowboy. To satisfy our curiosity he offered a casual account of how he had been handed the gun in payment for his role as lookout in the robbery of a neighborhood grocery store. A few onlookers near me expressed alarm about toying with guns, but the crowd jeered at gutless objections of this sort. The boy's account of the robbery stunned me. For the rest of the day I agonized about the gun, about every imaginable danger from its lethal misuse, and about the punishment awaiting him as an active accomplice in the robbery. I had begun to wonder, too, if anyone robust or persuasive enough could be located to disarm him. For he had a reputation for mulish defiance, once he had made up his mind about something.

From this distance in time I can attempt a few conjectures about my pre-adolescent state of mind. I recall my paralysis from indecision and worry. Perhaps I was gullible to swallow my friend's account of the robbery, for I had almost overlooked his class-clown reputation for tall tales, the more shocking the better. He might have found a discarded gun, purchased it himself illegally by mail order, or lifted it from his father's weapon collection, and then embellished the episode. The stress of peer conformity, too, began to unsettle me. All of us admired the boy so much we could not let so princely a character be brought down nor condone the thought that anyone would inform on him. No one wanted him hurt, shamed, expelled from school, or dragged away to reform school or prison. These omens of violence surfaced during the early 1940's in a small Pennsylvania Catholic grade school, a relative sanctuary where none of us could have foreseen the violent conditions of many urban schools today, with driveby shootings, schoolyard weapon-searches, and armed teenage vendettas. I feared that this boy, surely as inexperienced as I, might harm or kill himself, or take revenge on a crabby teacher, or entrust the weapon to children lacking even his minimal skill or discretion.

By now I had begun trying to imagine myself thrust into the alien role of informer. Reviewing my backstock of images from films, radio serials, comic book fantasies, however, I could only loathe the Judas snitch, the rat-fink, toward whom neither gangsters nor police showed any respect. Still less did I savor "the good boy" role, the sort of prissy Sunday-school wimp repellent to full-blooded characters like Tom Sawyer and Huck Finn. On the surface Huck's decision against betraying his friend contrasted blatantly with the decision to betray my own friend. At a youthful phase ripe for heroes I had not yet learned to appreciate the tacit heroism of trying to live out an ordinary life in an extraordinarily loyal and disciplined way.

Hunting for some exotic precedent, I cannot recall that the brave generosity of Jesus, caring and dying for others, touched my young imagination. Yet somehow I did want to be unselfish and kind—the moral ideals reaffirmed at school, the parish church, and especially in my family. I suppose I doubted that the everyday choices of Jesus could inspire a ten-year-old's choice for or against a friend. The nascent religious side of me had always felt resistant to legends about the boy Jesus, told as cautionary tales by our teaching nuns. With the exception of a brief adolescent interlude in the Jerusalem temple, the New Testament remains silent about Christ's everyday life from the manger to his public initiation about the age of thirty. In class we were once taught a ridiculous prayer I refused to utter, "Boy Savior, bless our behavior!" You might picture Jesus as a baby or an adult, but who could imagine him as a clumsy adolescent? Catholic spirituality, I knew, cherished a vast backlog of saints, intended to refract new aspects of Christ's life in various lands and eras. A few child saints paraded before me in fantasy, sappy and unreal, none of them offering a trace of illumination.

What other moral source within myself could I draw upon? In my heart I did not identify any motive specifically Christian. The best I could say for myself was that I wanted no one to be hurt, neither the boy nor the possible victims of this weapon. I could not bring myself to confront the boy directly because we all knew his fierce intractability to any interference, once he had set his mind on something. I tried to measure his well-being against the well-being of others, and puzzle to what extent a wolf's rights had to be respected alongside the rights of sheep victimized. I felt love and empathy for this boy, and preferred to be just that sort of person who would try helping him, showing a tough love, even if he might at first protest the actual steps I was taking.

In weighing my options I do not think I was just sizing up the social pressures, calculating the rewards and punishments that awaited an informer. Granted the likelihood I would inform, I had to inform the most suitable person, someone disposed to minimize harmful side-effects to my friend, and at the same time protect my snitch identity. Recognizing the presence of self-interest in my calculations, I still resolved that this factor must yield primacy to my care for the boy's dignity and future. For best advice or direct intervention should I approach my parents, the police, the teacher or principal, or maybe the Benedictine priests who managed the parish and grade school?

At length I ruled out teacher and principal, both of them Benedictine nuns, who I feared might overreact at the first hint of gangsterism and expel my friend. It baffled me that my father during these years of my childhood had thus far drawn more respect from my peers than he had yet earned from me. Mark Twain once remarked that as a boy he had thought his father a fool yet found the old man grew surprisingly wiser as Twain grew older. The parish priests struck me as avuncular, sagelike, trustworthy maybe, but too unworldly to cope with outright crime. My experience with the police in fantasy and real life, however, had soured me. Emerging from concealment, they used to stage terrifying ambushes, closing down our football games on a lot always closed off by no-trespassing signs. A stay at juvenile hall or a criminal police record could torpedo your later school and job prospects.

Like the three epic dissenting figures introduced at the beginning of this chapter I was searching for a transcendental realm beyond conventional wisdom. To my disadvantage I could not yet distinguish at this age between the moral absolute itself and my imagined ranks of adult rescuers. I was not sharp enough to foresee that my parents and the local priest might size up the police less critically than I or might show less compassion toward the boy than I. However, to my credit, I showed enough independence to curb my own feelings of insecurity. I did not itch for the tattler's reward or for approval as a "good boy" from nuns, police, or other authority figures. I wanted only to track down an adult resourceful enough to protect those who might be hurt by the gun.

What brought closure at last to my reflections was an instant of urgency and clarity. What sort of a son was I, hesitating in a crisis to confide in my parents? I wanted above all to prove myself a true son— someone worthy of decent parents, not just a dependent child trying to please them. I decided at last to try out both my father and mother, and ask them to join me in a visit to the local rectory. I was surprised to find them both immediately responsive. All three of us shared the astounding premise that any priest worthy of the name would confront and disarm my friend as humanely as possible. We would defer to the pastor's discretion, who after interviewing the boy could determine the pistol's source and decide whether to summon the police.

These are a few of the complex inner factors shaping my moral decision. Though distant in time my own motives then have a deceptive lucidity today, but the inward life of everyone else in this scenario can only be surmised. It is easier to give a summary epilogue of the outward events, which managed to avoid any obvious disaster. Even the teacher and principal showed more moderation than I had foreseen in my script. The following afternoon in class, the pastor, sweeping through the door on a surprise deus ex machina visit, asked the boy to rise from his seat, and hand over his pistol immediately. After the first shock this visit left an impression of quick justice, a gentle but firm imprint of authority, and a warning that this nonsense must never occur again. He then conferred quietly with the teacher and boy a little while outside the classroom.

My friend, obviously mortified, returned to class. Math lessons now resumed, with no noticeable reprisals from the teacher nor later moralizing on the scandal. I was never fingered as the informer nor did the heroic gun-slinger want to communicate anything further about the entire episode. It disappoints me, even to this day, that the boy refused to disclose details about an alleged meeting afterwards between his parents and the pastor. I never pinned down the gun's true origins, nor could any of us uncover the boy's reactions to the betrayal itself.

Right Questioning

The story catches a vivid enlargement of consciousness in my earliest years, shifting from routines of inactive compliance to a new threshold of proactive moral reflection. Though explored in a child of ten, most of the essentials in this decision, I believe, characterize not only one microcosm but mature moral choices anywhere.[4] So much anxiety in my narrative centers on finding a suitable confidant and mediator and evading peer censure against informers. Yet in the very act of sorting out likely consequences and trying to find the most trustworthy intervention I rediscovered my moral priorities. The values that marked my choice had to match up with the unselfish, responsible person I had been aspiring to become.

Two cautions must be kept in mind before any attempt to generalize from this narrative. First, I keep reminding myself not to fixate on an isolated, dramatic moment of choice. In other words, I should not convey the impression of reifying two separated realms of human consciousness, the amoral ordinary and the moral extraordinary. For the moral life is not a mere series of distinct moral acts but a living continuity. It may be acceptable, of course, to single out culminating, almost sacramental moments in such a life as morally exemplary, somewhat the way Camus does in the slave's crowning act of rebellion. It often takes a crisis, a break in ordinary continuity, to bring people to their moral senses, but they must try to reestablish continuity after the instant of disruption.

Standard ethical questions tend to take the following shape: how do I make a sound moral decision? How would such a process differ from making any mature human choice? Hard as it is to know that I know, how can I know that I am doing right? Yet it would be helpful, on the contrary, to redesign these questions so that doing good is the indispensable culmination of a life centered on being good. The key question should be, how can I live a deeper moral life? Thus, faced with an urgent dilemma of conscience on a jury, in a multi-national boardroom, or at a bedside, how would a person genuinely moral and wise handle it? I believe a problem well-stated is a problem half-solved. Once the questions are framed with care, attention shifts away from the sheer act of choice, and toward pervasive qualities of a good moral person, the inclusive moral dynamic.[5]

I am convinced that the moral act cannot be understood apart from the moral agent, and I will develop such an ethics of agency in my final chapter. My approach here can be summed up in a few terse lines by ethicist Stanley Hauerwas: "The question 'what ought I to be?' precedes the question 'What ought I to do?'... For the question 'What ought I to do?' tempts us to assume that moral situations come abstracted from the kind of people and history we have come to be." Moral dilemmas are not out there waiting to be assessed but created by the kind of people we are. "Those who are committed to living faithfully do not have to decide constantly whether to be faithful. They simply are faithful."[6] I back this premise but think its formulation needs better nuance and balance. Though tending to act in character, people may at times act worse or better than their habitual style. Their past is always present, fluid and incomplete, asking how it is going to be integrated into this particular deed right now. I trust that most people are basically free—never so entrenched in right that they cannot fall nor so entrenched in wrong that they cannot re-form.

I hope to steer away from what is called an ethics of crisis or quandary that tests the limits of one's fundamental moral principles. I side with a more routine sort of ethics, reminiscent of the ordinary science that Thomas Kuhn distinguishes from extraordinary science. In his influential work on scientific revolutions, Kuhn noticed that standard histories of the sciences tended to emphasize a series of exciting crises, radical paradigm shifts. They downplayed the relatively conservative patterns of routine science. The genuine science of everyday consists, not in inventing new theories, but principally in prosaic mopping-up operations, investigating some part of nature in detail and depth, all in conformity with the paradigm currently accepted. In a similar way I want to center on the "ordinary" ethics of a good life, the development of character and virtue within a relatively established ethical paradigm.[7]

This principle of ordinary moral continuity—doing that emerges coherently from being—is my first major caution. The second follows as an important corollary: a single univocal method of reasoning cannot bring clarifying simplicity to the messy tangle, the kaleidoscopic range of moral choice. Some moral philosophers, for example, are attached to a legal rationalistic style of reflection. They watch lawyers consulting civil law, say, on the issue of business liability, and then distilling a few principles of jurisprudence, or lining up past judicial precedents, as a context for interpreting this particular injury claim. Like a lawyer this type of ethicist might try first to dredge up a few relevant moral maxims. These might involve some list of prima facie obligations, like the Kantian moral imperative, which urges you to act as if your decision could serve as a moral precedent anywhere. Then by deductive reasoning these maxims are applied to some concrete problem, say, in medical ethics. Such an approach seems to guarantee certainty, for the axioms have a semblance of clarity, and the reasoning process can be double-checked, much like a geometric proof.

Analyzing my case-study of a young conscience above, I can sift out axiomatic principles of this sort guiding my choice. "Be as truthful as possible. Be loyal to your friends. At times true love demands tough love. Try to do the right thing but only after consulting others to help you examine every angle. You cannot please everyone. Since you are bound to step on someone's toes in any conflict of rights, try to do as little damage as possible." Truisms like these are indeed true and deserve wider respect. A coherent ethics that can be derived from moral maxims will contribute insight now and then. Yet the moral reflection process I described in this case-study involves much more than deductive reasoning. Reasoning is indeed present, but also the methods of active imagination, thought-experiments or inner dialogues with myself, empirical research and consultation, empathy for others' viewpoints, conjectures about relative rights and responsibilities, meditating, and mulling over some of the great moral stories. My major resource is not so much systematic logic as a long-evolving habit of being, an intuitive sense of kindness, equity, or common decency.

Mark Twain's novel would call such a resource the moral sentiment or simply the "heart"—feelings that Huck knows his guardians and church teachers tend to dismiss as too subjective and unreliable. I think an individual conscience often sorts out its priorities in the charismatic instant of engagement alongside others. For example, people may join in a civil rights march and catch fire from Martin Luther King or some other prophetic figure. Guided by this vision, perhaps at a later moment they may search to reclaim moral principles in their own religious tradition, which will authenticate and at the same time remain faithful to the vital prophetic experience they shared.

Standard influential ethical traditions, such as Aristotelian virtue ethics, the natural law ethics of Aquinas, the deontic or rational duty ethics of Kant, the consequentialist ethics of Bentham and Mill, are usually cited as rival systems destined to trigger endless moral disputes. However, I have learned to treat these and other ethical systems as limited perspectives that often overlap, complement, and correct one another. A specific model, or combination of models, may prove most suitable, depending on the particular issue, the intensity and complexity of public debate, or the temperament of a particular ethicist.

It will be helpful to illustrate how these classical positions may converge as differing strands of argument, say, against the death penalty. Here I will not argue my own moral stand but only point to three contrasting styles of reasoning against this penalty. Adopting the perspective of Aquinas' natural law and of Kant's deontic ethics, I might appeal to some universal premise of natural rights, such as this: "My own right to life must be treated as sacred and inalienable despite any apparent gesture of mine to forfeit this right." Kant offers an axiom of compelling simplicity: "Treat humanity in yourself and every other person as an end, never as a means." Once such an axiom is granted, I must next establish that capital punishment reduces the criminal's humanity to only a means. In other words, whatever privileges claimed by a society to exempt itself from backing this axiom strictly—such as its need to exact vengeance, protect future victims, or impose strict retribution measure for measure—must now be refuted one by one.

From a consequentialist rather than a Kantian perspective, arguing once again to abolish the death penalty, I could update Jeremy Bentham's evidence for needed reforms in the prison system of his own Victorian era. Utilitarian moral rules do not stem deductively from inherent rights or duties but surface as rules of thumb, summaries of my own case-experience, a provisional consensus in society. Today in America, the death penalty, as many sociological surveys confirm, no longer functions to deter the average criminal. It also targets a disproportionate and therefore unfair number of minority inmates, especially those too poor or ill-advised to find the best legal aid. In at least one society, then, the penalty is proving ineffective, unjust, and thus morally wrong.

From yet a third perspective, moral activists and mentors I know best seem to decide in fuzzier, less rationalistic ways than Kant and Bentham. Rooted in the virtue-ethics of Aristotle's *Nicomachean Ethics,* and also in later neo-Aristotelian natural law ethics, people will tend to focus less on the moral deed than the moral agent. They resist the death penalty because violent retaliation is an unthinkable option for the compassionate persons they are trying to become—compassionate first toward the killer's victims, of course, but more inclusively, even toward the killer's humanity, too. For instance, a student friend once confided that when astronauts reach the moon or scientists leap over one more knowledge barrier he had no trouble identifying himself with humanity at its peak. Now with someone condemned to die, even a depraved person, humanity at its nadir, my friend felt impelled to identify as well. He could no more approve this death sentence than approve his own death. Why kill a killer, who if granted a life-sentence without parole, might at least during imprisonment find a spiritual second-chance to repent?

In the actual decision process, tightening an argument proves less important than exploring a morass of empirical data and seeking advice from various specialists to get the issues in accurate focus. Soon people discover that the side-effects and implications of any choice grow more intricate after first scrutiny, and the rights of various parties seem now to collide, now to overlap. Also, many axiomatic natural rights which the Middle Ages and the Enlightenment Era found applicable everywhere, today stand demystified as Euro-American conventions, limited mostly to a specific time, social class, gender, or religion. To be specific, the right to "liberty," listed by the Declaration of Independence as an inalienable human right, even in 1776 did not extend to black slaves, women, nor to white males a notch below the class-imposed norm of land ownership.

Guidelines for Deciding

Thus far I have used the term *moral* to indicate the standards that human character and human interaction must follow in order to be judged good or right, at least in a particular culture. I add the final proviso about a limited context because I want to signal that discussion at this point will remain open about the alleged relativity of "good," "right," and "moral," as perceived in comparisons between cultures. I treat as synonyms the ethical and moral, the ethicist and the moral philosopher. A descriptive ethics will disclose or predict the laws or values as they simply exist, whereas a normative ethics will center on the values that ought to exist. I recognize that ethics as a study often connotes a systematic reflection on life's inherent moral dimension. Influenced by German usage, some writers distinguish between a lived ethic in the singular and a systematic ethics in the plural. My term *ethics* centers on a lived ethic and the practical steps needed to reduce the disparity between what is and what ought to be.

Examining the case-study from my childhood once again, I can piece together a check-list that gives shape to this one budding moral choice, and by extension, I am convinced, to any process of sound moral reflection. Each area of scrutiny on the list should have its impact but in no rigorous sequence.

My first aim, of course, must be to gauge the potential fall-out from each option open to me, especially its effect on the rights of others. Second, I must be willing to spend most of my reflection time discerning the "fit" of each available option. I can test this option's compatibility with my role as a preadolescent friend or son, say, or later as an adult teacher and counselor. More important, how compatible is this option with the character I have been shaping through years of effort to live a moral and spiritual life?

Third, throughout this decision process I can expect to seek inspiration from images and dialogue in model narratives that embody a wide range of experience. I mean stories about Christ or the saints in my own faith tradition, heroes and heroines of my own nation's history and mythology, scenes from literature and film featuring model characters like Antigone or Huck Finn, and the example of friends, teachers, and spiritual guides who continue to inspire the person I hope to become.

As my fourth aim I must at some point find out if a specific civil law already stands in place to address this particular moral situation. Fifth, the more pivotal the choice before me, the more prepared I must be to rehearse it with a wise confidant. This readiness to confer must also include consulting research libraries, community agencies, and specialists, notably on such knotty issues as medical or business ethics. Sixth and finally, since a serious decision is no mere private whim but an act open to public accountability, I must be prepared to offer a defense for my decision, once completed, by explaining its consistency and implications.

These are some of the overlapping concerns I am convinced should enter into a sound moral decision. They must not be mistaken for a diagram of sequential logical steps, for that sort of guidebook could only oversimplify or distort the multi-layered process of choice. I can promise no syllogistic certainty here but a confidence based on mounting probabilities, as each person deciding and acting continues to probe for the truth in every feasible way. The most effective apologia for any practical moral choice is therefore this effort to verify its coherence with the major roles, narratives, and values that shape each unique moral life.

2

RELIGIOUS AND MORAL FAULTLINES

I HAVE DEFINED CONSCIENCE AS A SENSE OF ACCOUNTABILITY toward God, or toward the moral-religious center that gives underlying coherence to each individual life. My own decision in childhood to inform on a classmate gave a simplified blueprint of shaping a conscience. However, not until my experience as a priest and draft-counselor during the psychedelic sixties was I introduced to the mystery of conscience in all its complexity and relativity. At that point my range of empathy had to stretch far beyond its earlier cultural and spiritual boundaries. I was prompted now to revamp my notion of religion and also to reinterpret the conventional barriers between religious and moral factors in experience.

The present chapter, after giving an account of this widening viewpoint in counseling, will explore conflicting versions about how religious and moral factors ought to interact. I will first single out two scenarios of their incompatibility—religious authoritarianism, triggering a stance of anti-religious rebuttal—and then their potential yin-yang compatibility in what I call an ethics of loyal scrutiny. The opportunities for either collision or congruence between the religious and moral factors will be illustrated in two contrasting biblical narratives about Abraham's encounters with God.

When moral reflection meets explicit religious experience, a familiar paradox arises. My neighbor and I may affirm the same Christian creed, for instance, but at the same time contradict each other on such vital moral issues as abortion and capital punishment. Yet conversely, the same neighbor and her husband might arrive at a single moral stand on environmental protection, though he happens to contradict her basic Christian premises. How can this discontinuity be explained—the fault-line that separates a given applied ethics from the religious heritage often claimed for its basis?

I have already implied some reasons why this sort of disparity might arise. The most common type of moral reflection, I claimed, is not so much deductive argument drawn from moral axioms, nor projections how to achieve best moral results for the greatest number of people. I think the prevalent type of moral reasoning is more intuitive and passionate than this—an overlapping ethics of story, virtue, or character, which will be addressed at length in my concluding chapter. In my experience people worry less often about moral brinkmanship, riding a tight-rope between good and bad, than about intensifying their present efforts to be unselfish. The more complex a given moral issue, I suppose, the less likely will someone's ethics derive in a simple logical chain from a recognizable official religious premise. The way an individual perceives a concrete problem will be conditioned by half-aware factors such as one's individual temperament, morally sensitized to some issues more than others, and to the prevalent moral consensus that crosses religious boundaries.

Case Study: The Dissenting Conscience

Most of the world's religious traditions view the moral and religious as distinct but inseparable yin-yang factors, complementary but not contradictory, each incomplete without the other. Yet in the United States today, on the contrary, the terms religious and moral continue to evoke two separate enclaves. There are first a set of religious laws to govern someone's vertical interactions with a personal God, and then a set of moral laws to govern someone's horizontal interactions with other people. Perhaps such a dichotomy reflects the so-called wall between church and state, between religious rights and socio-moral rights. Originating in a private letter of Jefferson the wall metaphor has long since been enshrined as an axiom of American public wisdom.

Stretch of the Law

I am convinced the most glaring divorce between religious and moral factors can be traced in the amended U.S. Congressional Selective Service Act of 1958. The law asserts that Conscientious Objector status will be granted only to cases "of religious training and belief." The term religious here is narrowed only to belief in "a Supreme Being, involving duties superior to those arising from any human relation." Exemptions from the military draft cannot be claimed for non-religious reasons, which the law spells out as "essentially political, sociological, or philosophical views or a merely personal moral code."[1] Split off from a personal moral code, where did such a restrictive concept of religion come from?

Since the Revolutionary War the basis for exempting dissenters for reasons of conscience from military service had always been specific membership in the Quaker, Anabaptist, or some other pacifist church. But during the Second World War cases of Conscientious Objection were beginning to surface, based not on specific church membership but on a dissent of conscience against all war. In other words many hoped to see conscience achieve parity with explicit religious guidelines like the Ten Commandments or other church teachings. By amending the Selective Service Act in 1958 Congress clearly wanted to extend the criterion for exemption beyond sheer membership in a pacifist church. It felt challenged to devise an umbrella broad enough to include the intricacies of more than two hundred sectarian creeds but restrictive enough to exclude the draft boards' nightmare of a million unique cases.

By 1965, however, this limited scope of religious exemption expanded by a quantum leap. This was the year of the momentous Supreme Court Decision *U.S. versus Seeger*. The Seeger Decision offered the following functional criterion for spotting a valid but concealed religious identity: "Does the claimed belief occupy the same place in the life of the objector as an orthodox belief in God holds in the life of one clearly qualified for exemption?" Speaking for the Court, Justice Tom Clark construed the notion of "Supreme Being" in the Selective Service Act broadly indeed. And as a corollary he interpreted any exclusions outside this scope as narrowly as possible. Congress had stated that "merely personal" moral values were not sufficient grounds. The Court now reasoned that the phrase "merely personal" means a "moral code which is not only personal but which is the sole basis for the registrant's belief and is in no way related to a Supreme Being."

It may help to draw upon my own perceptions as a volunteer draft counselor a few years later. As a theologian I could only salute the skillful research behind this legal presentation. The year of the Court's Seeger Decision also marked a pivotal moment within my own church. Texts of the Second Vatican Council were now promulgated in 1965, signed by the pope and all Catholic bishops convened in Rome. Among these declarations is an entire decree expounding the duties and privileges of conscience, religious freedom, and moral dissent. Most important, the Council condemns sheer undiscriminating obedience to civil law: "Actions which deliberately conflict with [universal natural law], as well as orders commanding such actions, are criminal. Blind obedience cannot excuse those who yield to them." And the Conscientious Objector is granted firm legitimacy: "It seems right that laws make humane provisions for the case of those who for reasons of conscience refuse to bear arms, provided however, that they accept some other form of service to the human community." According to another Second Vatican Council decree, the possibility of salvation is reinterpreted even to include non-theists, to the extent that they try to live out the imperatives of their own conscience. Catholics are encouraged to reject nothing that is true and holy in other world religious traditions. The God behind all these spiritualities is described, not merely in personalist terms but also as "ultimate and unutterable mystery," or "that hidden power which hovers over the course of things."[2]

Four years after the revolutionary Seeger Decision and Second Vatican Council I began work as a draft counselor volunteer. Though I knew many people of conscience who had dedicated their lives to military service I began to meet an increasing number drafted against their will and even against their conscience. My college students were yearning for some plausible moral basis to refuse induction into a United States-Vietnam guerilla war that by now seemed immoral—and incidentally, futile. It was appalling how few citizens during those war years were acquainted with basic draft procedures, the recent Seeger Decision, or their own human rights. Deciding to join an active Conscientious Objector network in the wider Detroit area I sought out registrants that might qualify for exemption. For each case selected I would interview the individual, offer help to complete a Conscientious Objector form and personal essay, and during later sessions, role-play in a tenacious Socratic coaching style to prepare candidates for their local draft board defense.[3]

Examining the text of the Court's Seeger Decision, I had not expected to uncover a few quotations from the Second Vatican Council. There is no doubt that the Court had done its theological homework. True to American legal custom, immunity for religious dissenters could apply only to those who repudiate all war, not just this selected present war. But the range of religious legitimacy had now widened to include the following situations: institutional or private faith, faith in one God or many Gods, faith that chooses personal or impersonal models of the Sacred. Moreover, the Seeger Decision cites specific descriptions of the Sacred—Hindu Brahman, Buddhist Nirvana, the "Hidden Power" mentioned in the Second Vatican Council, and theologian Paul Tillich's "power of Being, which works through those who have no name for it."

The religious label had now become humanely inclusive. Deploring the inadequacy of human language to deal with ultimate questions, Justice Clark cautions local draft boards and courts that they cannot "reject beliefs because they consider these beliefs incomprehensible. Their task is to decide whether the beliefs professed by a registrant are sincerely held and whether they are, in the registrant's own scheme of things, religious."

Range of Religious Identity

The Supreme Court's decision reinforced my openness toward an ever widening range of religious dissent as the interviews progressed. Behind their various disguises, there seemed many people of conscience trying to live a truly integrated moral-religious existence. Since then, whenever I use the term *religious*—or its synonym *spiritual*—I refer to whatever explicit or partially conscious drive, credo, or value system lies at the root of behavior marked by awe, commitment, ecstasy, and moral seriousness. The ideal religious person or society is one living, more or less, a religiously integrated existence. In this model situation the adjective religious and the adverb religiously would be so pervasive that no sector of life could be readily compartmentalized into the noun religion. A religious or spiritual quality would permeate that life as the Center from which everything else derives its meaning. I prefer to describe such an existence as a religious tradition, spirituality, or Way. Or reversing this perspective, if I could probe underneath daily behavior and values and language to find whatever ultimately underlies the life of a people or an individual, I would call the source religious. This center of ultimate coherence—whether person or force, imaged or imageless, named or unnameable—will be called the Sacred.[4]

By the simple act of defining controversial words like moral and religious, I have opted already for an abridged theory with its own claim to coherence and applicability. As explained earlier, the term *moral* indicates the standards that human character and human interaction must follow in order to be judged good or right, at least in a particular culture. I sidestep attempts to distinguish the spiritual from the religious, a misleading dichotomy that attempts to isolate the inner life from an outer life burdened by history, ritual, and community structures. The religious factor as defined above already includes the moral dimension. By mistake many people reduce the multi-layered religious factor to the sheer cognitive features of a creed. Yet a complete religious Way is also a value system, a committed meditative state of mind, an angle of vision toward the cosmos and other people. In fact, the world's religious prophets insist that belief must blossom into moral action, and they often rank the moral deed of a so-called unbeliever higher than the moral inertia of a so-called believer. As my definition implies, to be moral means to be implicitly religious, whereas to be religious means not just to be moral, but comprehensively far more. A combined moral-religious perspective will bring into focus distinct but inseparable overlapping dimensions of an inclusive human life.

A further advantage to my definition is its flexible calculus, adjusting to people's words and concepts mostly within their own ultimate frame of reference. It should be easier now to spot functional parallels between an individual spirituality, political commitment, and the ethos of an entire era or civilization. The God-image of a bearded patriarch makes room alongside it for more contemporary symbols, such as Mother Earth, the triumphant Proletariat, cosmological myths of entropy or evolutionary progress. Abandoning a strict Jewish or Hindu tradition, say, a person may turn to the Communist Party, Greenpeace, a 12-step recovery program, or some other secular ideology, still organizing hours from dawn to bedtime around an implicit religious vision.

Locating the religious factor almost everywhere may look suspiciously at first like locating it nowhere. But devout Hasidic Jews can turn even the study of mathematics into an act of worship. Australian Primal peoples link sacred originating forces "once upon a time" with every meaningful act performed in the present, whether hunting, mating, or sleeping. Zen enlightenment means being intensely present in each commonplace event—when someone is dusting a shelf, nothing is more important than dusting that shelf. What makes activities like study and dusting a religious activity, however, can only be determined according to a culture's specific worldview, not by the outsider's a priori categories of religious and nonreligious. Each religious manifestation within a culture is embedded in a particular world of everyday work and relationships. This is true, even more so, in the microcosm of an individual life.

To verify the subtle interweaving of moral and religious features that emerged in my draft-counseling, I turn back even today to the disclosures by Daniel Seeger, Arno Jakobson, and Forest Peter themselves, the three parties in the Seeger Decision. Their responses to the Conscientious Objector questionnaire show how cogent and yet inexpressible a private religious experience can be, especially when challenged to account for itself under fire. First question—do you believe in a Supreme Being? Peter answers that it depends on definitions. "Human life for me is a final value… I suppose you could call that a belief in the Supreme Being or God. These just do not happen to be the words I use." Jakobson recognizes an ultimate cause or creator of all existence, which he terms "Godness," and the taking of human life a contradiction of that Godness inherent in other people.

To this same question Seeger's response shows the most theological sophistication. "Of course, the existence of God cannot be proved or disproved," he says, "and the essence of God's nature cannot be determined. I prefer to admit this and leave the question open rather than answer yes or no." But then he introduces a shrewd distinction. Skepticism or disbelief in the existence of God does not necessarily mean lack of faith in anything whatsoever. For the martyrdom of Socrates shows that irony and skepticism may be consistent with positive faith. The Court of Appeals, in its earlier decision against Seeger, complaining of difficulties in pinning him down, conceded that perhaps there was almost no functional difference between Jakobson's devotion to a mystical force of "Godness"and Seeger's compulsion to "Goodness."

From Seeger's random affirmations Justice Clark construes the rudiments of religious legitimacy, much in the way I would help registrants organize their own draft board presentations. In summary, Clark thinks Seeger does in fact lay claim to a religious faith. Never overtly denying belief in a Supreme Being, Seeger holds that "the cosmic order does, perhaps, suggest a creative intelligence." Violence for Seeger becomes a "spiritual crime." Most important, this man's behavior seems to confirm the sincerity of his words. Raised as a Catholic, recently a close student of the Quakers, he had been serving currently as a dedicated hospital orderly under the American Friends Service Committee. "We think it clear," says Clark, "that the beliefs which prompted Seeger's objection occupy the same place in his life as the belief in a traditional deity holds in the lives of his friends, the Quakers."

The most rewarding hours of my own draft interviews were spent hearing out each value system, trying to grasp what touched a person most about happiness, love, work, and the purpose of life. Some of these applicants, identifying themselves with readily labeled sectarian pacifist churches, seemed to be religious insiders, secure both socially and legally. The majority, on the contrary, viewed themselves as religious outsiders, drifting in and out of legal recognition by the government. They referred to conscience or to a private religious world of their own, often dense and inarticulate. I was searching in their lives for any sense of ultimacy, a coherent ethics "in some way related to a Supreme Being," according to the Court's minimal demand. After an applicant was able to find words for his own idiosyncratic moral position, it was not difficult for me to help him trace its virtual religious implications. I was convinced, then as now, that the moral and religious dimensions, though distinct concepts, can never be separated in actual decisions about values.

Roots of Breakup

As interwoven religious-moral issues arose repeatedly in my interviews with religious dissenters I continued to wonder how and why this hyphenated adjective had been split apart in American history and law. Though heartened by my encounters with so many sincere pacifists I grew increasingly resentful against the historical sectarian rationale behind the religious exemption itself.

All versions of Selected Service legislation, and even the Seeger Court Decision, insisted that to merit an exemption the religious dissenter had to renounce all war and violence, not only this selected war at hand. Thus, just by certifying oneself an active member of the Amish or Jehovah's Witnesses, given their official stand on unconditional pacifism, an applicant met the requirements. Such a dissenter explained himself, not by moral reasoning but simply by an appeal to the authority of church tenets. War and other forms of violence were immoral, not because evil in themselves, but specifically because God had forbidden them. God's command had to be obeyed, no matter what its contents. The U.S. legal tradition seemed to anticipate only a single type of religious dissent, one based on what has been called a divine-command ethics. In its most popular form such an ethics treats actions as immoral *only* because God has forbidden them explicitly—by a direct public scriptural revelation or in a self-authenticated private vision.

Though mere proof of active pacifist church membership gained an automatic exemption, an applicant identifying himself as a Roman Catholic pacifist, on the contrary, met with immediate disapproval. Defending the moral feasibility of a justified defensive war, traditional Catholic ethics since Augustine in the fourth century tended to support only a selective pacifist position. Had I myself sought a draft-exemption during the Vietnam War, for example, I would have defined myself with honest complexity as a selective pacifist, evolving day by day into a total pacifist. Some draft-exemption applicants from the martial arts tradition explained their training in a range of tactics to disarm or immobilize an armed aggressor for protecting innocent victims, then themselves, and even their opponents from harm. Yet no draft board seemed ready to endorse such a subtle excuse as nonviolent. I thought peace advocates ought to back this rationale of proactive non-lethal defense as no less credible than the more familiar Gandhi style of heroic passivity.

It is no easy task to extend a pocket-size model of personal combat to the uncharted battlefields of modern technological warfare. For some years I could imagine an ideal scenario of limited justified combat— nation against nation, or forays across national borders to smoke out stateless terrorists—where soldiers had to obey the moral discipline of armed civilian police. Most important, those backing a war's initiation or continuance had to show compelling proof they had first explored every diplomatic solution, and would thereafter enforce all conditions limiting the range and severity of combat. Like civilian police, soldiers would be trained to track down criminal suspects not for revenge but for a just trial and punishment, to use no more force than necessary in pursuing or disarming their adversary, and to take no disproportionate risks that might harm innocent civilians. However, the more I have witnessed irrational public anger and mania in wartime, sales promotion by arms lobbyists, unreliable news coverage, the sweeping collateral damage caused by the latest weapon technology, and the deeper I examine past wars and their elusive prologues, the more I doubt that any military engagement today could fulfill the criteria for a fair proportionate response. It does not surprise me to read estimates that the proportion of civilian to combatant deaths has escalated from 5% in the First World War to 90% in the Gulf War. I will always dissent from the bombing of civilian targets or entire cities, the use of nuclear or biochemical weapons, or the strategy of driving adversaries to suicidal resistance by a demand for unconditional surrender.

Any Catholic peace advocate, then, has had to weather tough challenges under a longstanding U.S. legal tradition. To earn a draft-exemption the candidate must prove that all current warfare is unjust, say, because in practice it will erase the distinction between combatants and civilians, or because once conventional weapons fail, such a war will lead inevitably to a nuclear or biochemical holocaust. In my draft counseling years I watched this burden of argument fall not only on Catholics but on the majority of Christian dissenters, lacking pacifist church identity, and especially on agnostic humanists and others who had to frame their own moral position.

I could only conclude that existing civil law did not treat religious dissenters with equity, nor to my knowledge has that policy changed since then. Favoring the pacifist churches, draft legislation heated up almost everyone else's stand on nonviolence from moderate to absolutist, all or nothing. Each applicant's statement was first pried loose from a genuine personal ethics of story and virtue—a coherent ethics in its own right, which I will explore in a later chapter. The account of conscience had then to be repackaged for the draft board as an ethics of legal deduction. The process of preparing this defense brief seemed to deconstruct and devalue the original moral experience itself. The law appeared to imply that the authority of one's own conscience dared not compete with the authority of the Bible, nor with the authority of private revelations claimed by some pacifist-church founder.

Tilt toward Religious Extremes

Despite these grievances, during my years as a draft counselor I never lost respect for members of the so-called "peace churches"—

Mennonites, Amish, Hutterites, Quakers, and all those pre-Reformation, Protestant, and later millennial sectarians, historically sorted into the Far Left Wing of Protestant Christianity. Few other Protestants had applied so thoroughly to daily life the Reformation cry of "Only Scripture, only Grace." Mostly because of their stubborn religious dissent since the U.S. colonial era, all explicitly pacifist churches had earned a draft exemption which today could at least be extended to non-church members. From my youngest years I had mingled with quaintly dressed Mennonite families at department stores and the bus depot in my Pennsylvania home town and learned to appreciate their earnest, even if inconsistent, quarrel with modern technology. I had heard that during the Vietnam War some Mennonite communities boldly used to ship medical and food supplies to South and even North Vietnam, both sides of the conflict, a gesture reminiscent of their commendable historical opposition to slavery, oaths, and military service. I suspect today that contemporary society finds it easy to approve the white hot sincerity of these dissenters, provided they remain a quiet folksy minority.

After the Vietnam War, searching through radical Protestant sources with more rigor, I began to close in on a few key motifs I thought responsible for the wall between religious and moral realms. Like confessions by saints in most religious traditions, Anabaptist spiritual diaries tended to dramatize the soul's conversion experience as an enormous rupture between sin and grace, between the worldly past and the otherworldly present. In the most famous Anabaptist martyrology, Tieleman Jansz van Braght's *The Martyrs' Mirror*, composed in the sixteenth century, dialectical motifs common to the New Testament are boosted to feverish intensity—God and Satan, Christ and Anti-Christ, spirit and flesh, gospel and law, grace and good works, inner and outer meaning. From my own perspective, a fixation on these abundant polarities seems more Zoroastrian, Gnostic, or Manichaen than Christian. The history of the world "has been from the very beginning a conflict between God and Satan," Braght affirms, "the children of light and the children of darkness." Salvation history consists of two opposing forces, "two different peoples, two different congregations and churches, the one from God and from heaven, the other of Satan and the earth."[5]

The generic term *Anabaptist* underlines a common feature in various sixteenth century sectarian groups to welcome only adult converts for membership, and to rebaptize those already baptized elsewhere in infancy. Flourishing especially in Switzerland, Germany, and the Netherlands, this Calvinist-Anabaptist impulse when exported to England launched within the Anglican Church a range of separatist and non-separatist factions. Many of these groups later emigrated to the United States under the name of Puritans, Pilgrims, Anabaptists, Baptists, and others. Though the platforms of these small divergent communities varied, almost all Anabaptists treated the larger society as still unredeemed and corrupt. They saw their own small communistic cells as God's Elect in the final age, trying to live uncontaminated from other Christians and the world. Anabaptists hoped in their own covenant groups to live out the Gospel, adhering to the Sermon on the Mount as literally as possible, notably Christ's command and example of nonviolent brotherly love. "Love your enemies," he said. "Pray for those who hurt you" (MATT 5:44).

I discovered to my relief that not every early Anabaptist community taught total pacifism in the current U.S. legal understanding of the word. Many Anabaptists were actually selective pacifists, not the absolutists destined to serve in later U.S. law as the exclusive model for automatic draft exemption. Perhaps many of the first Anabaptists themselves, like most draft candidates today, including those from recognized peace churches, found themselves unable to reason out an ethics of unconditional pacifism. Majority governments may have found it easier to sweep all dissenters to the margins under a single label of cranky extremism, rather than cope with responsible moral debates about the legitimacy of each particular war. I imagine Anabaptist preachers, defending a literal interpretation of all biblical commands, must have strained to find consistency between Christ's commands of total pacifism and Old Testament commands to slay noncombatants in a holy war.

Historians explain that during the sixteenth and seventeenth centuries the combined church-state authority in Europe required a uniform feudal loyalty. Entire populations were expected to endorse the incidental religion of a particular region or current ruler. Some Anabaptists refused all obedience to both state-church and civil leaders, others only to the state-church, but others only to the state's demands for military service in religious wars. Some refused to serve in any war against fellow Christians, or in all wars. Some would not serve but paid war taxes, and others refused all forms of cooperation in any war. The most common rationale for passive obedience or nonobedience was a literal interpretation of Christ's pacifist message cited above, his own nonresistance to crucifixion, and the example of persecuted early Roman Christians.[6]

"Render to Caesar what is Caesar's, and to God what is God's." This biblical saying of Jesus would provoke a debate throughout Christian history about how two such contrasting realms could coexist. In the pre-Constantinian era and later, controversy focused on two favorite scriptural texts. Chapter 12 of Paul's Letter to the Romans states: "Let every person submit to the governing authorities. There is no authority except by an act of God, and the existing authorities are instituted by God. Consequently anyone who rebels against authority is resisting a divine institution... Pay tax and toll, reverence and respect, toward those to whom they are due." In this passage the conciliatory attitude of Paul toward Roman authority seems to parallel the assumption behind Acts of the Apostles, that the Pax Romana and superior network of Roman law and communications will offer a providential backdrop for dispersal of the Gospel. Martin Luther, always wary of Anabaptist extremists, interpreted this passage as a strict vindication of secular authority. Terrified of anarchy, he hoped that princes, not church authorities, would be the more trustworthy guardians of order. Yet later the princes, too, would disappointment him.

The antithesis to this text is chapter 13 in the Book of Revelation. If Paul's Letter took for granted an acculturated Greco-Roman, world-affirming, middle-class perception of the Roman empire, the Book of Revelation seems to have risen from a militant Jewish separatist tradition, speaking for the marginal and slave proletariat. Written most likely toward the end of the first century, during the reign of Domitian, its imagery is cryptic and bloody. Loathsome beasts assume political power and demand to be worshiped as Gods, mouthing blasphemy and filth, at war against God's people, "deluding all inhabitants of the earth, making them erect an image in honor of the beast... Rich and poor, slave and free, had to be branded... with the mark of the beast." Interpreted according to apocalyptic genre conventions, this work seems a disguised attack against the current totalitarian regimes of Nero and Domitian.

Now transformed into a satanic power, Rome must be endured or overthrown.[7]

Celebrated in the Book of Revelation this suffering remnant of saints and martyrs was the only true Church, as radical Anabaptist communities viewed themselves. They yearned to communicate directly with God and to shape their own individual conscience, untouched by the agents of an organized church or society. As apologists for disengagement from politics and war—despite rare outbursts of extreme militancy, as at Münster—Anabaptists would be targeted ironically as a threat by both Catholic and Protestant civil leaders in the Reformation era and persecuted with violence. They may have started out as good neighbors toward the surrounding majority. Yet opposition hardened them, sparking a martyr's sense of apocalyptic fatalism which disengaged them ever further from the social order outside.

The quintessential Anabaptist in American history was Roger Williams, founder and first governor of Rhode Island. In turns an Anglican, Calvinist, Puritan, Quaker, Baptist, and so-called Seeker, he kept hunting for a church so pure that it grew less and less visible to him. He became increasingly impatient with any civil or church authority that intruded upon his own internal relationship with God. While a minister in the Massachusetts Bay Colony he preached against the equivocal Puritan style of non-separatism. The covenant-theologian majority, convinced that Puritan Congregationalists alone belonged to the true internal Christian church, had abandoned Anglican liturgy and church authority yet still professed external Anglican membership. Banished by the Bay Colony for his separatist heresy in 1636, Williams carved out of the wilderness a new community where church and state could exist "separated," each realm stripped of all theocratic pretensions. No citizen would be persecuted or forced to conform against conscience. From that century's Christian perspective such a regime seemed an unworkable novelty.

Anabaptists throughout their history would claim the primacy of individual conscience as long as they were an oppressed minority. Yet once they in turn became the state majority many soon regressed to the rigidity of their former persecutors and refused tolerance toward any conscience dissenting from the new civil consensus. To Williams' credit, on the contrary, as governor of Rhode Island he continued to welcome

Quakers, Jews, and almost any type of dissenting Christian as citizens. In his experience church authorities, whether Catholic or Protestant, tended to fall into the same trap: "They are so partial as to persecute when they sit at the helm and yet cry out against persecution when they are under the hatches."[8]

Ironically the most brazen defense for this religious double-standard challenged by Williams can be found in the political theology of Cardinal Alfredo Ottaviani, leader of the traditionalist forces at the Second Vatican Council. He reasoned that when in the minority, Catholics should agitate for universal religious equality or even separation of church and state. Yet when in the majority, Catholics should restrict the rights of minority religious traditions in that society, for "error has no rights." Repudiating this mind set, the Council majority insisted that whereas error in the abstract may have no rights, individual persons acting in conscience do have rights.[9]

True to their separatist spirit most sectarians resisted being molded according to the laws of civil society or the abstractions of moral philosophy. Regulated in detail by God's biblical word, a life of service to God became increasingly walled off from service to the human community. Despite the brave independence of many Anabaptists, I think they have left a troublesome legacy. On the United States legal tradition, especially, they imprinted an ethics of divine command, a naive biblical literalism, and a harmful dichotomy between loyalty within the church community and loyalty beyond it.

Tilt against Religious Extremes

A one-sided religious ethics tends to provoke a one-sided anti-religious moral rebuttal, and both these extremes have raised a barrier between the religious and moral dimensions of experience. A number of my draft counseling registrants, identifying themselves at first as hostile to religion in general, soon narrowed their aversion mostly against a specific ethics of divine-command. They disputed any attempt to extol biblical or even private revelation at the risk of discrediting conscience and moral reason. Few of them had ever explored any alternate coherent form of religious-moral reflection. I would describe these critics mostly as *moral humanists*—people averse to traditional religious tags but pledged to defend and extend human values. To me their plausible complaints seemed to reincarnate voices of the great classical moral humanists, whom I had once dismissed as too carping. I was beginning to discover new appreciation for the wit and moral passion of figures like Socrates and Ben Franklin.

I could now imagine myself playing Socrates' role in the *Euthyphro*, one of Plato's earliest dialogues, which sets up a naive religious zealot as easy prey for Socratic irony. In Plato's Athens, an era evolving from *mythos* to *logos*, the traditionalist Euthyphro still treats his religious tradition mostly as a matter of oaths, oracles, ritual sacrifice, prayer formulas, avoidance of pollution taboos, and knowledge of sacred myth. Accepting the myths literally, he typifies the mentality of Socrates' public adversaries, scandalized by the efforts of Socrates to demythologize these treasured religious stories.

The exchange between Socrates and Euthyphro takes place on the steps to the court house, where Euthyphro intends to denounce his father to authorities for indirectly causing the death of an unruly servant. Euthyphro seems less disturbed about his father's actual guilt or innocence for manslaughter than about the ritual pollution spreading from this crime to his family and property. The chief motive given for informing on his father is that the Gods forbid murder and have decreed retribution for so serious a crime. He unwisely boasts of special skill at discerning between what pleases and what displeases the Gods. Listening carefully to Euthyphro's reasons, Socrates tries to undermine the man's self-confidence, first by prodding him to acknowledge a conflict in filial piety, directed now toward his father, and now toward the Gods. If piety means anything at all, should not his horizontal filial duty bear more immediate weight than his vertical religious duty?

Socrates' next attack is more cogent. Any polytheist trying to be moral but also obedient to the Gods has to face the quandary that two Gods might disagree about what is morally right. William James would later commend the polytheistic imagination in ancient Greece and elsewhere for tolerating so many colliding images, drawn from divergent religious experiences, unique to every person. For an orderly monistic or monotheistic system, he fears, succumbs to a craving for logical coherence and trims rich ambiguity from the mystery. But this ambiguity and obscurity are precisely what Socrates the moralist calls into question. If Euthyphro interprets the stories literally about Gods clashing with one another, then Socrates demands: "Now it appears that what is loved by the Gods is also hated by them." And thus, in denouncing your father, "you may be pleasing to Zeus but displeasing to Cronus and Uranus, pleasing to Hephaestus but displeasing to Hera, and so with any other Gods who differ from each other on this subject."

Less confident now, Euthyphro decides that murder is most likely the one crime declared wrong by a universal consensus of the Gods. After this admission Socrates introduces his third and most powerful critique. Since Euthyphro knows that human beings have already reached a consensus against murder, perhaps this sheer human precedent is the main reason why the man concludes Gods have reached a parallel consensus. "Consider this," Socrates now insists. "Is the pious loved by the Gods because it is pious, or is it pious because it is loved by the Gods?" In other words, is any impiety against his father or the Gods wrong in itself and thus unacceptable to the Gods, or wrong only because it is unacceptable to the Gods? As I interpret him, Euthyphro never answers this pivotal question.

The dialogue itself soon dissolves into tedious Socratic word-play, and Euthyphro excuses himself to escape further humiliation. But before the end, Socrates extracts a few more concessions from him. He acknowledges first that piety is only one part of a more inclusive human attribute, justice. Though human beings need our service, the Gods can manage without it. In conclusion Socrates implies that Euthyphro ought to focus not on the Gods' decrees but on human reason and direct his service, not to the Gods, but to his fellow human beings.[10]

Confronted by lightweight literalists of this sort, Socrates marginalizes, almost silences, the religious side of the moral-religious dialectic. This impulse to dethrone, demystify, or to secularize religion would reach its apogee in the eighteenth century. For then, as moral philosophers looked back at fierce religious wars of the preceding two centuries, they decided that the self-appointed interpreters of biblical sources had long discredited themselves. If each battling Christian sect could arrogate its own privileged revelation directly from God or preach its own idiosyncratic reading of one shared Bible, what authority but human reason itself could arbitrate between militant religious contenders? As a parody of this confident sectarian style, I recall a meeting of Jesuit teachers a few decades ago. A dispute arose whether or not to move an urban Catholic high school to a suburban neighborhood, more insulated from the encroaching ghetto. One older voice spoke with an air of devout certainty. It had been revealed to him in prayer, he said, that Jesus himself would never abandon the Inner City. This remark elicited a facetious rejoinder from a fellow teacher, contending that he himself had received a contrary revelation from Mary and Joseph, worried that their child would be endangered walking alone after dark in that neighborhood.

A widely acclaimed sage of the Enlightenment Era, Ben Franklin recounts his frustrated efforts in colonial America to tolerate intolerant sectarians such as Quakers, Dunkers, Anabaptists, and some mainline Protestant crusaders. While Socrates had to deal with religious conflicts personified as a rivalry between Gods, Franklin found Christian prophets disputing among themselves, each making exclusive claims about the same God. Every sect supposed itself in possession of all truth, he complains in his autobiography, and those who differ from the sect are heretical. Self-confident believers, traveling in foggy weather, are prone to view those ahead and behind as if wrapped in fog and only themselves in the clear. Yet everyone is actually engulfed in fog.

Therefore, applying his own Deist grid transparency to the creed of his local Presbyterian Church, Franklin salvages such doctrines as God's existence, providence, and the belief that "the most acceptable service of God is doing good to man." These essentials he winnows from the Calvinist doctrines of eternal election and reprobation, and "other articles which, without any tendency to inspire, promote, or confirm morality, served principally to divide us, and make us unfriendly to one another."[11] What survives after his critique is just the moral factor: "works of kindness, charity, mercy, and public spirit. Not holiday-keeping, sermon-reading or hearing, performing church ceremonies, or making long prayers, filled with flatteries and compliments, despised even by wise men, and much less capable of pleasing the Deity."[12]

Whereas Jefferson would push his confident rationalism to the limit by rewriting the New Testament, Franklin just composes his own prayerbook, an abridged liturgy, and a more coherent version of the Our Father. He reinterprets Christ exclusively as the great moral teacher. Christ "preferred the doers of the word to the mere hearers; the son that seemingly refused to obey his father yet performed his commands, to him that professed his readiness but neglected the work; the heretical but charitable Samaritan to the uncharitable though orthodox priest and sanctified Levite; and those who gave food to the hungry, drink to the thirsty, raiment to the naked, entertainment to the stranger, and relief to the sick, though they never heard of his name."[13]

One of the most playful and daring pages in Franklin is his forgery of an Old Testament tale commending tolerance even toward the unbeliever. Because the Bible can serve too easily as an arsenal for quotations to condone intolerance, Franklin the moralist concludes he might as well devise a few helpful passages of his own to undo the mischief. Accustomed to spring this quotation on credulous Bible zealots, he could trick them with such persuasive archaisms as "Lo, I have sinned" and "Nay, for I will abide." In this story Abraham invites an elderly stranger for a meal of unleavened bread in his tent, but quarrels with his guest for not offering table prayers to Abraham's God. After expelling this unbeliever into the wilderness, Abraham hears God calling him, "Abraham, where is the stranger?... Have I borne with him these hundred and ninety and eight years, and nourished him, and clothed him, notwithstanding his rebellion against me; and couldst not thou, who art thyself a sinner, bear with him one night?"[14]

Moral humanists like Socrates and Franklin have commonly adopted an antireligious rhetoric. They tend to distrust the self-appointed religious visionary anxious to meddle in the reasonable deliberation and compromises needed for a stable social morality. Yet behind the rebuttal of humanists against all religion I imagine them trying most of all to defend their own implicit religious ethics against an apparent religious counterfeit.

A Sound Religious Ethics and Its Counterfeits

Whether the religious-moral factor will retain its balance or split into two alienated realms depends mostly on the way people decide to interpret religious revelation. The biblical figure of Abraham offers a familiar illustration of two contrasting interpretations. In the first God's revelation overrides human values; in the second God's revelation both challenges and confirms human values. The shocking account of Abraham's readiness to sacrifice his son shows up in the Book of Genesis, and later, with significant changes, in the Quran. The version familiar to Jews and Christians confronts Abraham with a series of tests, each progressively more arduous. Asked to leave his parents and homeland for a site as yet unrevealed, and then to banish his concubine and her son Ishmael, Abraham is now directed to kill his son Isaac in a sacrificial ritual. This is the culminating test of a father's faith, for until now Isaac's birth had seemed a miraculous gift for Abraham and Sarah in their old age. With no complaint he obeys God by preparing the victim. At last a voice from heaven tells him: "Now I know you fear God. You have not refused me your son, your only son" (GEN 22:12). Abraham then locates a ram nearby, which he offers as a substitute sacrifice.

Conformity to the Divine Command

The summit of Abraham's faith has been reinterpreted in Soren Kierkegaard's most popular work, *Fear and Trembling*, as a "teleological suspension of the ethical." It is helpful to recognize in this proto-existentialist prophet a worthy heir to the sectarian Anabaptists of two centuries before. The theology of Kierkegaard raises a fist of outrage against the sterile "Christendom" of the Danish Lutheran State Church with its paid functionaries and triumphant steeples. Christians must return to true inwardness, to the faith of persecuted small communities idealized in the New Testament and the pre-Constantinian church of the catacombs. This genuine leap of faith has to be no less unquestioning and literal than the trust of Abraham.

Like Abraham, Kierkegaard's model sectarian Knight of Faith must turn against the moral law of conscience and especially against the law of rationalistic Kantian moral philosophy. It is ironic that both Twain's Huck Finn and Kierkegaard's Knight of Faith renounce what they call "conscience." Yet whereas Huck rejects only the complacent folk wisdom of his society, the Knight rejects the very certainties derived exclusively from a person's own reasoning and intuition. The Knight must adhere literally to God's biblical word, no matter how arbitrary and unintelligible it may appear. In other writings Kierkegaard would suggest the possibility that a mature conscience might be reconciled with God's grace at some later stage of Christian maturity. Yet pondering just the Kierkegaardian version of Abraham's faith presented in *Fear and Trembling*, I cannot imagine a more shocking parable for a dichotomy between the religious and moral life.[15]

A divine-command ethics, as described earlier, spells out the implications of this dualistic Kierkegaardian model—a passionate religious faith split off from moral reasoning. The believer condemns war and violence, say, not because these actions are inherently wrong, but only because God's direct revelation has declared them wrong. I concede that the weasel term "divine command" can refer to extrinsic dictates imposed by a tyrannical God but also point to my intrinsic conscience at its noblest moment of choice. With similar ambiguity the mother-image may function for some people as a superego-shrew or it can personify the ideal interpersonal values passed along to a mature daughter or son. In draft-counseling I tried to expand my limited horizons to welcome a generous range of moral deliberation, including logic, feelings, virtuous priorities, all the intricate reasons of the heart. Far from ruling out the hidden prompting of God's grace, I always presumed its presence. If an applicant happened to mention his explicit intent to follow God's will I interpreted him first to be searching for God's guidance by a careful sifting through the urges of conscience. However, a divine-command ethics, in its most popular form, makes more extreme claims than the need for this prayerful self-scrutiny. Every major moral decision has to certify its derivation from God's word, revealed either in sacred scripture or in a direct private vision.

One obvious motif runs through the anti-religious rebuttals of Plato, Franklin, Kant, and Freud—their shared antipathy, not against all religious ethics, but specifically against the ethics of divine command. Even a half-century before Kierkegaard, Immanuel Kant was attacking any literalist Christian defense of Abraham's obedience. Kant thought the biblical Abraham should have responded to God's alleged command by asserting his own moral dissent in the following way: "That I ought not to kill my good son is certain beyond a shadow of a doubt. That you, as you appear to be, are God, I am not convinced and will never be, even if your voice would resound from the heavens."[16] And elsewhere, Kant concluded, "The reason for regarding suicide and other transgressions of duty as abominable must be derived, not from the divine will, but from their inherently abominable nature... Suicide is not abominable because

God has forbidden it. On the contrary, God has forbidden it because it is abominable."[17]

Kant's contemporary, Ben Franklin, summons almost the same words of critique. "Vicious actions are not hurtful because they are forbidden, but forbidden because they are hurtful," he writes in his autobiography. "Revelation had indeed no weight with me as such. But I entertained an opinion that though certain actions might not be bad because they were forbidden by it, or good because it commanded them, yet probably those actions might be forbidden because they were bad for us or commanded because they were beneficial for us, in their own natures, all the circumstances of things considered."[18] And Freud, a twentieth-century stepchild of the Enlightenment, feared that conventional religious beliefs would soon disappear. The moral life must be based, then, not on religious sanctions with their vanishing halo of authority, but on inherent natural rights or, more clearly, on a consensus enacted into international law. "If the sole reason why you must not kill your neighbor is because God has forbidden it and will severely punish you for it in this or the next life," says Freud, "then, when you learn that there is no God and that you need not fear God's punishment, you will certainly kill your neighbor without hesitation, and you can only be prevented from doing so by mundane force."[19]

In some eras people grow so accustomed to the touchstone of imperious civil or church authority that they find it easy to imagine God in analogous terms of power. The King, the Party, the Pope, or God have spoken, and thus their might makes right. A current bumper-sticker expresses this attitude succinctly: "God has said it. I believe it. That settles it." The power of reason, undermined by sinfulness, has proven so unreliable a moral guide that it needs to be replaced by God's direct intervention. During the late Middle Ages especially, God was often imagined as the omnipotent sovereign, the Uncaused Cause, answerable to no moral criterion beyond God's own will. This viewpoint runs parallel to a voluntarist legal tradition emphasizing, not the intrinsic reasonability of a law's contents, but the extrinsic authority of the law-giver and the technical conditions needed for a law's valid promulgation.

Some theologians in one famous thought-experiment even suggested the Hebrew God could have decided arbitrarily to hand Moses an alternate set of commandment tablets, reading, "Thou shalt steal, lie,

and murder." It is ironic that a divine-command ethics, accepted by the
U.S. legal tradition as grounds for exempting religious pacifists from war,
could by the same capricious authority have turned their pacifism into
violence. Jean Calvin, for example, taught that everything God wills must
be thought righteous by the mere fact that God wills it. To my own
Catholic consciousness today, sensitized to the menace of totalitarian
regimes, under the banner of God or humanity, St. Ignatius Loyola's *Rules
for Thinking, Judging, and Feeling with the Church* looks like counter-
reformation hype, easily misquoted as an invitation to self-deception,
even idolatry: "What seems white to me, I will believe to be black if the
hierarchical Church so determines it."[20] At the extreme, believers of this
sort tend to genuflect before the slightest hints of the Sacred or to obey a
religious command merely because of its religious label, no matter how
unintelligible or unethical its import.

A one-sided subservience toward God's authority, I am convinced,
has several negative side-effects. In the previous chapter, describing the
emergence of my own preadolescent conscience, I tried to distinguish
between conscience and superego, between true guilt and mere guilt
feelings, between a mature selective obedience and an immature hunger
for approval. To the extent that the ethics of divine command calls my
decision immoral only because God designates it so, I cannot accept this
justification for a sound moral choice. Caught in a zero-sum game, it
instills an authoritarian mind-set—the scope of divine power enlarges, to
the diminishment of human reason and judgment. By fixating on God's
law revealed in one particular scriptural tradition, this ethics can
underrate God's law revealed globally, imprinted within every individual
conscience.[21]

An Ethics of Loyal Scrutiny

Unlike the ethics of divine command, my own theology treats the
religious and the moral, the Sacred and the Good as inseparable. God and
we ourselves, created in God's image, share one identical moral standard.
To determine which claims to moral authority might be plausibly divine,
or what moral implications ought to be drawn from any selected biblical
passage, I must first consult my own reflective moral judgments. If to take
something on faith means to accept it only on God's authority, still I must
try to resolve any apparent disparities between the various authoritative

modes of God's revelation—God speaking in my conscience, but also God speaking in Scripture, historical events, in wisdom from the evolving human sciences, and countless other ways. Thus, when God seems to command me I believe I must be ready to obey. Yet before obeying I have to determine the moral legitimacy of what seems to be commanded. I will call this frame of mind an *ethics of loyal scrutiny*.

The ethics of divine command can be epitomized in Dostoyevsky's oft-cited credo, written in a Siberian prison: "If anyone proved to me that Christ is outside the 'truth,' and this really meant that 'truth' is outside Christ, then I would prefer to remain with Christ than with 'truth.'" I want to replace this rationale with an ethics inspired by Meister Eckhart's no less famous credo: "Truth — so noble a thing, that could 'God' turn aside from it, I would cling to Truth and let 'God' go." Eckhart's manifesto echoes in Gandhi: "For me, God and Truth are convertible terms. And if anyone told me that God was a God of untruth or a God of torture, I would decline to worship God." My sort of ethics reaffirms the parliamentary custom of a Loyal Opposition party, which aims to keep political life honest, to remain vigilant toward any abuse, and never to break off mutual respect and dialogue. I find the prototype for these moral values in a less well known facet of Abraham's faith — the missing human side to his Knight of Faith compliance.

A few chapters before Abraham's ordeal about sacrificing Isaac, the Book of Genesis describes God poised to destroy everyone in the city of Sodom. Hoping to pare down the number of victims as far as possible, Abraham begins to bargain with God. "I trust my Lord will not be angry, but give me leave to speak," he says. "I am bold indeed to speak like this to my Lord, I who am dust and ashes." Surely, God would not want to punish righteous people along with the sinners? God is prodded gradually to revoke the original plan, if at least a few righteous can be located. Abraham's most forceful argument, I think, is the following: "Do not think of it! Will the judge of the whole earth not administer justice? (GEN 18: 25)"

In a midrashic commentary on this biblical text the rabbinic tradition imagines God's perspective in the dialogue over Sodom's fate. Abraham has argued that by agreeing to a Covenant after the flood God once promised never to destroy the earth again, but now would God indeed send a deluge of fire instead of water? "What else could I do?" says

God. "People cast aspersions upon me and say, 'He does not judge correctly'. Go, then, and examine my judgment, and if I have erred, you teach me!"[22] Here are the essential components for an ethics, not of divine command, but of loyal scrutiny. It is based on faithful I-Thou intimacy with a personal God, a partnership of familiar conversation, with room for mutual affection, candor, rough playfulness, audacity, and even anger. Abraham and God are bound by one identical moral standard to such an extent that God's own law can be quoted against God. God must be faithful to God's own word. God the judge must administer the same justice that human beings are expected to show one another on earth.

With echoes of the two contrasting Abraham stories already recounted, a contemporary short story by Hugh Nissenson, "The Blessing," introduces a young father stunned by his eight-year-old son's death from cancer. Yitshaak declares his refusal to say the conventional prayer, "Blessed art thou, O Lord," at the approaching funeral rites. For it would seem monstrous and humiliating to sanctify God's apparent crime. His Aunt Esther, on the contrary, whose own faith had been tested in the Belsen concentration camp long ago, presses him to say the words anyway, even if the familiar Hebrew God-image and verses seem to collide against his immediate grief and anger. Esther on their home balcony proceeds with evening prayers, as expected, addressed to the orderly stars. For she had never ceased blessing God her tormentor. But Yitshaak, rebelling against the orderly formulas and sky, feels excluded by the tumult of his heart.[23]

At risk of oversimplifying the character of Aunt Esther, I imagine her rooted in a spirituality of divine command. At this point of life her faith seems profound, seasoned by undeniable suffering, her very literalism a mark of resilience and fidelity. A spirituality like Esther's must stand as a caution against belittling or demonizing any person struggling to obey God's will. Yitshaak, on the contrary, cannot identify with this type of faith, which unfortunately looks like the only path to remain a faithful religious Jew. He seems banished from Esther's prayer tradition, with no perception that his tears themselves and the very wrestling with God might be his one truly relevant prayer. I suppose an abrasive gesture of loyal scrutiny would strike him as blasphemous. Yet even cursing God still seems faithful in its own way, never cutting off contact. God at least remains a living personal reality that people take seriously enough to blaspheme.

This pattern of confronting God with bold, impatient complaints pervades the biblical narrative of Jacob wrestling with an angel or Job invoking God as advocate to plead his case in court against God who is both the judge and the guilty defendant. It recurs in Jeremiah's outspoken lamentations and the various Psalms that indict God for being too aloof or half-hearted to answer prayers. Even the somber Prophet Muhammad, according to various narrative traditions, was prompted during his visionary night journey to bargain playfully with Allah for a reduction in the number of required times for daily prayer.[24] In the New Testament, Jesus tells a few parables urging a prayer of brash persistence, an attitude compared to waking up a friend to get food or hounding an unjust judge to fulfill his obligations (LUKE 11:5-8 and 18:1-8). His own cry of reproach during crucifixion repeats a complaint from the Psalms: "My God, my God, why have you abandoned me!"

None of these non-Jewish sources, however, seems to match the devout audacity of one Hasidic story about the tailor who confessed the following sins on Yom Kippur: "Today is the Day of Judgment. One must repent. But I didn't sin much. I took a little left-over cloth from the rich. I once drank a glass of brandy and ate some bread without washing my hands. These are all my transgressions. But you, Master of the Universe, how many are your transgressions! You have taken away small children who had not sinned. From others you have taken away the mothers of these children. But I shall forgive you your transgressions, and I ask you to forgive mine." Listening to this prayer in sympathy, the officiating rabbi insisted that if he himself had been the tailor he would not have forgiven God until God sent the Messiah.[25]

My favorite tale from the Talmud is "The Oven of Akhnai," where a group of rabbis argue to apply the Torah text correctly to Akhnai's problem of moral choice. Rabbi Eliezer is driven in exasperation to perform a few dazzling miracles to sanction his own interpretation. He even solicits a heavenly voice to say, "Halakhah is always as Eliezer teaches it." But Rabbi Yoshua cries, "The Torah says not even to trust voices from heaven!" Rabbi Yirma agrees, "You yourself, God, told us on Mt. Sinai to follow the community of those who agree on the truth." Then the heavenly voice is silent. Later, Rabbi Natan meets the prophet Elijah in the vicinity, who reports that God's reaction to the entire contest was only to laugh and exclaim, "My children have defeated me, my children have defeated me!"[26] As I interpret this story, God is a wise teacher and counselor, glad to be overruled at the hands of God's disciples who struggle by their prayerful initiative to discover the right moral decision themselves. God's will does not have to be imposed from the outside but can empower an emergent moral consensus within God's faithful community.

Though the obvious context for this ethics of loyal scrutiny is a prayer of confrontation addressed to a personal God, it can be adapted to the inner wrestlings with conscience in all religious traditions. Many examples of an iconoclastic spirituality come to mind, attempts to trim down the authority of a particular sacred text, saint, guru, or anything else that could be mistaken for the Sacred. A Zen Buddhist master warns, "If you meet Buddha on the road, kill the Buddha!" Gandhi treats the Bible, Quran, even the Hindu Vedas, all as imperfect representations of God's will, and insists he must "decline to be bound by any interpretation, however learned it may be, if it is repugnant to reason or moral sense." Searching for the ideal guru, he admits he has never found someone who could be thus enthroned in his heart. The throne has remained empty, and his search continues. With a similar attitude, the Hindu mystic Ramakrishna compares the quest for Brahman the Absolute to a thief's hunt in some dark chamber for a cask of jewels. Brushing up against article after article, he murmurs, "Not this, not this," but through these negations will gradually close in on the treasure.[27]

The average moral humanist I interviewed in draft-counselling showed a susceptibility to dreams about an ideal society, stripped of all conventional political and religious authority. The worst setback imaginable would be trading a person's hard-won mature independence for blind obedience within a religious sect or cult. Yet slogans about a humanist Golden Age, I think, no less than slogans about the Christian Millennium, can be misused by totalitarian societies to shut off inquiry and sanction violence. An insightful parody of this utopian vision can be pieced together from Aldous Huxley's familiar anti-utopian classic, Brave New World. To avoid overpopulation and the pathology shaped by dysfunctional family dynamics, people in such a society are cloned according to desired type in test-tubes. They are then reared for mass conformity, pacified by drugs, permitted no disruptive experiences of the moral or beautiful.

At the heart of Huxley's novel is a quarrel about the nature of the good life between the New World's technocrat dictator Mustapha Mond and John the Savage. John had been raised according to Old World customs on a reservation, a mesa kept as a cautionary museum for New World visitors — live scenarios of babies clinging to biological mothers, lovers intertwined, people reading Shakespeare or enjoying a flower. Rather than capitulate to the dehumanized utopia of Mustapha Mond, John reverts to the shocking Primal Way of his reservation homeland— self-whipping, mantra-chanting, ecstatic trance, in an orgy of purification and atonement that appears to end in suicide.

In his preface to this novel's reissue in 1946, Huxley makes a wise concession about its one crucial defect. "The Savage is offered only two alternatives, an insane life in Utopia, or the life of a primitive in an Indian village, a life more human in some respects, but in others hardly less queer and abnormal." If he could rewrite the book, Huxley would add a third alternative. "Between the utopian and the primitive horns of his dilemma would lie the possibility of sanity," he concluded. "Religion would be the conscious and intelligent pursuit of man's Final End, the unitive knowledge of the imminent Tao or Logos, the transcendent Godhead or Brahman."[28]

The present chapter has argued that subservience to an ethics of divine command so polarizes the religious and moral factors that it triggers the religious extremity of John the Savage, and as a corollary, the anti-religious extremity of moral technocrats like Mustapha Mond. As a replacement for this divisive rationale, the ethics of loyal scrutiny presumes a vital partnership between the religious and moral factors. Somewhere between religious authoritarian claims by Anabaptists or Kierkegaard, and the anti-religious rebuttal of moral humanists like Socrates or Ben Franklin, stands Huxley's third alternative, identical to my own. The religious-moral position I hope to formulate in subsequent chapters must be compatible with a complete human life, not cut off from it by an anti-rational leap of faith.

3

AN EARTH-CENTERED ETHICS

I N EARLIER CHAPTERS I TOLD THE STORY OF A GRAPHIC CHILDHOOD encounter, from which I tried to derive guidelines for moral reflection in general. Then I described a later phase, prompted by interviews with pacifist dissenters, which led me to probe for the roots beneath disparities between religion and ethics in the U.S. legal system. A one-sided religious ethics, provoking a one-sided anti-religious moral rebuttal—these two extremes have driven a wedge between the religious and moral dimensions of experience. In the present chapter, however, it is time to explore prospects for religious-moral collaboration that will prove more encouraging. Rather than start from experiences of my own and then generalize, as I did before, I will now reverse this process and sketch an overview on the broadest canvas imaginable—four chapters toward a social ethics of the environment and human rights. My concluding seventh chapter will scale down in scope to an individual ethics of virtue, social character, and story, the necessary spiritual counterpart to a public ethics of minimal legal protection.

At the head of this book's Prologue I have chosen an epigraph summing up Albert Einstein's guiding vision, and also my own. Posted on the Internet in several different versions, this quotation serves today as a popular motto. The words were allegedly written in 1950 in reply to a rabbi's plea. Overwhelmed by the death of his daughter, the man pressed Einstein for some form of consolation that did not smack of conventional religion. "A human being is part of the whole, which we call 'Universe,'" Einstein explains, "a part limited in time and space. We experience ourselves, our thoughts and feelings, as something separated from the rest, a kind of optical delusion of consciousness. This delusion is a kind of prison for us, restricting us to our personal desires and to affection for a few persons nearest to us. Our task must be to free ourselves from this prison by widening our circle of compassion to embrace all living creatures and the whole of nature in its beauty."[1]

What I appreciate about Einstein's credo is its immense inclusiveness, spanning humanity, the Sacred, all the animate and inanimate environment. The man of science speaks from a seasoned perspective that is holistic, alert to spiritual, moral, and aesthetic reverberations. He suggests that most human failures arise, not so much from willful malice as from self-delusion and a nearsighted spirituality. He implies the myth of a lone self, yearning for solidarity with other splinters of the cosmos, which despite its fragmented appearance has never lost an interrelational coherence. Such a tale could be inserted easily into a context of modern process and quantum thought, the philosophy of German Idealism and American Transcendentalism, British Romantic poetry, but especially the teaching of Hindu Vedanta, and the Buddhist and Taoist Ways. The liberation Einstein longs for must begin in an interior awakening. Yet it soon translates into compassion, an activist impulse to change the external world. He looks for an ethics both individual and social which views human rights as part of a wider ecology.

Despite conflicting opinions among individuals, cultures, and religious traditions about specific moral dilemmas, I think it possible to locate a persuasive consensus on the broadest fundamental issues. To line up moral teachings of the world's principal religious Ways for comparison, I will select a single focus as the touchstone, an *ethics of social ecology*. By this term I mean an inclusive moral vision that embraces humanity, the cosmos, and the Sacred. From this perspective every religious, scientific, social, educational, economic, political, military, urban, agricultural issue must be treated, not in isolation, but holistically—insofar as it supports or undermines the overall ecosystem. The terms ecological ethics or environmental ethics will be used interchangeably.

Similarities from the major extant religious Ways grow more evident, once the Ways are sorted into distinctive family units, some of them sharing a more or less common historical legacy. One obvious unit is the Abrahamic or Semitic cluster, which includes the Jewish, Christian, and Muslim Ways. Reserved for more detailed study in the next chapter, this unit will be called the heritage of historical prophecy. In the present chapter, however, I will focus on a large variety of Ways under a single group label, the heritage of perennial wisdom. This heritage includes first the Primal sub-family, represented notably by Native American Ways; second the Chinese-Japanese sub-family of Taoist, Confucian, and Shinto Ways; and third the sub-family of India, including the Hindu, Jain, Buddhist, and Sikh Ways.

This medley of differing global Ways all seem to be converging today toward a shared recognition of environmental apocalypse. In his dream interpretations Carl Jung learned that when outer life becomes one-sided, the unconscious life in individuals often generates a compensatory dream to help the mind correct this imbalance. Analogous to the law of conserving physical energy, a similar balancing process occurs, he suspects, in the macrocosm of human history. At the peak of the Enlightenment Era in Europe, for example, the French enthronement of the Goddess of Reason in Notre Dame became a symbolic gesture of great import to the Eurocentric world, much like the hewing down of Wotan's oak by the Christian missionaries a millennium earlier. During the Goddess' reign, however, you could spot a widespread interest in all sorts of psychic phenomena, manifested in the growth of spiritualism, astrology, theosophy, and an introduction of the Hindu Upanishads into Europe. Jung conjectures that no psychic value can disappear without being replaced by another of equivalent intensity.[2]

One massive symbolic reversal of this sort, I think, occurred with the Greening Revolution of the 1960's. In 1972 a group of scientists and industrialists calling themselves the Club of Rome published a devastating conclusion. Their words, buried since then among so many protests against acid rain, toxic waste, global warming, today no longer convey their first terror: "If the present growth trends in world population, industrialization, pollution, food production, and resource depletion continue unchanged, the limits to growth on this planet will be reached sometime within the next one hundred years."[3] In order to understand how the world reached this frightening nadir, a few moments of reconnaissance are necessary.

Analytic Reason and Its Aftermath

Socrates and his Greek contemporaries, reinterpreting the traditional sacred stories, as mentioned earlier, helped to ease the momentous transition from *mythos* to *logos*—from a perspective centered on ritual and story to one centered on calculative reasoning. History has situated Plato and Aristotle in Greece alongside Confucius and Lao Tzu in China, Zoroaster in Persia, Gautama Buddha and Mahavira and the Upanishad teachers in India, and the major Hebrew prophets in Israel. With little or no proven horizontal contact, all these religious founders and teachers flourished during that era of remarkable spiritual and moral insight from 800 to 300 B.C.E., which Karl Jaspers has called the Axial Period. Almost in unison, all five centers of civilization registered a pivotal shift, turning away from religious rite and legend that had lost their vitality. The conscientious believer was now summoned to demystify the old religious myths and to recover a vital balance between ritual sacrifice and ethical responsibility.

It is misleading, in my opinion, to reduce this Axial shift just to the quirks of a reified universal Mind. In more empirical terms I prefer to record a transformation occurring within a few gifted sensitive individuals confronting similar existential situations in different lands. These leaders then inspired the foundation or revitalization of large spiritual communities. As Jaspers says, picture here and there a few revered hermits, wandering teachers, and sages in caves, forests, or mountain tops, all seeking the Absolute as Atman, Nirvana, Tao, or the will of God.[4] At that time and maybe even today, most other people in each of these five civilizations, especially those in rural settings, and the rest of humanity continued to live relatively close to the earth and the communal past. Again, the Axial shift is oversimplified by calling it a transition from mythos to logos. I prefer to view mythos and logos as a balanced yin-yang dialectic, much like the religious-moral dialectic described in the previous chapter. Both factors are distinct but inseparable, each needing the other for completion. In pre-Axial times, the mythos-logos balance tilted toward a relatively uncritical adherence to religious myth and ritual. Now in the Axial Period the dialectic tilted opposite, toward interiorizing and ethicizing this religious factor.

At any rate, this Axial shift achieved a mixed gain and loss. Sacred groves were often stripped of nymphs and taboos, and many sacred ties to the earth were left abandoned. "The unquestioning grasp on life was loosened," says Jaspers, "the calm of polarities became the disquiet of opposites and antinomies." People would prove capable of contrasting themselves with the entire universe, and transcending themselves. "What were later called reason and personality were revealed for the first time during the Axial Period." One penalty for this human advance was that some thinkers erected conspicuous boundaries that have persisted— between scientific reason and imagination, the material world and the supernatural, the liberated individual mind and human kinship with the earth. This is the same rift T.S. Eliot calls the dissociation of sensibility, with harmful repercussions on literary creativity, especially after the Renaissance Era in Europe. In some gifted personalities, the power of reason would combine with aggressive individuality to reign almost unhindered in Europe and then to overflow in radiating circles of conquest. According to Hegel, for instance, by his century Europeans sailing around the world had encircled it. Whatever had not yet fallen under their domination would soon do so, or was not worth the trouble.[5]

Most Euro-American modernist historians view the eighteenth and nineteenth centuries as the apogee of modern science, industrialism, capitalism, global imperialism, and secularity. As enlightened thinkers emancipated themselves further from their pre-Axial origins, alchemy would be transformed into chemistry, astrology into astronomy, traditional cures into pharmacy and medicine, shamanic exorcism and priestly absolution of sins into psychotherapy. A wry summary of this scientific triumph is given by the main character in *Roger's Version* by John Updike: "Whenever theology touches science, it gets burned. In the sixteenth century astronomy, in the seventeenth microbiology, in the eighteenth geology and paleontology, in the nineteenth Darwin's biology all grotesquely extended the world-frame and sent churchmen scurrying for cover in ever smaller, more shadowy nooks, little gloomy ambiguous caves in the psyche where even now neurology is cruelly harrying them, gouging them out from the multifolded brain like wood lice from under the lumber pile."[6]

Yet prophets continued to surface, religious in both the traditional and broader sense, ready to point out the cost of any proud overreaching in human knowledge. It is not wrong to know but to misuse what you know. Cautionary tales describe Eden's tree of forbidden knowledge, the Tower of Babel, Prometheus, Daedalus and Icarus, Faust, and even the Sorcerer's Apprentice. At the midpoint of Mary Shelley's *Frankenstein: The New Prometheus*, written in 1816, the monster recounts for Victor his painful stages of self-education and self-awareness: "Increase of knowledge only discovered to me more clearly what a wretched outcast I was." Victor Frankenstein, a Prometheus figure punished for usurping God's exclusive power to create human life, advises his friend Walton, "how dangerous is the acquirement of knowledge, and how much happier that man is who believes his native town to be the world, than he who aspires to become greater than his nature will allow." Before dying, Victor reaffirms this caution: "Seek happiness in tranquility and avoid ambition, even if it be only the apparently innocent one of distinguishing yourself in science and discoveries." [7]

In 1990, two decades after the Club of Rome declaration mentioned before, Victor Frankenstein's warnings revived with a gruesome new urgency. Thirty famous international scientists, led by Carl Sagan, issued a document, "Open Letter to the Religious Community," which condemned environmental "crimes against creation." Such problems "must be recognized as having a religious as well as a scientific dimension ... Efforts to safeguard and cherish the environment need to be infused with a vision of the Sacred." These scientists urged the global religious community "to commit, in word and deed, and as boldly as is required, to preserve the environment of the Earth." [8]

The apocalyptic style of Carl Sagan's message might have been expected from a shrieking prophet but not from a cool professional scientist. At any rate, the quick response by theologians to this plea has been astounding. I suppose most theologians, after being trained so long to generate answers, often cannot hear the actual questions raised by specialists from another discipline. Yet within just a few years environmental issues have become a central theme of global conferences, courses on all educational levels, new periodicals and newsletters, and many books—an interdisciplinary dialogue that includes representatives from all the major global religious traditions.

Revealing the desperate extent of their alarm, many environmentalists from the scientific community even seem ready today to replace the logos-centered, mechanistic premises underlying the modern industrial era. They yearn to turn back and reexamine pre-industrial attitudes and values, allegedly best preserved in the Primal and Asian Ways of Wisdom. In his widely influential book, *Small Is Beautiful*, for instance, Ernst Schumacher turns without hesitation to Gandhi's village communities and the "right livelihood" command in the Buddhist Dharma to locate his model of a small-scale frugal economy.[9]

Or again, representing the Native American traditions, a Comanche student of mine believes that at death she will be joined more closely to the cosmos and experience all that is now closed to her. She hopes to explore the inside of the sun and stars, travel to the edge of the expanding universe, experience the inside of a mother's womb, see through the eyes of a bird, a whale, a guppy, a male human being, and reconnect with her ancestors. In the rest of this chapter I will examine a few ecological motifs prominent in these Primal and Asian Wisdom traditions, and compare the different religious-moral visions that sustain them.

Primal Wisdom of the Land

"What is this you call property?" Massasoit, chief of the Wampanaog tribe asked his seventeenth century Puritan friends. "It cannot be the earth. For the land is our mother, nourishing all her children, beasts, birds, fish, and all men. The woods, the streams, everything on it belongs to everybody and is for the use of all. How can one man say it belongs only to him?" A similar complaint would arise three centuries later from a California Wintu medicine woman: "When we Indians kill meat we eat it all up, when we dig roots we make just little holes… We shake down acorns and pine nuts. We don't chop down the trees. We only use dead wood. But the White people plough up the ground, pull down the trees, kill everything. The tree says, 'Don't, I'm sore. Don't hurt me.'… How can the spirit of the earth like the White man?… Everywhere the White man has touched, it is sore."[10]

By Primal Ways I mean the religious traditions of various indigenous peoples scattered especially through Central Africa, northern Australia, Melanesia, Siberia, the Arctic, the Amazon basin, and the reservations of North America. To represent this Primal perspective on environmental ethics I have chosen the Native American Way, an umbrella label that includes the Wampanaog and Wintu just cited and more than 600 other extant indigenous tribes in North America alone. All generalizations about Native American spirituality, of course, must be adjusted flexibly to correlate with the particular myths, rites, and outlook of each tribe, not to mention the unique spirituality of each individual.

Indigenous people throughout the Americas have even more reason than the large nation-states for anxiety about environmental abuses. Their present misery stirs up ominous rumors of the future that may await us all—the Arctic oil spills, demolished rainforests along the Amazon, pollution and reduction of game and fish sources on U.S. reservation territory, or the reckless mining for rich oil and mineral deposits on land colonists once devalued because it seemed worthless to farm. A disproportionate number of U.S. Native Americans today suffer cancer and radiation poisoning from labor in uranium mines, or from contact with nuclear and toxic waste dumps near reservations.[11]

A few blocks from the University of San Francisco where I teach stands the home of an outspoken army veteran of the Vietnam War, an Apache descended from the Mescalero and White Mountain tribes of the southwest. I first met him in a parking space dispute and thus from the start have heard out his beliefs on the sacred earth and the fallacy of private ownership rights. He likes to remind me with irony how my white people tried unsuccessfully to conscript an indecently large number of black people to fight Vietnamese yellow people in order to protect my white land stolen from his red people. You can anticipate at least one angry Apache environmentalist veto whenever we cut down a tree on the university campus or tamper with the neighborhood skyline by adding one more building. He has tried repeatedly to make his tribe's own territorial burial sites accessible for pilgrims from neighboring tribes who also hold these locations sacred. Employed by his tribe as a full-time real estate agent, he invests their assets in shrewd land purchases throughout California. His most passionate complaints center on shortsighted tribal elders anywhere, greedy to rent their sacred land to Mafia-types for casinos or to the U.S. government for nuclear waste disposal.

Combining his fiery temperament, Apache heritage, and experience in property deals and hi-tech warfare, my friend represents, not the ancient noble savage, the vanishing Indian, or the stone-faced frontier Indian, but a bracing juxtaposition of two recent Native American stereotypes. He mixes the urban guerrilla Indian with some features of the New Age Indian, exemplary artist and visionary and environmental activist. Defining his religious Way, he talks like St. Francis of Assisi about a family relationship with the powers of thunder and sunset, calling them Brother, Grandfather, and Mother Earth. His words evoke a cosmos charged with sacred energy, a worldview that could be interpreted one moment as theological pantheism or panentheism, another moment as polytheism, animism, or diffusive monotheism.

In an effort to grasp Native American and other Primal Ways I have adopted the so-called African Triangle premise. At the apex of this triangle is the Sacred, viewed as a personal or transpersonal Source, a mystery so unapproachable that it is often left unnamed. Two legs of the triangle can be imagined radiating from this apex—ancestral spirits and nature spirits, accessible to popular devotion. Interested in moral implications, I prefer to associate these two triangle legs, first with human rights of all living people and the ancestral dead, and second, with a shield of environmental taboos and rites to preserve the natural world. Navajo artist Carl Gorman offers a convincing explanation why his own Primal Way does not name the Sacred. His people feel too insignificant to pray directly to the Great Power, the incomprehensible. "Nature feeds our soul's inspiration, and so we approach the Great Power through that part of Nature which is close to us and within the reach of human understanding... As every form has some of the intelligent spirit of the Creator, we cannot but revere all parts of the creation."[12]

Today many people, convinced that modern civilized life has only complicated the simple existential questions, turn back to Native American Ways for the forgotten ancient answers. To be specific, how can those already living *on* the earth become more genuinely *of* the earth? According to Lakota theologian Vine Deloria the old traditional Native Americans were in tune with the rhythms of life. They stood at the center of a circle and brought everything together there. In wisdom and skill human beings rank not at the summit but just halfway up the ladder of created life. For they are surpassed in flight by the eagle, in sight by the owl, or in hearing by the lark. "The special human ability is to communicate with other forms of life, learn from them all, and act as a focal point for things they wish to express," he explains. "It is believed that birds and animals give up their lives and bodies so that human beings can perform the proper ceremonies by which every creature is blessed." Thus, by performing the sacred rituals at sites designated as holy places, a Lakota shaman, for instance, can mediate between all physical and spiritual forces of the cosmos in an exchange of gifts. "As gifts are given and responsibilities accepted, the world as we know it is able to move forward to completion of its possibilities."[13]

Here it is possible to gather the ingredients for an ethics of environmental affinity, wonder, and responsibility. The Ways of Native Americans and other indigenous people show particular awareness of our indebtedness to invisible spirits, the dead Ancestors and the forces of nature. The natural world is a "Thou," animated with spiritual forces flowing back and forth, and the most worthwhile achievements depend on access to the source of this power. Sacred power must be balanced and replenished for individuals and the community by the regular performance of ritual. When people hunt and kill a deer, pick an ear of corn, or even dig up a cactus button, they must somehow return that gift. Those who take must give back. To keep things in balance people exchange gifts with one another, and give ritual offerings back to the spirits, so that power will continue circulating from the invisible to the visible world.[14]

This reciprocal kinship with the natural world pervades "The Man to Send Rain Clouds," title piece in a story collection by Leslie Silko, the distinguished Pueblo novelist. The plot gives a simple account of family members finding old Teofilo's body near his sheep pasture, then cleaning and dressing the corpse. Only then do they inform the Franciscan mission priest about Teofilo's death and insist, somewhat obsessively, that the priest sprinkle as much holy water as possible on the wizened bundle before burial. Over the body his gathered friends pray, "Send us rain clouds, Grandfather."

The story centers on an implied quarrel between two religious perspectives, Catholic and Native American. Expecting to perform a Catholic sacramental anointing of Teofilo and a funeral Mass, the priest shows bewilderment and impatience at the way his role is reorchestrated. Keeping the news of this death concealed from him, his parishioners seem to belittle the more vital Catholic rituals by exaggerating the near-magic of holy water. As the story progresses, all the ancient Native American rites show up, performed defiantly in secret. Thus, family and friends succeed in sidestepping the outsider's Way, perceived as intrusive and alien. They devoutly paint Teofilo's face, tie a feather to his hair, bring out their candles and medicine bags, sprinkle sacred pollen and corn meal on him, and at the climax, flock to the priest's holy water gravesite blessing. From the Native American perspective, this sacred water seems to fall on the earth like August rain, almost evaporating before it touches the wilted squash flowers. In their prayers, they are offering Teofilo back to the earth and sky as a return gift, hoping his spirit will in turn send them back rainclouds for their crops.[15]

By an irony of history Native Americans, once treated by early colonists as mere nomads and thus with no title to the land, are revered today as the most enduring presence, identified somehow with the sacred land itself. Like many other Primal peoples, they embody a superior environmental ideal. Grounded on faith, land, ethnicity, gender, and language, most of these communities show a rich density of kinship relations, bonds with ancestors, interpersonal communication, and a disciplined appreciation for their natural and cultural surroundings.[16]

Though committed to live in harmony with nature, however, it must be conceded that many Native American individuals and tribes have indeed abused their environment. Reluctant to cut Mother Earth with a plough, the Lakota, for instance, would still set range fires to drive buffalo herds over a cliff, or in times of plenty eat only the choicest animal parts but waste the rest. One reason that so many tribes remained nomadic throughout their history is the rapid soil erosion and firewood depletion in each area they touched. The renowned cliff dwellings at Mesa Verde overlook the remains of a vast rubbish dump, where people for generations continued to toss their garbage.[17] I noticed a recent ecological dispute between some California resident ranchers and the Campo Mission sovereign nation, a barren terrain east of San Diego. In an admirable attempt to free themselves from federal dependency this small group of Native Americans have tried to lease a hilltop dumpsite for garbage shipped by train from distant cities. Against this plan non-Campo neighbors brandish environmentalist warnings of seepage into water reservoirs beyond reservation borders.[18]

A typical critique of the Primal environmental record occurs in the recent novel *Thinks* by David Lodge. During a dinner party conversation Lydia deplores Euro-American environmental abuse and conjures up a Primal utopia, where people treat the earth, not as belonging to them but as something to which they belong. Ralph, on the contrary, argues that the earth belongs to us because we are the shrewdest animals on it. "Only the limitations of their technology have prevented primitive peoples from destroying their environment on a scale that would appall us... The Polynesians wiped out half the bird species on the Hawaiian islands long before Captain Cook ever got there. In New Zealand the Maoris butchered the entire population of giant moa birds and left most of the carcasses uneaten. To this day the Yuqui Indians in the Bolivian rainforest chop down trees to get at the fruit. Conservation is a concept of advanced civilizations."[19]

Yet many Native Americans, embedded today in their assigned locale, actually possess an intimate knowledge of the environment, almost as if no boundaries could separate them from nature. Scientists often treat them as models for sustainable use of natural resources and as a storehouse for knowledge about nature that today's larger civilizations have overlooked. The obvious nomads today are not these indigenous people but the U.S. majority, lacking community roots, moving from city to city for jobs, with little prospect to be buried in the place they were born. Readily ignoring the bond of people to the land and their family past, contemporary society offers almost no ongoing community to which people can pass along stories and memories. As Deloria observes, without an enduring community to come and return to, no one can personalize the land. Most appreciation for the land is just aesthetic, a momentary warm feeling invoked by the uniqueness of place. Though this warmth may inspire an individual, it does not sustain communities nor a prolonged relationship with the land.[20]

Mere aesthetic tourism is the accusation by Deloria and other Native American critics against many ecologists, especially those too facile at identifying with indigenous beliefs. Often outsiders content themselves with a cursory sampling of a few venerable moral admonitions. Prone to reduce the ancient rites to mere New Age magic, they mistake the meticulous performance of some ritual as a profound experience of the Sacred. As evidence of these distortions today, consider the number of visitors claiming honorary adoption into various tribes, shamanic ordination, or the legacy of exotic herbs, sweat-lodge secrets, and peace-pipe rituals. Gullible anthropologists have been exploited in turn by paying hundreds of dollars to sit on the ground, with tom-toms thumping and corn flour thrown into their faces, and to copy down from phony medicine men the gospel that all things live in circles. Purchasing credentials of this sort, many religious tourists leave, boasting they now possess obscure authority within an old tradition without the need to live a committed religious life.[21]

Though at first proud to watch the Primal Way stirring so much outsider enthusiasm, some perceptive Native Americans have had second thoughts about the careless, patronizing manner in which their Way has been appropriated. Must they be treated as a twice-conquered people? First they were stripped of their land; but now their pipes, drums, feathers, prayers, and even their thoughts have been adapted at the conqueror's whim. In her famous poem, "For the White Poets Who Would be Indian," Wendy Rose complains about the outsider's forays of "temporary tourism" into her Hopi tribal culture. People try to snap up words "fish-hooked from our tongues." Anxious to grab hold of any roots, merely sitting back and trying to become primitive, such "instant and primal knowledge" will only prove sterile.[22]

An Asian Wisdom of Interconnecting

Besides Native American Ways the second most stimulating religious source for the environmental scientist today has been the wisdom heritage of Asia. Its influence can be sampled in a well known Zen Buddhist lecture by Daisetz Suzuki. He contrasts a nature poem by Basho in seventeenth-century Japan with a nature poem by Alfred Tennyson in nineteenth-century England. Basho simply admires a flower blooming by the hedge, but Tennyson plucks out his flower, root and all. By pondering it, Tennyson tries to understand the nature of God and humanity. Suzuki underlines a huge disparity in viewpoint here—between East and West, between the receptive integrative mind and the active analytic mind. Basho does not pluck the flower but only looks at it. "He lets an exclamation mark say everything he wishes to say. For he has no words to utter; his feeling is too full, too deep, and he has no desire to conceptualize it." Tennyson, however, does not identify with the flower but stands apart from it. Nature exists mostly to be used by human beings. "In Tennyson, as far as I can see, there is in the first place no depth of feeling... He is an advocate of the logos doctrine. He must say something, he must abstract or intellectualize on his concrete experience. He must come out of the domain of feeling into that of intellect, and must subject living and feeling to a series of analyses that give satisfaction to the Western spirit of inquisitiveness."[23]

Alongside Suzuki's graphic contrast between two poems I want to explore a similar contrast between paintings. Imagine first a Chinese landscape scroll-painting. Its focus is a mountain scene or calm lake, and somewhere you can uncover an almost concealed hut, boat, perhaps a few tiny human figures, all melting into the landscape. Are the figures sketched in, only to suggest the momentous contrast in scale? Here human beings and their daily affairs are dwarfed by natural beauty. They do not stand apart from the natural world but are immersed in it as an integral part. For a contrasting picture, imagine an eighteenth-century portrait by Thomas Gainsborough, John Copley, or some earlier painter. The face and clothing of the central figure are sketched in loving detail, playing up each oddity of character and style. Perhaps over the person's shoulder or through a side window, a fragment of the natural world may appear, a barely noticeable backdrop to the central drama, which is only the human figure. The observer suspects that this slight trace of natural beauty is used mostly to suggest context in time and locale or to relieve a dull surrounding monotone. In the first painting the natural world is integrated with the human. In the second it is scaled down as if a mere tool, ornament, or framework for the human center.[24]

East Is East?

Much current environmentalist curiosity about the Asian Wisdom Ways, I think, can be boiled down to variations on the lopsided contrasts I have just outlined. Ecologists seek a fresh rationale for contemplation rather than manipulation. It is arbitrary to attribute to the West only activism, analysis, power, rugged individuality, logos; and to the East only a speechless awe, holism, creative receptivity, and a mythos-logos synthesis. By stacking the cards in this manner critics determine in advance to idealize the East as a screen upon which they will project, and then recover, all the endowments missing from their disparaging critique of the West.

My synopsis has omitted so many nuances from the contrasting poems and paintings above that the outline seems at second glance a caricature. In the history of art Neoclassical portraiture in Europe was followed by breathtaking Romantic landscape paintings by Constable and Turner or the lucid still-life canvases of French Impressionists. Parallel to this contrast within Europe is the contrast of yang and yin within Chinese civilization itself, between a Confucian Neoclassical concern mostly about human society and a Taoist Romantic concern mostly about the natural world. In other words, human-centered and cosmos-centered tendencies can be located in both West and East.

This East-West dichotomy, I find, pervades the work of Max Weber, Carl Jung, Joseph Campbell, and other Euro-American students of comparative spiritualities and ethics. They divide religious Ways into Eastern and Western. The East specializes in mysticism, contemplation, a world-transcending asceticism; the West, in calculative analysis, power relationships, and a world-centered social activism. Yet I insist, on the contrary, that the East, too, has its Hindu political activists and the bodhisattvas of so-called Engaged Buddhism. And the West, too, has not yet disowned its contemplatives, such as the Jewish Kabbalists, Muslim Sufi, or Christian Rhineland and Spanish mystics. Counter to this faulty East-West premise it is clear that West and East are geographic misnomers for the deepest currents in everyone, no matter what the individual's spiritual heritage. A religious imbalance or distortion anywhere—in an era, an entire civilization, or some phase of an individual life—can be rectified by drawing mostly upon resources yet untapped within that respective heritage.

Before an environmentalist of Euro-American background can learn from the Asian Wisdom Ways it is essential to weed out another fallacy—a subtle variation on the East-West premise just criticized. *Orientalism*, as described by Edward Said and others, implies a bias that treats the Hindu Way and the civilization of India, say, as just a mirror for Euro-American projections. Sociologist Ramachandra Guha complains that varying images of the East are raw material for political and cultural battles being played out in the Euro-American mind. People of Asia allegedly exhibit a spiritual dependence on nature. This is interpreted first as a symptom of their prescientific and backward selves; but second, as a symptom of their ecological wisdom "Both views are monolithic, simplistic, and have the characteristic effect—intended in one case, perhaps unintended in the other—of denying agency and reason to the East and making it the privileged orbit of Western thinkers."[25] The orientalist fallacy is just one more illustration of smug intellectual imperialism.

Exporting their agenda to India and elsewhere, many U.S. environmentalists hope to construct huge natural parks throughout the developing world like those in North America. Such a program may be effective at home because of North America's unique environmental and economic history. The very concept of nature as wilderness, pristine and untouched, is not a universal archetype but a notion peculiar only to some urban cultures. Cloning this achievement abroad, however, seems to reduce a range of vital environmental reforms into mere wilderness protection, with minimal concern about the side-effects of park construction on local work and livelihood. Projects of this sort may turn into sheer amusement parks, living museums, or hunting reserves for the wealthy elite, both foreign and local. Though designating a few spots as biodiversity reserves, a nation could still continue to plunder everything outside that location.

Guha and his Indian colleagues point out how large developmental programs, such as dams and roads, displacing peasant farmers from their land to the already overpopulated cities, spur industry and urban centers to make even heavier demands on the forests and arrable land. His own position approximates that of the German Greens, rather than either the U.S. conservationists or the more radical so-called deep ecologists. Emphasizing links between industrial growth and military imperialism, the German environmentalists argue mostly for an ethic of renunciation that tries to limit consumption levels by the developing world. Most Indian ecologists demand that their own government conserve natural resources, but more important, decide with equity who will use the environment and profit from it. It is necessary to balance conflicting land-claims—regional and national governments, green imperialists viewing the land as an international heritage, and the people traditionally living on it.[26]

My own experience of land, plants, animals, and the ecology of Asia stems from living almost a year with Jesuit colleagues and the families of my former students in Nepal, India, Sri Lanka, Thailand, Malaysia, Indonesia, Taiwan, and Japan. I recall the marvelous spectrum of natural beauty in mountains, forests, and countryside, but also the near-lethal pollution in sprawling overpopulated cities. In a small Madras home the birds were invited to fly in and out of open windows to share leftovers from our supper. In Katmandu at night, dogs rummaged for food offerings at an outdoor Shiva shrine next door. In Katmandu, too, the comatose body of a sacred cow once blocked a busy bridge passage for hours because no one had the audacity to budge it off the road. Affable monkeys wandered freely among visitors at a small Buddhist temple in rural Sri Lanka and also at a Hindu sacred grove in rural Bali.

Travel brochures play up scenes like these but edit out the clouds of diesel and kerosene fumes that blackened my face and lungs on roads near Katmandu and Colombo. I could not overlook the exposed raw sewage in open Bangkok canals, the high percentage of reported parasitic worm disorders in Nepali villages, the scarcity of potable water in rural areas almost everywhere. For me it is silly to romanticize those trying to live the Asian or Primal Ways of Wisdom, as if they have already attained an ecological Shangri-La. I watch them cope—earth-victims and earth-abusers no less than I—with the same international ecological crisis.

According to geographer Yi-fu Tuan the many U.S. environmentalists chasing after the Asian Ways of Wisdom today tend to overestimate this wisdom. Enraptured at China's Taoist and Buddhist Ways, they like to compare Asia's quiescent and adaptive approach toward nature with the aggressive masculinity of Euro-Americans In complex historical empires, on the contrary, a benign institution can introduce jarring effects that were not part of their original purpose. The building of so many Buddhist halls and temples in China and Japan, tiny oases of green in a brown background, actually caused massive deforestation in nearby areas. Timber reserves were wasted, too, by firewood cremation, a rite introduced into both these nations by Buddhist monks.[27]

The environmentalist is tempted to imagine ancient China as a forest utopia built on Taoist ideals. Instead, Chinese historical records indicate a widespread devastation of forests and farm land during almost every war and dynastic upheaval. A civilization's publicized rationale about its environment tends to mirror just a fraction of its actual environmental attitudes and practice. Unfortunately among forces motivating those who govern the world, aesthetic and religious ideals seldom play a major role. The Communist government in China today has begun intense programs to reforest and control erosion. Those who admire the old religious Ways can only regret that this so-called "mist of green" today does not derive from the traditional Taoist and Buddhist values. Instead, the present government has carried out its environmental reform in explicit denial of these values.[28]

Cosmic Internet

Two themes at the heart of most Asian Wisdom Ways seem especially engaging to contemporary environmentalists. The first is an interdependent cosmos; the second, a worldview that is more life-centered and cosmos-centered than human-centered. Focusing on both themes for closer study, I will exemplify them mostly in the Buddhist Way, but also when useful, in the other Ways of India, China, and Japan. Unlike the Jewish, Christian, and Muslim Ways with sharp boundaries separating each tradition from the other, the Asian Wisdom Ways readily converge and overlap. In Japan, for instance, with true spiritual integrity, the same person may live by a Confucian ethic and a Taoist aesthetic, get married at a Shinto wedding, and be buried at a Buddhist funeral.

When environmentalists are introduced to Asian Wisdom their first hope is to grasp the religious rationale for viewing the cosmos as interconnected or holistic. Most Chinese, especially Taoists, describe the Sacred not as a personified Supreme Being separable from everything created but as the originating process itself. It is an electromagnetic field of yin and yang, people interacting with their natural environment, physical with spiritual forces, dead ancestors with the living, microcosm with macrocosm. Hungry ghosts or cycles of stars might tamper with an individual's destiny. A single moral choice today could temporarily disrupt or reconfirm the evolving harmony of the universe. This ordered process and the plan regulating it are a handy definition of *Tao*. The *I Ching* or Book of Changes, the art of geomancy, and astrological charts are consulted regularly by many families of my Chinese students.

The concept of an interrelated cosmos is best demonstrated by the mutual respect and intimacy between human beings and animals illustrated above. Guiding me though the Tokyo Zoo, for example, a former student of mine pointed out a small, quiet cemetery with flowers and food offerings. He identified this as a Shinto shrine venerating the zoo's dead animals, the *Kami* or sacred spirits of a bear or parrot, say, that many visitors had long befriended. By emphasizing karmic rebirth Hindus, Buddhists, and especially Jains have been persuaded to treat stray animals as potential reincarnated human relatives and thus worthy of nonviolent respect. Many devout Buddhists take the bodhisattva vow, a promise to postpone their own Nirvana liberation until they have succeeded in helping, not just other people, but all living creatures to attain Nirvana.

To help evoke an experience of interconnectedness, many Buddhists imagine the Net of Indra, a favorite visualization technique in the Hua-yen or Kegon Buddhist tradition. Stretching throughout the universe, this net extends vertically in time and horizontally in space. At each point of connection between threads is a crystal bead, standing for an individual existence. By examining any single bead a person may catch also every other bead reflected, and then reflections of reflections, all forming an endless flickering totality.[29] As a comparable metaphor of interdependence I imagine the computer global web, which seems to decentralize power and extend it to the farthest horizon. Solidarity within the web is so tight that a computer virus introduced at a single link can rocket through the entire circuit.

What blocks the mind from translating this visualization exercise into an ingrained perspective is our automatic tendency to divide the perceived world into individual and separate things, static entities confronting our isolated ego. The Einstein credo cited before describes this splintering effect of our deluded consciousness. One aim of Buddhist meditation, on the contrary, is first to heal this subject-object dichotomy, and instead to perceive all reality as relational. Only then are we ready to penetrate beyond appearances and reach Nirvana, a condition of liberation from all selfish desire. Like a Whiteheadian process-philosopher, everyone must view the cosmos as a dynamic continuum.

The traditional Buddhist word for this cosmic process is *pratitya-samutpada*, interexistence or an evolving interdependence. Such a concept offers an insightful foundation for an ethics of mutual responsibility and interconnectedness in the ecosphere. Am I my brother's keeper? More than this, says the perceptive Buddhist. Somehow I *am* my brother and sister. As meditation deepens, yielding to the flow of consciousness, and blurring the distinction between subject and object, I become more disposed to de-reify the self, the world, anything given public validation as a separate *the*. Buddhist teaching offers an assortment of linguistic tools to unfreeze the fixed conventional notions of the mind—Sanskrit and Pali words translated as no-self, no-permanence, no-knowledge, and emptiness. Reality itself transcends the pitfalls of common linguistic usage. I aim to dissolve my conventional self-definition as a separate monad. Once this is accomplished I can then learn imaginatively to exchange identities between myself and others. A common visualization exercise among Mahayanist Buddhists is called the Great Compassion meditation. I try to imagine the sufferings of all living creatures, one by one, engulfed in flames of sadness. And then singling out particular individuals and their anguish, I try to feel for them, the way I would feel for my own suffering children or parents. Then I ponder how I could help them find release.[30]

The present Dalai Lama has often pointed out the dynamic interconnection between environmental activism, contemplation, and living a deeper moral life. In the final pages of his latest autobiography, *Freedom in Exile*, he says, "I am especially encouraged that the belief in consumerism as an end in itself seems to be giving way to an appreciation that we humans must conserve the earth's resources... Human beings are in a sense children of the earth." Though long tolerant about her children's abuse of the earth, our common Mother now gives proof that she has reached the limits of her tolerance. "As a Buddhist monk I feel that belief in the concept of karma is very useful in the conduct of daily life. Once you believe in the connection between motivation and its effect, you will become more alert to the effects which your own actions have upon yourself and others... We need to cultivate a universal responsibility for one another and for the planet we share, based on a good heart and awareness."[31]

The Buddhist renaissance that greets a current visitor to Taiwan, for example, is just the first wave of an activist Buddhist moral revival throughout Asia. Innumerable organizations, such as Buddhist Compassion Relief or the Dharma Drum Foundation, are sponsoring antinuclear protests, ecological awareness, drug rehabilitation, and disaster relief. Yet one ingredient that stamps this so-called Engaged Buddhism as distinctively Buddhist is a revitalized interest in meditation. The change in one's own consciousness and a change in the surrounding world are vitally interconnected, as suggested in the Buddhist concept of pratitya-samutpada mentioned above. Like Vedantist Hindus many Mahayana Buddhists hold that consciousness itself is not a product of the world but the world a product of consciousness. People live in just the universe they have created and thus deserve. The art of life consists less in escaping the world or saving the world than reaching a profound self-enlightenment. Buddhist manifestos for environmental ethics, nonviolence, and political change presume a direct link between reform of outer structures and a self-conversion within.[32]

Beyond The Imperial Ego

Asian Ways fascinate the environmentalist because they emphasize an interdependent cosmos but also a perspective life-centered or cosmos-centered, transcending mere human self-centeredness. To appreciate this second theme the outsider is invited to consider the attitude of a devout Taoist artist, reluctant to impose a self-willed pattern on the natural world, but hoping to compose a picture that lays bare some inner dynamic not usually perceived because of distractions. This same receptive creativity can be observed in the sculptor who tries to carve with the grain, the poet whose meaning springs uncharted out of half-conscious wordplay, the ballerina whose body dances almost by itself. Evoking a scenario of simplicity and harmony, the Taoist classics introduce an extensive cast of self-effacing fishermen, farmers, and contemplative dropouts. Most similes in this literature can be traced back to worlds far removed from civilized human life—silence, baby and savage, wild horses, wood and stone and water.

Often called the Natural Way, the Taoist art of life tends to exclude attributes like the mechanical, industrial, over-civilized, and the will to manipulate, possess, or intrude. In one famous Taoist tale a sculptor is employed by his sovereign to carve a mulberry leaf out of precious stone. He takes three years just to shape a leaf with texture and color, delicate enough to draw the incongruous compliment that it looks almost natural. A comparable tale, "The Nightingale," by Hans Christian Andersen centers on the Chinese emperor, enraptured by a real nightingale's song, even if disappointed by the bird's drab appearance. He soon discards it for a wind-up artificial bird of silver and gems, mailed him as a gift. Far more beautiful on the outside, the new bird sings almost as well, but just a single repeated song. Still, it proves more dependable than the natural bird whose songs and concert times occur at random. After a year, however, the mechanical apparatus runs down and cannot be fully repaired. The emperor falls ill and, yearning to hear music again, turns from the inert artificial bird to a tune outside his window, sung now by the real nightingale now, a voice of compassion and hope.[33]

"Chrysanthemums," a subtle story by Chi-tsai Feng, explores the friendship between a simple gardener and a refined artist. This unusual, one-sided relationship manages to survive all the unpredictable upheavals in Tang's fame as a painter during the communist Cultural Revolution and afterwards. Fan the gardener is old, ugly, a clumsy silent mountaineer type, intimate with the world of flowers—obvious kin to the typical old Taoist seer, with an intuitive charism hidden beneath apparent ignorance. After Fan shows appreciation for a specific pipe carved by Tang, the artist offers it as a gift because he thinks it too simple and unfinished, almost worthless. At first Tang had turned to creating pipes as just a hobby, during the depressing times when his paintings had lost favor. Gradually, through Fan's encouragement, the elaborately sculpted pipes prove more authentic art than his paintings. For each finished pipe is unique and inspired. "Some he fashioned out of gnarled old roots, letting the natural shapes guide his carving… He preferred to capture the spirit of things rather than their precise outlines." Fan brings a repeated gift of chrysanthemum plants to Tang, but barely notices that his flowers and friendship are taken too much for granted. Not until Fan dies, insisting he be buried with the pipe Tang gave him, does Tang begin to sense the impact of Fan's love and perceptiveness.[34]

The Taoist Way has seldom matched the interest of Confucians and Buddhists in the explicit details of moral teaching. As Masao Abe explains it, Buddhists, Jews, Christians, and Muslims all concern themselves primarily with human liberation. To this extent, then, the four can be called human-centered Ways. However, the difference between them lies in the fact that among the first three personal salvation is based on a personal relationship between human beings and God. Among Buddhists, however, that personal salvation is based on the "transpersonal, cosmological dimension common to human beings and to nature." As a Mahayana Buddhist Abe hopes to reach a Nirvana enlightenment while still immersed in this present samsaric cycle of births and rebirths. "However, if one remains in Nirvana," he fears, "one may enjoy the bliss, but forget the suffering of his or her fellow beings who are still involved in the process of samsara." It is necessary, then, to become a bodhisattva, "in a dynamic movement between samsara and Nirvana without any attachment to either, without any reification of either."[35]

Though the Buddhist and Hindu Ways are often misinterpreted simply as unworldly or otherworldly spiritualities, even the profound Hindu mystic Ramakrishna did not want to withdraw from his immediate surroundings. Caught up in a prolonged ecstatic Brahman-Atman unitive experience he still pleads with the Goddess Kali not to sweep him away from the company of his friends and the natural world: Give the "knowledge of Brahman to those who want it!... Let me remain in contact with men. Don't make me a dried-up ascetic. I want to enjoy Your sport in the world."[36]

The Hindu scriptures offer a bold image of God's immersion into everything created, a mythic parallel to the Einstein insight of my epigraph. The Satapatha Brahmana text describes the god Brahma, weary of self-contemplation and yearning for companionship, in this decision: "Let me sacrifice myself in living things, and all living things in myself." And the world begins to take shape. But after creation this sacred Oneness breaks apart: "When he had fallen into pieces, his breath departed from the midst of him, and the Gods abandoned him." Then Brahma begs Agni, God of fire, "Put me together again." Thus, the Creator has surrendered his primordial unity so that our multiple selves and the natural world could come into existence. Now in reverse, our lives and ritual offerings, transformed by Agni's purifying fire, will help reunify the sacred cosmos.[37]

Ramakrishna's key disciple Vivekananda feared his Ramakrishna Order of disciples would get trapped by a dichotomy between the higher realm of meditation and the lower realm of social action. Adhering to his Advaita Vedanta premise that the world is mere appearance, how could he still preach an activist mission to the world? "Know through Advaita that whomever you hurt, you hurt yourself," he concluded. "They are all you. Whether you know it or not, through all hands you work, through all feet you move. You are the king enjoying life in the palace, you are the beggar leading a miserable existence in the street. You are in the ignorant as well as in the learned, in the weak as in the strong. Know this and be sympathetic."[38] Vivekananda did not hesitate to extend this empathy to the rest of the cosmos. "Where do you seek our God," he asked, "overlooking God in various forms in front of you? The person who serves God best is kind to all God's creatures."[39]

A renowned Hindu activist, Vivekananda also described himself in Buddhist terms as an aspiring bodhisattva of the earth. Those who today call themselves Engaged Buddhists speak of a culminating return to the immediacy of concrete time and place. Once awakened spiritually, you will still weed the garden as before, but you now do so, fully aware and engaged in the weeding. As the Zen koan expresses it, "Before enlightenment tea is merely tea, then tea is no longer tea, but after enlightenment tea is indeed tea." The following abridgement of Dharma wisdom has been attributed to Gautama himself: "Whenever you see a form, simply see. Whenever you hear a sound, simply hear. Whenever you smell an aroma, simply smell. Whenever you taste a flavor, simply taste. Whenever you feel a sensation, simply feel. The 'you' will no longer exist. Whenever the 'you' does not exist, you will not be found in this world, another world, or in between. That is the finish of suffering."[40]

Perhaps the most familiar of all Zen tales introduces a man chased by a tiger. Cornered near a precipice, he grabs a wild vine and swings himself down over the ledge. The tiger sniffs at him from above. But far below, another tiger waits to eat him. With only the vine to save him, he watches as two mice gradually gnaw at the vine. Suddenly he spots a ripe red strawberry nearby. Grasping the vine with one hand, he plucks the strawberry with his other hand. How sweet it tastes!

I would be taking Daisetz Suzuki too literally if I imagine his version of this tale demands that the Zen victim only admire the strawberry without plucking it. What a flexible environmental ethics requires is a true Zen sense of wonder and awareness. An awakening so profound can inspire both a life of contemplation, and also a selfless, disciplined management and use of the natural world.

4

A GOD-CENTERED ECOLOGY

T HE FIELD OF ECOLOGY HAS FOUND AN ENCOURAGING partnership with the Primal and Asian Wisdom Ways described in the previous chapter. Yet many environmental scientists feel uneasy as they broach the religious Ways I shall now examine—the Jewish, Christian, and Muslim Ways of historical prophecy. Stemming from a single Abrahamic source, believing in one personal God, these Ways also venerate as God-sent intermediaries many of the same prophetic voices, interpreted uniquely within each respective tradition.

I pointed out a few actual merits and flaws in Native American and Asian Wisdom ecology, which must be distinguished from the air-brushed Primal Eden projected on these Ways by many Euro-American environmentalists. Similar strengths and limitations will now be examined in the Jewish, Christian, and Muslim ecologist, who must first be distinguished from the familiar stereotype of a plundering religious activist. I hope to identify on both sides the extremism and misinterpretations that hinder collaboration between ecological science and these three particular Ways. A favorite cartoon of mine suggests that a surprise awaits the environmentalist skeptical about rapport. A few devils are pictured debating suitable torments for the latest arrivals in hell. "I can identify all the usual sins," says one devil. "But what are these dreadful new 'sins against the earth'?" An unlikely new moral sensitivity is shaking up all three religious Ways.

Greening of Abraham's Legacy

Scanning the last half-century in my own church, only a few years ago did I first hear thunder from the pulpit about Nietzsche's so-called sins against the earth. Mark Twain once drew an analogy between the clergy and pharmacists, both of them anxious about clients dropping away and dabbling at their own self-medication. To lure them back, the pharmacies tried sugar-coated medicines, and the churches began prescribing weaker doses of damnation, stronger doses of empathy and love. Preachers had long condoned slavery and witch-burning on the basis of just a few biblical citations. Now they updated their message about slavery, witchcraft, hell, and damnation of the unbaptized. "More than 200 death penalties are gone from the law books," Twain says. "But the text remains. It is the practice that has changed. Why? Because the world has corrected the Bible. The Church never corrects it. The Church also never fails to drop in at the tail of the procession—and take credit for the correction."[1]

Brute Kinship

As Twain predicted, today I watch Jewish, Christian, and Muslim leaders claiming that their own Scriptures and prophets not only foresaw the present ecological crisis centuries ago but already outlined its remedy. What I recall about my own Catholic childhood, however, is a casual insensitivity to the animate and inanimate environment that I suspect was the more typical attitude. One nasty episode in my memory dates back a few years before the pistol story recounted in the first chapter. To my shame now, I remember that period as an aggressive phase of torturing small animals, perhaps to compensate for feeling so small and powerless myself. One by one I would fry a trail of ants with a magnifying glass. Also, in certain years a stormcloud of mayflies would blow with the north wind from Lake Erie, overwhelming my hometown of Erie, Pennsylvania, with millions of inch-long insects clinging to windowpanes and clogging the fans. Just as people blame elm rot on Dutch Elm disease, or flu on the Asian Flu, we nicknamed these insects Canadian Sailors. One day I was interrupted in a sadistic campaign of tearing off papery wings and pelting mayfly bodies against a store window. An elderly stranger gently urged me to stop and reconsider. Surely I could recognize that even these insects were God's creatures, she said, and no less alert to pain than I. Though unconcerned about their feelings, at least I must realize how much my ruthless behavior was brutalizing me. The woman's words did not touch me at that moment but later.

After some reflection I determined to confess this particular sin next time I approached the Sacrament of Reconciliation at our local church. Through the opaque screen of the confessional I watched the shadow of the priest snap back startled, both of us certain he must have misunderstood this tale about killing aunts and many Canadian sailors.

When I at last explained myself, he laughed off my bug crusade and left me with the shortsighted impression that this sort of violence had no moral import. If I confessed these same sins today, however, I predict the average priest would confirm my expression of guilt, and encourage a maturing sensitivity and responsibility.

Fortunately near this time I joined the Friendly Indian Club at the local YMCA, led by a young college student who, if I recall accurately, claimed descent from the Oneida or Iroquois tribes northeast of us. A small troop of budding naturalists and trekkers, we would journey every few weeks to nearby woods or sometimes a remote state forest, and pick up litter, explore trails, dig for flint arrowheads, and listen to wisdom and legend passed down from our Native American ancestors.

I must admit that my image of a Friendly Indian at that time was shaped in counterpoint to the 1930's Hollywood stereotype of a Hostile Indian. I could not imagine a cowardly Indian, nor for that matter, one that was fat, runty, or near-sighted. In my watch-pocket I began carrying a sacred arrowhead to which I attributed the power to guarantee me at least a one-base hit whenever I fingered it during a softball game. I think these Primal rites of passage were my first crucial lessons in appreciating animals and the natural world. I learned how to listen intently to sounds in the woods, see with keen scrutiny, befriend the animals, trees, and ancestral spirits of the land.

A Scientist's Initiative

The virtual Native American in me, then, once felt impelled to turn from my explicit Christian heritage in search of a wiser ecology. For this reason I can feel some empathy today for those puzzled by the oxymoron of a Christian ecologist. In a simple zero-sum estimate, by emphasis on the otherworldly and transcendent, Jews and Christians and Muslims seem at first glance to undervalue the natural and the human. Few have proved more alert to this grievance than the poet Rainer Maria Rilke: "What madness, to distract us to a beyond, when we are surrounded right here by tasks and expectations and futures. What fraud, to steal images of earthly rapture and sell them to heaven behind our backs. It is high time for the impoverished earth to claim back all those loans which have been raised on her bliss to furnish some future-beyond!" Rilke recognized that his earlier poems used to speak with familiarity to and about God. Yet by

1923 he acknowledged that "now you would hardly ever hear me refer to God... God's attributes are taken away from God, a name no longer utterable, and returned to the created universe."[2]

To underline the mutual wariness that affects environmental scientists and theologians I will single out one representative book, published in 1997, accessible and provocative. Here sociobiologist Connie Barlow samples various conversations and interviews launched with key ecologists, biologists, and New Age theologians—all interwoven as an implicit dialogue among members of an ideal scientific community. In the first dozen pages community members and their families are introduced by casual snapshots, mostly to suggest that the scientist is no disembodied technocrat smelling of formaldehyde but a complete human being.

Though offering religious leaders a cordial welcome into conversation with scientists, the author soon discloses a preemptive dress code. All participants must be sufficiently greened. In other words, they should care passionately about the environment. Yet they must also strip themselves of "superstition and supernaturalism" and irrelevant historical baggage. In the spirit of Joseph Campbell and other New Age guides Barlow has endorsed "the mythic metaphors of diverse religious heritages, while savaging those who corrupted the metaphor by claiming its material truth."[3] She conjectures with sociobiologist Edward Wilson that the human body at present is encoded with evolving archetypal needs, a tropism reaching out for spiritual metaphors.

Those religious traditions she finds most congenial, as anticipated, are the Wisdom Ways of India, China, and Japan. Impatient to intervene in the political process she supports the activist wing in each Asian Way against a mere narcissistic quest for higher consciousness. The Primal Ways are an ideal resource, too, especially Native American and Australian Aboriginal rituals. Euro-American or Afrocentric believers dissatisfied with their own current religious heritage are encouraged to burrow deeper for Earth Goddess roots in the Celtic and Yoruba past.

The Ways of Jews, Christians, and Muslims, however, do prove an annoyance to Barlow and many of her colleagues. Riveted on actual historical events, these traditions refuse to be reduced to sheer metaphor. What frustrates her most about all historical Ways is that those encouraging "the most brotherly love may not be so good for sisters.

Those that stress compassion may not always be the best at getting the fields plowed and warding off ill-intentioned intruders. Those that promote peace and harmony within the group may be bloody terrors without."[4]

What looks most promising about Barlow's work and similar environmental manifestos is the scientific community's determination to seize a fresh initiative, no matter how flawed its gestures of inclusion. I think convincing motives lie behind this reaching out. First, ecologists and other members of the scientific community have a genuine attachment to the natural world and thus feel actual panic about an environmental apocalypse. They intend to enlist every potential supporting voice, no matter what the source. Second, within the last century the history of science has shifted emphasis from atomistic particles, physics, and objectivity, to holistic field theory, biology, and relativity. Some of the old certainties and professional arrogance have eroded, therefore, especially within this postmodern era which opens up the exploration of alternate worldviews. As mentioned earlier, many scientists have discovered a resourceful new perspective in Taoist physics, a Buddhist interdependent cosmos, or a Zen awakening to the wonders of nature.

Perhaps the most significant reason for this fresh lead taken by the scientific community is an attempt to reinstate the lost balance between mythos and logos, described in the previous chapter. Ties with the soil, the fertility cycles of nature, the dimension of feeling and imagination and spirituality, all subordinated for centuries to the triumph of scientific analysis, now demand their compensation. For this reason, I can understand how a scientist might be tempted to reduce this freshly reclaimed religious factor simply to its neglected mythos function— viewed now as merely a ritual, an emotional story, or inspiring metaphor. Such a bias will alienate many theologians. However, the scientist's attempt to sensitize or green these theologians might send them back to transform the environmental ethics of their respective religious traditions. A shift in the moral priorities of these communities might then animate a true development of doctrine. Or perhaps traditionalists among them will insist that their own ancient texts and symbols only needed a fresh revisiting and reinterpretation.

To ignite environmental activism, then, Barlow treats the global religious traditions as mythic metaphors, some preferable to others—all useful as inspiring motives yet stripped of their historical facticity. My own perspective differs from hers in a few important features. To me, the traditional religious Ways represent many plausible visions of meaning. By the term *meaning* I refer to a coherent sense of worth or purpose which gives confidence to both the individual and community when they face daily discouragement. Why are some environmentalists prepared better than others to endure all the frustrating evasions from legislators, agency bureaucrats, corporate managers and shareholders? Perhaps because they count on an eventual Marxist proletarian millennium, or an advent reconciliation between Christ and all living things, or an ever mounting advancement of scientific discovery. These moral visions are more than just a spark of archetypal magic. Each has cognitive content— a program for action, motives to sustain achievable change, criteria to measure success or failure. I want all Ways, religious and moral humanist, heard out with equity, and thus guarded from partisan editing. Any vision will have to be discounted eventually, of course, if refuted by events and thus conducive to despair, or if proven idolatrous and thus self-destructive.[5]

God within the World

The core of environmental ethics in the Jewish, Christian, and Muslim Ways can be condensed to two essential affirmations. First, the basis of respect for the earth is not a cosmos-centered nor even human-centered perspective but God-centered. And second, the environmental crisis must never be treated in isolation but interconnected with a range of other moral concerns, including industrial greed, neglect of the poor and oppressed, war and other forms of imperialism. Each of these two assumptions will now be explored in turn.

To begin with, a God-centered ecology cannot be persuasive unless based on a God-image that is multi-faceted and coherent. It is true that the Bible and Quran can depict God as utterly unlike the created world —a sovereign judge or architect usually disengaged except for rare miraculous intrusions. Yet prayers and mystical literature in the Jewish, Christian, and Muslim Ways perceive God not only as a remote transcendent power but also as a vital presence immanent to all the earth. God's reality is so huge that nothing can encompass it, but so small and pervasive that Luther is amazed it can be "substantially present in a grain, on a grain, over a grain, through a grain, within and without, and although a single majesty, nevertheless entirely in each grain separately." 6

Many Sufi poems meditate on a single refrain: in the desert twilight, in the instant of quiet between question and answer, in the grace of the graceful, the dance of the dancer, in the flame and the burning, Allah is there. Allah and each of Allah's creatures are entwined like two chemical ingredients transformed by alchemy or like two lovers utterly lost in each other. Some Jewish Kabbalist mystics imagine the world's creation as the instant that God's glory shattered into fragments of light, scattered throughout the universe. Profane life now is filled with these many separated hidden sparks yearning to be freed from their constricting shells and reunited to the completed Godhead. By each loving deed we uncover the sacred particles and by releasing them with reverence help God restore this primordial unity. 7

Humanity, the Measure of All Things?

Challenging the environmental awareness of Jews, Muslims, and especially Christians, ecologists at times express hostility against any human-centered ecology, framed in either religious or secular terms, even when it is balanced and self-critical. During his Sermon on the Mount, for example, Jesus assures people that God our father cares for the birds of the sky. Then he asks his audience, "Are you not worth much more than they?" To this question, one famous environmentalist, insisting on an even-handed life-centered perspective, once answered a thundering "No!" Thus, a sound concern for humanity can be easily misinterpreted as a fixation on humanity to the point of disregard for everything else.

The wisdom traditions of Native Americans and Asians, as described before, teach respect for the web of interdependence that links everything in the universe, especially all living beings. Yet lordly human egos are tempted to poke into the vital network without foresight for others, even for their own grandchildren. This situation has become a favorite theme in contemporary science fiction. T.C. Boyle's story, "Top of the Food Chain," captures the arrogant way self-appointed American experts sweep into a poorer nation and first of all hose down the inhabitants, build latrines, and disinfect the crops. After expressing his contempt for the hop-head birdwatchers at the Environmental Protection Agency, the narrator tries to explain to an unspecified committee why his scientific rescue-mission to Borneo failed. His team had been sent to spray DDT on malarial mosquitoes. But the insecticide also killed off a type of wasp, needed to keep down the caterpillar population, which soon proceeded to eat the palm leaf roofing of people's huts. Mosquitoes were then outrivaled by a plague of flies, multiplying to such an extent that geckos gorged on them and died, a feast for an increasing plague of rats, controlled in turn by importing Australian cats, which eventually served as a novel diet for the starving people. "No one could foresee the consequence," the narrator protests. "It was like all nature had turned against us." [8]

Ray Bradbury, in "A Sound of Thunder," tests the implications of this same interdependency, violated by the insertion of a man from present time back into an early phase of evolution. Eckel pays thousands of dollars to join a Time Safari Inc. hunt for a live dinosaur. Transported back through centuries by a handy time machine, he lands in a primeval jungle, where he accidentally steps on a butterfly. On return to the present, Eckel is dismayed to find the Time company's logo has changed its spelling, a somewhat different clerk sits at a different desk, and a hated rival of the nation's president governs in his place. Destroy a mouse, and you destroy the wild boar needing it, and then the cave man grandchild of Adam that needs the boar. The trampled butterfly, Eckel decides, could upset balances and knock down a line of ever larger dominoes across time, so that George Washington might have never crossed the Delaware.[9]

At this moment of writing I pick up daily press accounts that mirror the Boyle and Bradbury stories about intrusions into the tightly interwoven ecosystem. The death of five hundred Kentucky prized mares and their fetuses may perhaps be traced to a cyanide spray used on cherry trees, the leaves of which are eaten by a species of tent caterpillar, whose droppings have somehow tainted the grass diet of horses. According to another article, a recent siege of rolling power blackouts in Northern California will prompt greedy energy-merchants to raise prices, which might be mitigated by construction of new public generators supplied with dwindling resources of oil and gas and by the use of more private tractor-size generators run by dirty diesel fuel, all of which will require heavier regulation by environmental agencies. The pending energy bill of Alaska Senator Frank Murkowski has drawn censure from environmentalists for its plan to submit part of the Arctic Wildlife Refuge to oil drilling—and thus to invade the northern breeding ground of the caribou, homeland also for the indigenous Gwich'in people and their sacred burial sites, and also a refuge part of the year for almost two hundred species of migratory birds from the United States.[10]

When environmentalists hunt for a religious target to blame for abusing the natural world, they often settle on a distorted logos-centered or human-centered ethics which seems to thrive in the Jewish and Christian Ways. Does an alleged Christian axiom not claim that nature has no reason to exist except to serve human beings? Such an attack elicits a characteristic rebuttal: "The evidence for the existence of that axiom, which exists in no creed known to me, seems at times to consist of Ronald Reagan's throw-away remark that 'when you've seen one redwood tree you've seen them all,' uncritical quotation of the biblical injunction to have 'dominion,' and an equally uncritical conviction that Christianity, being dualist, anti-materialist, and founded on the idea of a transcendent, male deity, must be opposed to nature, animals, and women."[11]

One of the most widely lampooned adversaries of the ecology movement within recent decades has been James Watt, Secretary of the Interior during the Reagan administration. Various cartoons have portrayed him as a fox in the hencoop, a wild sheep dog terrifying the sheep, or a brown-robed St. Francis of Assisi, not communing with the birds, but armed with a heavy bat in the midst of animal carcasses and lopped off trees. His political and economic views have tended to favor private industry, more development of mineral resources on public lands, and an increase of commercial concessions in national parks. By citing the Bible and his Christian beliefs often, Watt has given adversaries the impression that his environmental policies are based on an explicit Christian geo-ethics, treating the earth as just a temporary pit stop on the way into heaven. The Lord gave his people the earth to subdue for profitable use in order to pass unspotted through a corrupt, dangerous world on their way to eternity.

Though I think articles written by Watts himself show moderation, his feisty media interviews have generated the most outrageous remarks.

One moment he would call national parks "cathedrals to the wonder of nature and to the glory of the Creator" and insist we identify ourselves as God's servants who "cannot waste or despoil that which we've been given in the Earth because we don't know our tenure here." Yet he has spelled out this concept of limited tenure in a prickly way: "Build a road, build a latrine, pump in running water, so you can wash dishes. Most people think if you can drive in, walk twenty yards and pitch a tent by a stream, you've had a wilderness experience. Do we have to buy enough land so that you can go backpacking and never see anyone else?" Or "America's resources were put here for the enjoyment and use of people, now and in the future, and should not be denied to the people by elitist groups." Watt could seldom resist a baiting contest.[12]

In my opinion the environmental crisis stems indeed from a human-centered perspective, but only a distorted form of it. Jews, Christians, and Muslims all emphasize human salvation or liberation first —yet not exclusively—and through humanity the rest of the cosmos. This human-centered worldview has often been warped, especially by what eco-feminist theologians, using the language of gender stereotypes, call *andro-centrism*. Such a distortion could be defined as a hierarchical and domineering sensibility in either a man or a woman. The tendency includes domination of human by human, women by men, the young by their elders, one ethnic group by another, homosexuals by heterosexuals, society by the nation-state, the individual by bureaucracy, one economic class by another, a colonized people by colonial powers, the natural world by humans. Any ecological revolution at its most profound must develop into a comprehensive social ecology.[13]

The Jewish, Christian, and Muslim Ways, on the contrary, are not primarily human-centered but God-centered. For they affirm one personal God as creative source of an evolving cosmos that culminates in human life. As Muhammad Talbi affirms, "God also has rights. 'Anthropolatry' is so pervasive that we tend to forget this. And human beings have more than rights. They also have duties, in a horizontal ethical relationship with one another, but also in a vertical relationship with God, a relationship of hope and free and trusting adherence. For me as a Muslim any ethic which does not integrate this vertical relationship, this transcendental dimension of my humanity, is untenable."[14]

Far from permitting human exploitation of the world, God instead sets limits on the human use of it and will hold our use accountable. Exemplifying this accountability motif, one widely accepted hadith attributes the following aphorism to Muhammad: "When doomsday comes, if you have a palm shoot in your hand, you should plant it." Thus, even if there seems no earthly future, the planting of life should continue because such planting is good in itself and pleasing to God. And according to another hadith, "All creatures are God's dependents, and the best among them is the one who is most useful to God's dependents." [15]

Reading Creation Right

Among environmentalist charges against the Jewish and Christian Ways in particular, the same few conspicuous misreadings of the Bible continue to resurface, almost like a karate exhibition of flimsy exegetical skill. Perhaps these errors could be dispelled by a more resourceful examination of the text. I will focus on crucial Jewish and Christian Scriptures first, and treat the Quran later. The Book of Genesis introduces two narratives about God creating the cosmos—the Priestly account in chapter 1, the Yahwist account in chapter 2. The Priestly account depicts a cosmology contrasted with the religious cosmologies of nearby cultures, where the sun, moon, even certain animals, if not deified, had at least been considered superior to human beings.

In this Hebrew Priestly creation story of chapter 1, on the contrary, all other creatures exist to serve human beings, the lords of creation. These lords in turn have been given "dominion" (GEN 1:28) over the fish of the sea, the birds of heaven, and all living animals on the earth. Even more clearly the matching Yahwist creation account in chapter 2 says that human beings are given the earth "to till and care for it" (GEN 2:15). The Book of Wisdom describes again how God has given us dominion, but adds an illuminating phrase about this role: "to govern the world in holiness and saving justice" (WISDOM 9:2). Reflecting on these texts, the Talmud imagines God taking Adam and Eve aside in Eden to remind them, "See my works, how excellent they are! All that I created, I created for you. Consider that and do not corrupt or destroy my world. For if you corrupt it, there will be no one to set it right after you." [16]

As Rabbi Norman Solomon remarks, the concept of dominion in the Priestly creation story cannot mean a despotic rule of exploiting and destroying. But human beings, created in the image of God, are stewards, "summoned to share in his creative work, and to do all in their power to sustain creation." [17] The renowned first-century Jewish moral philosopher Philo of Alexandria taught a similar responsibility. "No mortal can in solid reality be lord of anything," he says. "God alone can rightly claim that all things are his possession... You have no good thing of your own, but whatever you think you have, Another has provided. Thus, we infer that all things are the possession of him who gives... Even if you take, take not for yourself, but count that which is given a loan or trust, and render it back to him who entrusted and leased it to you." [18] This attitude of loving reciprocity echoes the teaching in Primal Ways that whatever you take from the sacred earth must somehow be returned.

Perhaps the most imaginative sketch of a Hebrew cosmology with plausible implications for an environmental ethics occurs in the Genesis flood narrative and the Covenant with Noah. Once the flood subsides, God says to Noah: "I set my bow in the clouds and it will be a sign of the covenant between me and the earth. When I gather the clouds over the earth and the bow appears in the clouds, I will recall the covenant between myself and you and every living creature..." (GEN 9:13-15). Here God is portrayed as taking a fresh start, granting a new covenant, not just with human beings but with all living things, all the creatures saved two by two aboard the ark. The rainbow and other imagery suggest a cosmology more life-centered or cosmos-centered, not so emphatically human-centered as elsewhere. [19]

Throughout both the Old and New Testaments a range of motifs emerge—earth as partner with human beings in a sacred covenant, and even earth as sacrament or icon of an immanent God. By their own selfishness human beings tend repeatedly to alienate themselves from God, from one another, and from the original Garden of Eden. And as a consequence the earth rebels against them. As Hosea and other Hebrew Prophets later picture this alienation, "Therefore the land mourns and all who dwell in it languish, and also the beasts of the field and the birds of the air and even the fish of the sea are taken away"(HOS 4:3). In this text environmental disaster is linked once again to a profound moral alienation. From a Jewish perspective the future messianic era of justice and peace, however, will restore the Garden to its original utopian design. According to the Prophets wolf and lamb will lie down together, a human child can play near the lair of snakes. God will pour water on the thirsty soil, renew a covenant with all the earth, and replace our hearts of stone with true human hearts. "You will be my people, and I will be your God... I shall increase the yield of fruit trees and of fields... This land, so recently a waste, is now like a garden of Eden" (EZEK 36: 28, 30, 35).

Building on this Jewish world-affirming vision, the Christian Way adds a Christ-centered sacramental dimension which again reaffirms the inherent presence of God. By viewing the cosmos as a sacrament, I mean that material reality, worthy of awe simply as matter, participates in the sacred reality it symbolizes—a window to the Sacred. Christ's combined incarnation-death-resurrection somehow restores the whole cosmos to God's original creative plan. From the beginning, God has intended to become the God-Man, the pivot and goal of everything that God is continuously creating. The earth thus has within itself a gyroscopic dynamism leading everything toward this culmination. Paul's Letter to the Ephesians tells of "the mystery which God set forth in Christ as a plan for the fullness of time, to unite all things in him, all things in heaven and earth" (EPH 1:9-10). Paul's Letter to the Romans even shows "the entire creation from the beginning, groaning in one great act of giving birth," longing for this fulfillment (ROM 8:22).

Christian mystics and poets have tried every means to suggest the impact of Christ's incarnation, not just on humanity, but also on the rest of the earth. St. Gregory of Nyssa depicts Jesus immersing himself in waters of the Jordan, which symbolize all forces of the earth. As he emerges, Christ sanctifies and elevates the whole world by means of the water which runs off his body. "Mighty Matter," the famous prayer of Teilhard de Chardin begins, "the hand of God, the flesh of Christ." Teilhard reveres this natural world as "the divine milieu," an ocean "stirred by the Spirit, clay molded and infused with life by the incarnate Word." [20] In Dostoyevsky's *Brothers Karamazov* the monk Zossima pauses on a warm July night, so quiet that he can hear the splash of fish and identify each separate bird call. "Every blade of grass," he tells his peasant friend on their forest journey, "every insect, ant, and golden bee, all so marvelously know their path... Christ has been with them here even before us... The Word is for all. All creation, every leaf is striving toward the Lord, singing glory to God, weeping to Christ, even unconsciously." [21] For this reason Zossima, Alyosha, and so many other mystics of the soil drop down in reverence to kiss the earth, beg its forgiveness, and enjoy a life of solidarity with all living creatures, even the unseen spirit world.

A Comprehensive Social Ecology

Besides a God-centered view of the cosmos, Jews, Christians, and Muslims introduce a second key premise into their teaching on ecology. They refuse to perceive the environmental crisis in isolation but only interconnected with a range of other moral concerns. After all, a genuine ecological perspective implies a cosmos so organically interrelational that people cannot change their own individual lives without affecting first their immediate neighbor, and then successively, entire nations, all living beings, and all reality.

A Moral Cosmos

"A Handful of Dates," by Tayeb Salih, a Sudanese Muslim, hints at the wider moral implications of any actual crime against the earth. Centered on a young boy's consciousness, the story begins by describing the respect and affection the narrator has always felt for his grandfather. Yet it culminates in such hatred against his grandfather that the boy vomits up the few dates the man has fed him. What experience has reversed the boy's attitude? Before, they both used to read the Quran and pray together daily. The boy had won respect in the mosque for devoutly memorizing large portions of the Quran. He yearned someday to resemble the older man's tall, slender stature, his composure, and other conjectured moral features. In his daydreams he tended to associate his grandfather with an imaginary tribe of giant spirits that looked like him, all living behind his family's date palms and other trees along the Nile.

One day his grandfather recounts for the first time that Masood, an irresponsible neighbor, having inherited all these trees long ago, now owns only the last third of this legacy. To pay off his debts, mostly for womanizing, the contemptible man has sold the trees gradually to the boy's grandfather, who hopes soon to grab up the rest of them. The narrator has never attributed much value to ownership for its own sake nor does he welcome this expression of greed and disdain. He had thought the trees belonged to his grandfather "since God's Creation." He tells himself, "I don't care who owns those date palms, those trees or this black, cracked earth. All I know is that it's the arena for my dreams and my playground." He begins to fear for Masood, whom he now views in a fresh way—a man like himself, endowed with a sense of humor and warmth that his grandfather lacks. He recalls how Masood had once shown extraordinary pity toward those very trees on a day the boy had played carelessly with a young palm branch. "Palm trees, my boy," Masood told him, "like humans, experience joy and suffering."

Next, the boy and his grandfather are invited to the date harvest by Masood, where workers with long knives, carelessly hacking huge bundles of dates that crash to the ground, pay no attention to Masood's painful cry, "Be careful you don't cut the heart of the palm." After the harvest, various neighbors examine the date sacks and cart away their allotments, and the grandfather takes his five sacks, with a gruff reminder to Masood about the money he still owes. Given a fistful of dates to eat by his grandfather, the boy fixes his attention instead on how Masood must be feeling. The man seems overwhelmed, lifting a few dates to his nostrils but then returning them to the sacks. A sound escapes from his throat, "like the rasping of a lamb being slaughtered." Not just the heart of these date trees, but the heart of Masood himself is being sacrificed, ravaged by the boy's grandfather. The boy feels a tightening in his chest, a secret lodged inside him. Does he taste intimations of a symbolic cannibalism? The boy runs away and forces himself to cough up the dates, trying to renounce any complicity in this crime.[22]

Salih's story alerts the reader to an allegedly irresponsible harvesting of the date crop, hacked away for an immediate windfall without foresight to protect the growing stalk for future harvests. It would be morally superficial to pause over sheer details of the harm to palm growth and crop outcome or the chemical and social management remedies. Masood grieves that first he himself, and now others, too, are mishandling not only the palm trees, but also his vanishing heritage and his own soul. Here are the wider repercussions of a symbolic crime against the earth—an abuse of living plants, but more important, the abuse of a human person closely associated with them. The young narrator is a fervent Muslim who associates the trees first with God's Creation and with a world of his own free appreciation and fantasy but only secondly with any sort of actual ownership. Accustomed to superimpose on these trees the image of his grandfather, by the story's conclusion he superimposes the image of the pitiable Masood. By greed and selfishness the boy's grandfather has abused his ownership, no longer holding the orchard in trust as part of God's Creation or showing the mercy and compassion enjoined by the Quran. Thus, interwoven with this man's sin against the earth is a sin against Masood, his grandfather's deeper self, and God.

The boy's ruminations in this story touch on a major prophetic theme in the Quran. Allah will judge us, not by empty ritual observance but by a sound religious life committed to social justice: "Righteousness does not consist in whether you face toward the east or the west. The righteous man is he who believes in Allah and the Last Day, in the angels and the Scriptures and the prophets; who for the love of Allah gives his wealth to his kinsfolk, to orphans, the needy, wayfarers and beggars, and for the redemption of captives; who attends to his prayers and pays the alms-tax; who is true to his promises and steadfast in trial and adversity and in times of war" (2:177).[23] In the Quran Allah always acts with a single didactic moral purpose, making one attempt after another to shape human beings into more worthy disciples. Each moment of beauty in creation does not exist in its own right but elicits the refrain, "Can't you connect this with my mercy," or "Don't you realize I'm showing here how much I care about you." A characteristic passage reads: "Do you not see how Allah sends down water from the sky and covers the earth with vegetation? He is wise and all-knowing... Do you not see how He has subdued to you all that is in the earth? He has given you ships which sail the sea at His bidding. He holds the sky from falling down; this it shall not do except by His own will. Compassionate is Allah, and merciful to men"(22: 62-6).

The Quranic creation narrative shows many parallels with the Hebrew Genesis narrative discussed before, but this later account has its own distinctive emphasis. Echoing the problematic conferral of dominion mentioned in Genesis, the sura above says Allah has subdued all the earth to human management. Yet there must be no misunderstanding about the basis and limits of this power. Whereas Adam names the animals in Genesis and thus shows some independent creativity, Allah himself in the Quran teaches the animals' names to Adam. Adam in his pre-earthly existence, flanked by the angels, learns why he is about to be created a human being: "I am placing on the earth one that shall rule as my deputy"(2:30). According to the Muslim scholar Nomanul Haq, the word used here is Khalifa or Caliph, meaning vicegerent, custodian, or trustee, and must be interpreted in the context of recurring passages that insist Allah alone has sovereignty and full knowledge.[24] Prone to exaggerate our self-importance in the universe, we are cautioned, "The creation of heaven and earth is greater than the creation of man, yet most men do not know it"(40:55). Tempted to mistreat the subhuman world, we are reminded, "All the beasts that roam the earth and all the birds that wing their flight are communities like your own. We have left out nothing in Our Book. They shall all be gathered before their Lord"(6:39). And again, "God intends no injustice to any of His creatures. To Him belongs all that is in the heavens and the earth" (3: 108-9).

The Quran recounts how Adam and Eve disobeyed Allah and left Eden, but their fall is not the cosmic calamity depicted by Paul in the Christian Scriptures, nor does the present world yearn for cosmic redemption. Christians view the natural universe as a sacrament, a window into the Sacred. From a comparable Muslim perspective Allah communicates in two ways—first through the created universe, and second especially through the Quran, which spells out the moral meaning of these natural symbols or emblems. As Allah's caliph each of us is expected to construe these signs, preserve the preestablished balance of the universe, and treat it with reverence. Not only a human being but every created being has its own unique relationship with Allah, all of them prostrating themselves in *islam*, which means literally submissive worship: "Do you not see how all who dwell in heaven and earth do homage to Allah? The sun and the moon and the stars, the mountains and the trees, the beasts, and countless men—all prostrate themselves before Allah" (22: 18).

To Allah is attributed "knowledge of all that land and sea contain. Every leaf that falls is known to Him. There is no grain of soil in the darkest bowels of the earth, nor anything green or sear, but is recorded in His glorious Book" (6:59). The Quran and the Bible are filled with hymns of praise to God the Creator, notably in the biblical Psalms, celebrating a rich poetic inventory of the magnificent earth, sky, sea. St. Francis of Assisi evokes this panorama in his famous Canticle of Creatures: "Praise to you, my Lord, through Sister Moon and the stars; in heaven you formed them clear and precious and beautiful." And praise "through Brother Fire by whom you light the night; he is beautiful and playful and robust and strong." And praise "through our Sister Mother Earth who sustains and governs us and produces various fruit with colorful flowers and herbs." Meditating especially on the Psalms, Pope John Paul II in his 1990 address on the environmental crisis commends the restorative power that results from contemplating the beauty of nature. He hopes the next generations will be trained in aesthetic sensitivity and ecological responsibility from childhood onwards. Their education should include an appreciation for human artifacts, too, such as cities—wise urban planning, for instance, and respect for the natural contours of the land. A sound environmental ethics, he thinks, "must not be based on a rejection of the modern world, or a vague desire to return to some paradise lost." [25]

This ecological awareness, however, must be expanded into a wider moral vision. The pope asserts that "mere utilitarian considerations or an aesthetic approach to nature cannot be the sufficient basis for a genuine education in ecology. We must all learn to approach the environmental question with solid ethical convictions involving responsibility, self-control, justice, and fraternal love." We are only God's junior managers of the earth, not its absolute masters. "Human beings must not make use of nature against their own good, the good of their fellow human beings, and the good of future generations." To achieve a more rational management of the earth's resources is not enough. We must confront "in its entirety that profound moral crisis of which the destruction of the environment is only one troubling aspect." [26]

Humanity under Siege

Though defending the Jewish, Christian, and Muslim Scriptures against misreadings, I must acknowledge the validity of a few environmentalist objections against some widespread Christian misinterpretations of the New Testament. I have already singled out a dualistic fixation in early Anabaptist sermons, martyrologies, and hymns. Labeled Zoroastrian, Gnostic, or Manichaen, the heresy under different names tends to recur so frequently throughout Christian history that I conjecture at times about cultural limitations in the biblical formulation itself. In various eras this dualism has fostered an asceticism of combat against material possessions, the beauty of the human body and natural world. Much of the New Testament, I concede, shows a preference for dramatic polarities—God and Satan, Christ and Anti-Christ, spirit and flesh, gospel and law, grace and good works, inner and outer meaning. Many Christian sectarians and fundamentalists have tended to inflate these polarities into shocking dichotomies. Beginning as nonviolent and kindly neighbors, many Anabaptist communities, as I explained before, grew rigid under persecution and cut themselves away from the dominant social order outside, viewed more and more as an apocalyptic enemy.

The early Christian Church experienced a similar hardening process during its gradual repudiation by the Roman World. Mirroring this alienation, Christian opposition congealed against the religious mystery and fertility Ways of the Greco-Roman majority. And thus one more vivid polarity surfaces, especially in the Fourth Gospel, the Epistles of John, and the Book of Revelation—not just darkness versus light, evil versus good, death versus life, but the world versus Christ. This "world," which includes the Greco-Roman socio-religious milieu and more, is often perceived as evil, a threatening horizon set against the true Christian Way. Some New Testament passages mythologize the world as a domain under control of dark principalities and powers. To the average Puritan sectarian in colonial America, for example, forest and wilderness did not connote a primeval paradise, as it would for Transcendentalists like Emerson, Thoreau, or John Muir. Puritans treated it as the realm of otherness, a screen upon which the majority could project all they were not. This symbolic space might hint at what good Christians had once been, what they now repressed, what they could yet become. Wild nature was identified with ostracized sinners, a world unredeemed, the kingdom of Satan, including the Primal people living there.

The environmentalist banner, to no one's surprise, has also generated its own extremists—a worthy shadow-image of the Christian dualistic world-haters just described. To a moderate environmentalist viewpoint, the so-called monkeywrenchers, committed to the "earth-first" protest movement, prove a rude embarrassment. In order to block timber-cutting, overgrazing, mining, and powerline construction, for instance, they devise various weapons of sabotage to clog the gears of inanimate tools capable of harming people or other forms of life. As a result, slicing into insidious nails hidden in the timber, buzz saws have sometimes injured the hands or eyes of workers. Often a strategic annoyance to companies because of consequent delay, hassle, and expense for repairs, this activist movement claims to be nonviolent toward other human beings.[27]

Unlike monkey-wrenchers, the Earth Liberation Front, a loosely organized secret movement under current FBI scrutiny, supports direct violence. Backing a policy of "Burn the Rich" and "Stop Urban Sprawl," they claim responsibility for vandalism and arson against any property perceived as a conspicuous symbol of environmental profiteering. ELF targets have included thirty sport-utility vehicles in an Oregon sales lot, a Nike store dealing in shoes allegedly manufactured by sweatshop labor, farms raising mink and fox for luxury furs, newly built homes in Long Island and ski lodges around Vail in Colorado. At present they seem to be sabotaging research by the very scientists from whom they might have won grudging support for their green ideology. Recently arsonists gutted a lab building at the University of Washington's center for Urban Horticulture, and left the following graffiti—"You cannot control what is wild" and "ELF." Apparently they are protesting against research into the genetic modification of forests, a project financed by various large corporations. According to one conservation biologist employed at the lab, the fire unfortunately destroyed her carefully nurtured samples of the rare Showy Stickseed plant, one quarter of the world's remaining specimens.[28]

Vindication of the eco-terrorist cause may seem important enough to require the destruction of someone's property or even a human life. This misanthropy suggests a memorable cartoon, featuring three men and a dog adrift on a raft. Pointing to one cowering man, his colleague tells him, "The vote's three to one, so you'll have to jump overboard." For some ecologists the disparagement of human overpopulation as "the people plague" or "a planetary disease" seems an acceptable pastime. The acclaimed naturalist Jacques Cousteau wonders what can be done to eliminate suffering and disease. "It's a wonderful idea," he admits, "but perhaps not altogether beneficial in the long run... World population must be stabilized, and to do that we must eliminate 350,000 people per day." Another critic laments that "our humanist concerns about the poor of the inner cities of the Third World, and our near-obscene obsession with death, suffering, and pain as if these were evil in themselves—these thoughts divert the mind from our gross and excessive domination of the natural world." [29]

To treat the human community as an overpopulated beehive or termitarium, I am convinced, is a prelude to ecological fascism. Joined to attacks against the human-centered teaching of the Bible, green activism at this intensity becomes a caricature of Malthus and Darwin. One of the most persuasive critiques of radical Social Darwinism, on the contrary, can be found in Charles Darwin himself. Throughout his career he tried to hear out all the ethical arguments on eugenic intervention, pro and contra. "We build asylums for the imbecile, the maimed, and the sick," he wrote in *Descent of Man*. "We institute poor-laws; and our medical men exert their utmost skill to save the life of everyone to the last moment... If we were intentionally to neglect the weak and helpless, it could only be for a contingent benefit, with an overwhelming present evil... Nor could we check our sympathy, even at the urging of hard reason, without deterioration in the noblest part of our nature." [30]

I think many environmental moderates share Darwin's misgivings. They will not let their comprehensive social ecology be reduced to a narrow ideological battle against U.S. overpopulation—the political catchwords of anti-growth, anti-sprawl, anti-fertility, or anti-immigration. For example, the Sierra Club, one of the most influential U.S. environmental organizations, held a famous 1998 referendum. Members were polled to determine if the Club should adopt a stricter anti-immigration policy than it promoted in the previous three decades. What is the root of environmental problems? Losers of the vote targeted U.S. overpopulation and urged the Club to lobby for a tighter U.S. anti-immigration policy. The 60% winning majority, however, wanted neutrality on the immigration issue. Instead they specified a broader range of causes—the loss of wilderness; pollution from irresponsible mining, timber, and oil interests; and worldwide overpopulation, of which local immigration is only a symptom. Nativists since then attack the majority's "environmental justice" position for pandering to ethnic minorities, and proving unpardonably human-centered rather than eco-centered.[31]

In my opinion, the environmental idealist, vigilant to save threatened rainforests and animal life, needs exposure to a more realistic perspective on humanity—what Reinhold Niebuhr calls the human paradox of our combined nobility yet insecurity. The biblical narrative about Original Sin, a "sin of origins," is reinterpreted by Niebuhr as the universal human tendency to act from distorted self-centeredness. Environmental activists must never blind themselves to the hidden self-interest in their own idealism. Niebuhr thinks the will to power will prove increasingly more demonic and intense, as its perimeter widens from individual to family, race, church, and nation. Even the nation-state is tempted to seek false security by amassing land and natural resources. Longstanding power structures in society will not yield to rhapsodic appeals for wildlife preservation. Only to the extent that people are liberated from greed and selfishness are they enabled to love humanity and the natural world.[32]

As proof of entrenched self-interest and power, or at least their apparent side-effects, I can point to a series of recent protests at different world economic summits. Why has the very mention of globalization sparked such furious opposition, first at the 1999 Seattle World Trade Organization meeting, then later in Quebec City, Genoa, and elsewhere? To globalize means to de-regulate tariff boundaries, impose uniform standards, and incorporate small local economies into an international laissez faire market system. For many developing nations a global free market means that Euro-American textile, agriculture, and pharmaceutical products will lose their protectionist advantage. Yet free-market catchwords, on the contrary, may disguise a takeover by the multinationals, a Euro-American cultural invasion from Pepsi, McDonald's, Disney—with most news packaged worldwide eventually through CNN, music through MTV, sports panoramas through ESPN. Pressured by the International Money Fund and World Bank to pay off a ruinous spiral of debt, governments of developing nations could be tempted to discount social responsibility toward their own domestic economy, the environment, the education and health of their neediest citizens.[33]

Hoping to avert this sort of globalized damage, then, a rare coalition of student and labor protesters at the Seattle summit prodded business leaders to guard the economic and cultural integrity of poorer nations. U.S. delegates aimed to impose humane environmental and labor standards on all trade partners, rules that claimed to guarantee the well-being of local workers and the wider environment everywhere. However, the very nations destined to benefit from such proposals ended up frustrating the idealists. Delegates of some developing nations suspected that behind this humane smokescreen lurked a plot to protect First World jobs by inflicting their own affluent standards on poor economies that lacked the capacity to implement them.[34]

Confirming this Third World distrust, a ruinous piece of evidence was cited repeatedly. This was an internal memo of 1992 leaked from the World Bank, written allegedly by Lawrence Summers, the bank's chief economist, Secretary of the Treasury in Clinton's administration, and current president of Harvard. He wanted the World Bank to encourage more migration of "dirty industries" to less developed countries. "A given amount of health-impairing pollution should be done in the country with the lowest wages. I think the economic logic behind dumping a load of toxic waste in the lowest-wage country is impeccable and we should face up to that… I've always thought that under-populated countries in Africa are vastly under-polluted; their air quality is probably vastly inefficiently high compared to Los Angeles or Mexico City." [35]

The Wider Human Rights Context

A balanced religious environmental ethics, then, has to confront more than one form of misanthopy—ecological extremists, greedy industrialists and financiers, and anyone promoting indiscriminate application of advances in science and technology. As Pope John Paul II observes in his address, "The Ecological Crisis": "Respect for life, and above all for human dignity, is the ultimate guiding norm for any sound economic, industrial, or scientific progress." Often interests of production and the economy prevail over concern for the dignity of workers and even for entire peoples. "In these cases pollution or environmental destruction are the result of an unnatural and reductionist vision which at times leads to a genuine contempt for human beings." [36]

A compelling advocate for poorer nations, the pope is convinced that newly emerging economies cannot be asked to apply restrictive environmental standards, unless industrialized economies first apply those standards within their own boundaries. Yet he acknowledges that the developing nations are not morally free to repeat errors made by the developed nations in the past, errors now recognized to cause such global damage. The environmental crisis cannot be disconnected from the moral issue of war itself—and the manufacture and selling of new war technology—which has ruined crops, poisoned the soil and water, and dislocated entire peoples.

He urges those living secure in an industrialized economy to take a candid second-look at their own life-style and recover a spirit of simplicity, moderation, and sacrifice. "Today, the dramatic threat of ecological breakdown," he says, "is teaching us the extent to which greed and selfishness, both individual and collective, are contrary to the order of creation, an order which is characterized by mutual interdependence." The earth is essentially a common heritage, given for the benefit of all. "The concepts of an ordered universe and a common heritage both point to the necessity of a more internationally coordinated approach to the management of the earth's goods. In many cases the effects of ecological problems transcend the borders of individual States. Thus, their solution cannot be found solely on the national level."[37] For these and other reasons, the pope is an ardent sponsor of the United Nations and its Bill of Rights, a topic I will develop in the next two chapters.

Astronaut cameras on the moon registered the first glimpse of our planet earth from outside itself. At that symbolic moment we could grasp more clearly than before that rocks, water, atmosphere, life, and consciousness are not only juxtaposed but also interrelated. If we could now imagine the earth itself as a blue spaceship floating in interstellar space, then, we must also realize that a fifth of the earth's population occupy the passenger seats, consuming 80 per cent of the journey's provisions. The other four-fifths travel in the cargo hold, suffering from cold and other deprivations, groaning over the inequity. Leonardo Boff, the Brazilian liberation theologian, demands a new revolution in consciousness so that we "see one another as members of a great earthly family together with other species, and find our way back to the community of other living beings, the planetary and cosmic community."[38]

5

HUMAN RIGHTS—THE HUMAN MINIMUM

THE ETHICAL TEACHING PRESENTED IN THE PREVIOUS TWO chapters asserted that no moral problem can be resolved in isolation, but only as one strand in a web of many interwoven moral issues. Any greening crusade true to its purpose, therefore, must also address the moral crisis of industrial greed, neglect of the oppressed and poor, war and other forms of imperialism.

I have met a few militant ecologists so hostile to human-centered rhetoric that they refuse to support human rights. Even the renowned moral humanist Bertrand Russell, responding to a questionnaire once sent him by *Humanist* magazine, felt reluctant to identify himself with the humanist tag. He confessed he had been finding the nonhuman part of the cosmos much more interesting and satisfactory than the human part.[1] Reacting to grievances of this sort, I have tried to persuade my environmentalist friends that no single-issue ecologist could achieve durable reforms without a wider human rights agenda. To advance programs of legislative change any self-designated democratic society needs a protected, open political arena. All citizens must be guaranteed the right to organize, protest, and take political action; and the rights to life, liberty, and a fair trial. Otherwise, powerful industrial and economic interests will be tempted to crush the least opposition with violence, triggering perhaps a violent counter-revolution in turn, not a moderate civil reform.

Even more urgent than these human rights is the right to an adequate standard of living and the right to a rudimentary education — both steps prerequisite before hoping to raise the level of awareness about health and the environment. As described before, the Primal Ways, for instance, tend to be idealized as models for sustainable use of natural resources and as an authority for knowledge about nature that modern scientists have neglected. Yet simply to survive, indigenous people need legal protection first against terrorism and genocide, then against robbery of their lands and against pressures to give up their traditional Way.[2]

The human rights and ecology movements share many similarities. International and interreligious in scope they both emerged after the Second World War and today attract wide support from progressives and also traditionalists. While human rights activists have managed to teach ecologists a broader rights perspective, so ecologists have left their imprint on the human rights agenda. The right to a suitable living standard must include protection against hazardous industrial and sewage wastes. The right to food and employment must be achieved in an environmentally beneficial way. Non-human animals — and a more controversial claim, even the natural environment itself — have rights of their own which must somehow be balanced against the rights of humans.

In a dramatic editorial of 1991 Hans Küng and Leonard Swidler announced for the first time that representatives from the world's religions would try to formulate a new Declaration of Global Ethos, modeled on the UN Bill of Rights. It is significant that both theologians chose the following theme as pivotal to their intended document: it will "have to center on care and reverence for all humans—and therefore, be anthropocentric. But it will also have to go beyond, to the care and reverence for all reality—and therefore, really be cosmo-anthropocentric."[3]

Sometimes it takes an immersion experience in another society to rouse someone's conscience, long deaf to cries about human rights abuse within one's own country. In spring of 1987 I walked in upon a brutal governmental crackdown in Singapore. On a visit there shortly before, I had been introduced to Fr. Edgar D'Souza, young editor of the Singapore Catholic diocesan newspaper, who told of various thriving local projects in human rights, including the Gaylang Catholic Center, which offered sanctuary to imported Filipino domestic workers complaining of employer abuse. At a neighborhood recreation center I happened to meet a lawyer released after two years in jail without trial, the punishment for his allegedly malicious public remarks about the dominant People's Action Party. At the time I thought this man's story a weird anomaly, maybe a paranoid fantasy.

After an absence of two months from Singapore I returned to find the Gaylang Center shut down, D'Souza replaced and deported, and Vincent Cheng, former chair of the Catholic Justice and Peace

Commission, jailed for leading "a Marxist conspiracy." Twenty-one Protestant and Catholic workers had been imprisoned without trial, under sanction of the Internal Securities Act, a leftover emergency statute from the British colonial era. Prime Minister Lee Kuan Yew remarked that his government "will not allow any foreign or regional organization... to meddle in the internal affairs of Singapore." For hours I watched terrorized faces on television in ritual public confessions, succeeded by patriotic editorials in the government-sponsored *Straits Times.* For me, these scenarios looked as contrived as the notorious staged purges and show trials in China and the Soviet Republic. [4]

To this day I have been trying to place my Singapore experience in context and to take soundings from all sides. The study must begin with an investigation of modern human rights theory, notably its influence on major legislation at the United Nations. After reviewing what I have discovered I will size up some perceptive critiques of rights universality from two religious traditions, Primal and Neo-Confucian. The first critique argues that the existing UN Bill of Rights does not extend far enough, the second claims it extends too far already. In the next chapter, continuing this study of human rights, I will shift from these two historical Ways to a more diffuse context of religious postmodernity. After an effort to understand that setting I will then explore religious and ethical implications of the final draft for a Global Ethic, endorsed by the 1993 Parliament of Religions at Chicago.

Rise of International Human Rights

Current talk about human rights is plagued by imprecise language, a muddle that at times appears almost calculated. Lengthy catalogs of rights are issued each year by various regional and international conferences. Unlike a formal philosophical treatise the manifesto genre permits a list of separate dogmatic assertions, without pausing to show their logical justification or to define major terms. In such lists each single right is often declared inalienable and absolute, whereas in actual practice one right must always be balanced against another. Yet this very imprecision of language, on the contrary, may prove a paradoxical advantage. Andrei Sakharov, creator of the Soviet atom bomb and later a defiant "refusenik," observed in 1983 that "the ideology of human rights is probably the only one which can be combined with such diverse ideologies as communism, social democracy, religion, technocracy... It can also serve as a foothold for those who do not wish to be aligned with theoretical intricacies and dogmas, and who have tired of the abundance of ideologies, none of which has brought humanity a simple happiness." [5]

I find it crucial in discussing rights to distinguish between human dignity as an end in itself, and human rights as just one means to attain this end.[6] *Human rights* can be defined as a set of minimal claims to equal freedom, claims applicable worldwide and binding in courts of law. Such legal claims are just one means to protect and foster this core of human dignity. Thus, distinguishing means from ends, someone averse to rights language in general may decide without hypocrisy to sign a particular rights manifesto that backs human dignity.

Despite the divergent value emphases in trying to describe it human dignity is an absolute. In other words, I believe human life deserves the utmost respect and protection, just because it is human. For some critics the notion of human dignity now proves too narrow, now too broad. I have already cited some radical ecologists who repudiate this human-centered worldview, even in its moderate forms, and teach reverence toward all living beings and all reality. A quick scan of history shows how often self-described secular and religious humanists narrow the perimeter of genuine humanity to exclude slaves, colonial peoples, all those of darker skin, religious heretics, women and children, the mentally and physically impaired, or any outsider.

In defense of human dignity, then, most people today use the term *human* to imply an inclusive social ecology—the human race with its ambience of all animate and inanimate beings. I am convinced that the appropriate conditions for a complete human life must be derived, not from a fixed concept of natural law or abstract humanity, but from an evolving perception of what it means to be truly human. It is common to think of human dignity as a universal self-evident value. Yet it must not be forgotten that only in recent decades have rights advocates themselves widened the scope of their radar to pick up human cries from racial minorities or abused women and children.

Concern for human rights in recent centuries can be divided into three main phases, often called the first, second, and third eras. Rights of the first era coincided with a widespread Atlantic revolution at the end of the Enlightenment Age—extending from the United States in 1776, to Switzerland, the Low Countries, Ireland, and then to France in 1789. Bills of individual and political rights emerged in this phase, designed to protect an individual against an oppressive nation-state. Prevented from violating life and property, governments also ought to support free speech and democratic suffrage. These rights focused on the isolated bourgeois individual, engaged in a legal adversarial relationship to society. Government power was treated by philosophers like John Locke as a potential Hobbesian Leviathan, to be restrained by contractual safeguards. Henry David Thoreau in his *Essay on Civil Disobedience* would push this minimalist principle to the extremes of the Abolitionist Movement and secession: "That government governs best which governs not at all."

Rights of the nineteenth century, the second era, centered on social and economic rights, more collective than individual. Here new protections were needed, not just for vulnerable individuals against government power, but also for entire social classes against impoverishment and injustice stemming from the industrial revolution. Marx believed that first era rights and freedoms, now invoked so glibly by the bourgeois second era, could be reduced mostly to the right of laissez faire and private ownership, a disguised self-justification for the rich and powerful. In the *Communist Manifesto* he and Engels address the leaders of this society: "Your very ideas are but the outgrowth of your bourgeois production and property conditions, just as your jurisprudence is but the will of your class made into a law for all… The ruling ideas of each age have always been the ideas of its ruling class."[7]

Inaugurating a third era of rights, the United Nations would reach an immediate consensus of revulsion against outrages of the Second World War. Did no higher law exist to restrain a sovereign national government from enslaving and exterminating its own citizens? The UN would raise previous first and second era rights to the status of international law. UN membership tripled over the next half-century to embrace many new postcolonial developing nations and ethnic minorities. Parallel to this increase, the collective rights catalog added the right to development and to a healthy environment, both issues clearly reaching beyond national boundaries.[8] The renowned UN Universal Declaration of Human Rights in 1948, prepared under the committee leadership of Eleanor Roosevelt, has inspired since then a flood of regional and international rights manifestos.

Shrewdly interwoven in the original UN Universal Declaration of Human Rights in 1948 were two lists of rights—first era rights, backed mostly by the capitalist democracies, and second era rights, backed mostly by the socialist welfare nations. As the Cold War developed in the fifties and afterwards, this composite inventory was split into two separate lists. Both lists were now debated again, spelled out with more legal vigor than before, and at last endorsed fully in 1976 as the International Covenant of Civil and Political Rights and the International Covenant of Economic, Social, and Cultural Rights. After this, I will refer to the combined 1948 Universal Declaration and two 1976 Covenants as simply the UN Bill of Rights.

The first covenant centers on civil rights of individuals against their own sovereign governments. These include rights to life, equal protection under the law, freedom of religion and opinion, and protection against torture, arbitrary arrest, and discrimination because of race, creed, or gender. The second covenant addresses only member states themselves. Governments must protect the rights of their people to free choice of employment, to security in case of sickness or unemployment, to adequate food, housing, and medical care, and to education and leisure time. Most people can recognize that political-civil rights are more easily translated into demonstrable measures fixed by law, and thus monitored. The economic-social rights sound more vague and utopian, rights applauded by everyone but harder to verify or monitor. The responsibility to spot rights abuses depends especially on various nongovernmental international organizations, such as Amnesty International, Helsinki watch, and the International Commission of Jurists.

Ethicists would like to pin down a single coherent ethical theory as the basis for current rights concern. Yet as Sakharov explained earlier, the language in all these documents tends to capitalize on its inexact pedigree, drawn from so many overlapping philosophical, ethical, and legal sources. Phrases in particular lists of human rights are clearly lifted from the preamble to the U.S. Declaration of Independence, from the U.S. Bill of Rights, and from the French Declaration of the Rights of Man and Citizen—a matrix of British common law, the scholastic natural law tradition, social contract theory, and countless Deist and Humanist manifestos. In international dialogue today I am convinced the notion of human rights has become so elusive and flexible that its connotations cannot be limited to the first-era texts of Euro-American individualism.

Though many people today have expanded human rights into a comprehensive Way of moral humanism, I count myself among those who treat these rights merely as minimal moral standards for acceptable governance. As moral philosopher Heiner Bielefeldt observes, human rights do not represent an all-encompassing way of life, nor do they offer a yardstick to evaluate cultures and religions in general. Human rights are not necessarily the highest ethical ideal in human history either, because they are not intended to replace, say, Christian demands of love, Islamic solidarity, or the Buddhist ethics of compassion.[9]

Rights at Home — A Primal Critique

I have discovered that opposition to human rights agreements, especially the UN Bill of Rights, comes in unexpected shapes. The initial draft for the United Nations charter of 1945 asserted lofty aims. Through uncanny foresight at least forty-two nongovernmental global rights organizations had been invited to share in framing the UN charter and the later Universal Declaration. These groups, lobbying for the insertion of human rights language, prodded seasoned diplomats to focus on human persons, not just on treaty obligations between sovereign governments. Charter provisions backing national self-determination and racial equality, however, would soon be watered down by the anxiety of major delegates. At that moment in history Soviet Russia, Britain, France, and the United States were especially touchy about potential interference in their internal affairs. Russia still had its Gulag, Britain and France their Asian and African colonies, and the U.S., two decades before our own civil rights revolution, still condoned regional racial segregation. After the war I was so outraged over Nazi tyranny and the Holocaust that I never imagined my own nation would hold back over universal pledges to protect the rights of victims anywhere. With continued disappointment I have watched U.S. courts reluctant even today to implement treaty-based codes of international human rights.

A few decades ago an attorney friend of mine recounted her efforts to defend a Salvadoran refugee's plea for asylum in the U.S. The young man, if repatriated to El Salvador, could at that time offer plausible evidence for later retaliation by death squads against himself and his family. Though familiar with precedents in U.S. immigration law, she thought the surest defense for her client's right to sanctuary could be argued from UN rights agreements signed by the United States. The U.S. Constitution has been acclaimed as the first constitution in history to specify that international treaties must function as federal law in our courts. Yet this lawyer felt poorly trained in the legal system of international rights and feared that the judge would prove even more ignorant than she. Would she have to instruct the court about a specific treaty text and base her interpretations on a drafting history of the decree? If I recall, senior colleagues urged her not to risk her defense by citing an international precedent. Adhering to their advice, she fortunately won her case. Her mentors presumed that any worthwhile universal rights were already anticipated in our own legal tradition.[10]

During Carter's presidency many people at first saluted his efforts to make human rights the centerpiece of foreign policy. Yet I found myself increasingly embarrassed by his self-righteous accusations against abuses abroad yet blindness to alleged abuses in America's own internal rights record. It is instructive that nations of the European Union, having signed the European Convention on Human Rights which bans the death penalty, refuse to extradite someone facing a death penalty in the U.S. Again, some banks of the European Union have declined to share financial information on their clients with U.S. institutions because of our allegedly inept standards for protecting consumer privacy rights. Fearing interference in our own internal court system, the U.S. Congress has hesitated for years to ratify a treaty establishing a permanent international war crimes tribunal.

George Washington's farewell address warned his new republic against foreign treaties and entanglements, a caution that apparently guided the current G.W. Bush presidency through most of its first year. Among international agreements rejected by his administration were the Kyoto pact on global warning, some constraints of the 1972 Anti-Ballistic Missile Treaty, the Comprehensive [Nuclear] Test Ban Treaty, and the Ottawa Treaty eliminating anti-personnel land mines. Then came the traumatic World Trade Center and Pentagon bombings, however, which exposed drastic limitations to our policy of unilateral militance. It is fortunate that Britain, NATO allies, and other nations rallied to America's side so quickly after the catastrophe, for they helped redefine an attack against America the superpower into a crime against humanity everywhere.

As this book goes to press, more than six months after the bombings, I witness the Bush administration's drawn-out official silence, mirrored by an uncommonly docile press. The news blackout covers civilian casualty statistics for the Afghanistan campaign, the names of terrorist suspects rounded up in our federal detention centers without specific criminal charges, and what Amnesty International perceives as U.S. defiance of the Geneva protocols for treatment of war prisoners. Despite my lack of privileged hindsight and archival evidence, I must protest this rash expansion of emergency powers granted the president by Congress. Yet I still hope America will learn a global collaboration worthy of the name—patiently to reinforce a fragile world consensus against terrorist networks, and to consult the United Nations not for its rubber stamp but for an informed legal sanction.

Human rights seem protected so effectively in the United States that the majority of our citizens think most international rights covenants redundant. Yet some U.S. minorities, especially Native Americans, will testify otherwise. Two opposed reactions to the current UN Bill of Rights will now be examined. The Primal critique demands that the rights revolution widen to include the collective rights of minorities inside the UN's member-states. The Confucian critique, which I will develop in the next section, argues for subordinating individual and collective rights more rigorously under each state's collective purpose.

Native American Rights

The Primal Ways have been singled out in an earlier chapter for their distinctive attachment to kinship, solidarity, ancestral spirits, and the sacred land. According to current UN estimates these peoples number about 300 million, living among ruling majorities in 70 sovereign nations. My own empathy for the wider spectrum of indigenous rights arises from close-up reflections on the abused rights of Native Americans.

Some of America's sixteenth-century European conquerors once debated if indigenous peoples of the Americas were truly human.

Ironically from their own perspective, on the contrary, many Native Americans have always extended a highly differentiated concept of humanity beyond the human species to animals and the rest of creation. I am convinced that this vulnerable minority, America's own half-colonized, need even more rights protection than the majority. They have had to cope with exploitative land developers, unresponsive school boards imposing an alien language and culture, and mainstream church activists trying to suppress the Native American Church. They can point to a history of violated treaties with the U.S. government. The same government, signing international covenants for decolonization and self-determination, has scarcely begun to extend these global rights toward its own interior indigenous colonies. Conclusions of the U.S. census in 1980 spelled out the disastrous side-effects of this failure. On a national average Native Americans have the shortest life span of any ethnic group, the highest suicide and infant mortality rate, the highest unemployment and school dropout rate, the poorest housing and health care. "Many factors account for these conditions," the report stated. "Unproductive land; lack of capital; lack of education; a cycle of poverty difficult to escape; and cultural dislocation and depression caused from an existence as a conquered people within an historically alien culture." [11]

Today Native Americans find passionate advocates, not only among environmentalists, but especially among human rights leaders. It is common for a well-meaning anthropologist, international jurist, ethicist or theologian, even an agent from the U.S. Bureau of Indian Affairs, to speak for Primal interests, often without consulting the people themselves. I think the average Native American tribal government has plausible reasons to be wary of human rights advocates, especially those aligned with the tradition of first era individualistic civil rights. In order to protect each individual, such a bill of rights limits all governmental power, including that of tribal leaders. Equality of each individual before the law and equality of access to essentials of daily life sound at first like two wise moral principles. They outlaw discrimination on grounds of race, color, creed, age, gender, and physical disability. Yet in practice these legal claims seem to prompt an individual to dilute tribal loyalties. Life beyond the tribal reservation will look more tempting, once discrimination barriers in the majority society have been leveled. And if the time comes to raise a rights claim even against someone's own tribal authorities, this act of dissent against tribal law will confer legitimacy on the dominant society's government that imposed the human rights law.

Many Native Americans have long doubted the wisdom of international human rights as a legal system. Such commissions tend to achieve their results through adversarial legal proceedings, whereas the Native American Way favors conciliation and compromise. African Primal traditions, too, prefer mediation and consensus, an inclination that pervades the 1981 African Charter on Human and Peoples' Rights.[12] U.S. rights advocates would often be hired by one arm of the government, yet another arm kept indigenous people heavily dependent on federal money or other entitlements. Initiating a rights complaint against one government bureau, plaintiffs were often fearful of retaliation against their family or themselves somewhere down the line.

One recurring complaint, often left discretely tacit, arises from the patriarchal family customs of most Native Americans, except for tribes that are matrilinear or even somewhat matriarchal. They bristle at the potential collision between traditional distribution of roles within the family, and anti-discrimination law or feminist equal rights. According to the Indian Law Resource Center, a leading activist group in international arenas, "many Indians believe that the group rights of Indian peoples are the most important and most endangered of all Indian rights." These rights would include the right to self-government, to maintain communal ownership of land and resources, to determine their own relations with other nations and other peoples, and to preserve their culture, language, and religious tradition.[13]

World Forum for the Half-Colonized

Throughout most of their history Native Americans and other indigenous peoples have remained voiceless. Often denied access to the process of education and persuasion, they have seldom been invited to sign international rights covenants. However, in the last decade the United Nations has suddenly reversed this repressive legacy by opening up a global forum for them. The General Assembly declared 1993 the international year for indigenous peoples, launched in 1994 a decade committed to indigenous rights, and upgraded the stature of a subcommission on this topic which had been meeting since 1984. The reversal in policy stemmed from steady lobbying by indigenous people themselves but especially from an outspoken 1977 document circulated for discussion by Native American leaders about abuses throughout the Americas. Managing to survive nine years of meetings, UN lawyers and various indigenous group representatives, including a large percentage of nongovernmental agencies, composed the *UN Draft Declaration on the Rights of Indigenous Peoples*, a text intended for discussion and eventual ratification by the General Assembly.[14]

Though still in draft form the text itself merits a careful reading. Since its first appearance in 1994 the document has raised both extraordinary hopes and antagonism in UN debates and the press. Daring and far-reaching, many of its claims cannot help but disquiet a number of UN founding member-states. This is not a text of mere aspiration, gauged to result in a few treaties, followed later by detailed legal implementation. Itemizing the rights of these groups to control their own land, resources, culture, religion, and government, it already spells out particular demands in 45 articles, sorted under nine headings.[15] Its major premise is based on a debatable analogy—just as the UN once condemned the exploitation by colonial powers of their colonial populations, so it must now adapt these same measures to address each post-colonial individual state's discrimination against its indigenous peoples. Do UN member-states seek equity and democratic process in their treaties with one another? Then let each sovereign state within its own borders promote government of, for, and by indigenous peoples themselves.

A few illustrations will show the comprehensive reforms expected. In their efforts to ward off cultural genocide, indigenous peoples oppose capricious population transfers, enforced assimilation, removal of their children for whatever cause, and any form of propaganda directed against their culture. For example, "No relocation shall take place without the free and informed consent of the indigenous peoples concerned and after agreement on just and fair compensation and, where possible, with the option of return." They want thorough control of their own media and access to all levels of education in their own language and culture: Media control includes the right of "equal access to all forms of non-indigenous media. States shall take effective measures to ensure that State-owned media duly reflect indigenous cultural diversity." They demand full legal ownership of their own land—"including the total environment of the lands, air, waters, coastal seas, sea-ice, flora and fauna and other resources which they have traditionally owned, or more correctly, occupied or used. This includes the right to the full recognition of their laws, traditions, and customs, land-tenure systems and institutions for the development and management of resources…" [16]

The most specific passages in this document address abuses by the state's military establishment. No military activities and no storage or disposal of hazardous wastes shall take place on indigenous lands without explicit consent. State governments must never force indigenous people into military service, nor "recruit indigenous children into the armed forces under any circumstances." These groups have a right to "their traditional medicines and health practices, including the right to the protection of vital medicinal plants, animals, and minerals." Most crucial of all will be the right to practice and teach "their spiritual and religious traditions, customs, and ceremonies; the right to maintain, protect, and have access in privacy to their religious and cultural sites; the right to the use and control of ceremonial objects; and the right to the repatriation of human remains." Vindicating their own intellectual property rights, too, they expect "restitution of cultural, intellectual, religious, and spiritual property taken without their free and informed consent or in violation of their laws, traditions, and customs." [17]

These selected claims should indicate why the document has generated so much controversy. Its most obvious weakness, in my opinion, is an ambiguous use of the term *indigenous*. The document intends to single out a land's original inhabitants subjugated by later immigrants. These Primal inhabitants today prefer to view themselves, not as mere minority populations in a sovereign state, but semi-autonomous peoples with their own language, culture, and history. China's representatives, for example, could accept the entire text if the term was narrowed so that it did not apply to contemporary Asia, or China in particular: "The question of indigenous peoples is the product of European countries' pursuit of colonial policies in other parts of the world." Malaysia added that such peoples exist only on so-called reservations, not in nations whose original inhabitants now live harmoniously in one society. Bangladesh insisted its own tribal peoples were treated no differently than their non-indigenous fellow citizens. The indigenous crisis referred only to the "unique case of injustice" in the

Americas and Oceania, where original inhabitants had been dispossessed and exploited.[18] It is apparent that framers of the text want to leave this concept as vague and inclusive as possible, so that no victim communities would be omitted. Many delegates, on the contrary, have tried to limit the concept so that indigenous claims cannot be invoked by each state's dissatisfied minorities.

The text often mentions financial reparation for violated treaties and other injustices of the past. Indigenous peoples also presume the right to recover burial sites and remains, and also art or archeological artifacts. Those communities that span existing national boundaries want the right to pass freely across borders and also the right to broker their own international covenants. If they expect these controversial demands to be implemented realistically, they must count on an international oversight board to adjudicate daily friction with existing national law. Claims of this magnitude suggest the text's second major vulnerability, which can be spotted in its preamble: "nothing in this Declaration may be used to deny any peoples their right of self-determination."

The concept of *self-determination* dates back to the original UN Bill of Rights: "All peoples have the right of self-determination. By virtue of that right they freely determine their political status and freely pursue their economic, social, and cultural development." The context for this right was a time of post-war decolonization, the right of an identifiable people by democratic vote to choose independent nationhood, freedom from foreign jurisdiction. However, the UN member-states today have declared this decolonization era concluded. Deaf to accusations of neo-colonialism, most of them are wary of any possible territorial secession. Straining to establish a regime of individual rights in their societies—equality of every individual before the law—they have yet to fathom the legal implications in acknowledging special collective rights of large racial, gender, age, religious, and cultural populations. Various international covenants in 1970, 1989, and 1993 have reaffirmed that the right of self-determination no longer includes a right to secession from a recognized independent nation, provided a people is not subjected to gross and continuous rights violations.[19] It is significant that indigenous delegates refuse to replace the legally restricted term self-determination by less provocative claims to self-management or self-development. They want to retain a right to secession if their more immediate human rights continue to be ignored.

The outcome of these high-profile demands cannot be predicted, specifically as formulated in the present draft. Framers of the document thus far insist they will never trim down their claims. At the same time some veteran member-states recognize that even if the General Assembly approved the present text, perhaps from a hidden intent to embarrass particular superpowers, the Security Council's veto would follow inevitably. Maybe the very existence of such a draft document will accomplish its major purpose. Threats of intrusion from a global forum and oversight agency might spur member-states like Australia, Canada, Brazil, and the United States to respond more favorably to indigenous lobbyists within their own national capitols.

Rights Abroad—A Neo-Confucian Critique

If the Primal critique of current rights coverage argues for wider inclusiveness, the Neo-Confucian critique represents a protest against an inclusiveness already too wide. I recounted earlier my disturbing visit to Singapore in 1987 and the rights abuses I witnessed abroad—especially the official self-justifications and implausible show-trials. An impressionable guest, perhaps I had mistaken the efficient, prosperous, work-oriented life of this small republic for that of an enlarged U.S. suburb, and overlooked some vast differences in history and structure between the two nations. My former students and their parents were quick to challenge the indignation I expressed over the peremptory sentencing and the degrading confessions. They and their friends tried to persuade me to adjust the ideal of universal rights to a regional Neo-Confucian context of family and society. Singapore, as a small vulnerable sliver of land, ever on the military, economic, and political defensive, could not risk communitarian upheaval, especially any disturbance with a hint of communist revolution.

Ready to acknowledge in my own nation the widespread racial and gender discrimination, police brutality, political corruption, and unjust distribution of wealth, how could I presume to criticize a flawed Asian society? My friends argued that Singapore's first aim must be economic stability. Only by first reaching a suitable level of economic development could this fledgling ex-colonial nation be expected to support the democratic political structures that make human dignity possible. Once

Singapore proved as powerful in weapons and wealth as the U.S., they taunted me, it could then choose whether to support a genuine democracy based on human rights or to remain a U.S.-style plutocracy, with most citizens too apathetic to vote. In a comparable scenario, during the aftermath of terrorist bombings in New York and Washington and the anthrax sabotage scare, I have watched my own government debating how far civil liberties must be restricted for the sake of national security. Invoking the civil rights ideal, a democracy claims to prefer that ten guilty might escape than that one innocent person be punished unjustly. Yet what if one of the guilty released has access to bioterrorist weapons?

Two decades after my visit there I notice that Singapore has ratified almost none of the UN rights treaties that require enforcement by outside monitors, a mechanism Prime Minister Lee would have viewed as "meddling in internal affairs." Bilahari Kausikan, a member of Singapore's Ministry of Foreign Affairs, has explained that "good government may well require, among other things, detention without trial to deal with military rebels or religious and other extremists; curbs on press freedoms to avoid fanning racial tensions or exacerbating social divisions; and draconian laws to break the power of entrenched interests in order, for instance, to establish land reforms. Those are the realities of exercising authority in heterogeneous, unevenly modernized, and imperfectly integrated societies with large rural populations and shallow Western-style civic traditions." [20] Singapore diplomat Kishore Mahbubani, however, concedes the need for a binding core of basic universal human rights. He insists this foundation must be distinguished from "private" rights about which international law is less definitive, more open to interpretation and debate. The basic core includes "no torture, no slavery, no arbitrary killings, no disappearances in the middle of the night, no shooting down of innocent demonstrators, no imprisonment without careful review." Rights advocates have to make complex political distinctions, then, restricting their protests just to those rights violations that will draw a sure international consensus. [21]

Regional Rights, Global Rights

This Singapore incident, and the Foreign Minister's vigorous defense, typify the protests expressed by some of the East Asian industrial powers today against international human rights law. Leaders of Singapore, Malaysia, and China have been especially outspoken, but I am sure many of the same doubts are shared in Indonesia, Taiwan, South Korea, Japan, and elsewhere. The complaints carry particular weight because of the region's huge population, its venerable moral traditions, and its confident leadership backed by recent economic prosperity. It would be more correct to say that most of these nations essentially endorse the aim of the UN Bill of Rights. Yet they distinguish basic from provisional rights, or embrace a rights sequence implemented in controlled phases. Echoing the precedents from China and the Soviet nations of past decades, they clearly subordinate individual rights to social and economic rights.

From the viewpoint of the global majority of nations, however, such provisos offer a screen behind which totalitarian nations can hide their abuses. An immediate international rebuttal against this Asian waffling was adopted by the 1993 UN World Conference on Human Rights at Vienna. It stipulates that civil human rights of the first era and socio-economic rights of the second era must be implemented simultaneously, and that neither set of rights will take precedence over the other. Whereas 48 nations endorsed the UN Universal Declaration in 1948, now 172 nations signed the Vienna Declaration, which repeats the following principle in various forms: "All human rights are universal, indivisible and interdependent and interrelated. The international community must treat human rights globally in a fair and equal manner, on the same footing, and with the same emphasis." [22]

Like the rights delegate of Singapore, however, I also recognize a primary core of human rights that should be addressed before other rights, mostly because such a nucleus would elicit immediate crosscultural support. This includes the crime of genocide, the use of torture and starvation by foreign invaders and local governments, enslavement of populations through forced labor, deliberate separation of children from their parents, and the attempt to wipe out basic religious and ethnic identity.[23] Recent incidents of ethnic-cleansing and civil war give unquestioned proof that these rights violations persist. Moreover, I have already hinted at my own impatience with the imprecision of rights language, and also with the mushrooming lists of rights churned out by international and regional groups, generating a minefield of easily violated hidden taboos. Alert also to the reluctance of U.S. courts to honor international law precedents, I have no difficulty grasping why any government should be apprehensive about the Trojan horse that might undermine its national sovereignty.

Some claims in the UN Bill of Rights sound absurdly broad, such as the right to self-determination which heads both UN covenants. I have already explained how this claim against colonialism, if left unrestricted, could trigger endless compound secessions within each newly constituted nation. The right to life seems to function as a salad bowl concept that covers a medley of particular rights. The gravity of particular rights varies, of course, in different societies and religious Ways. For many moral traditions of the world, rights to abortion or assisted suicide, for example, are by no means self-evident and are expressly condemned. A crucial right, such as the right to unemployment insurance, may be listed alongside something I think relatively gratuitous, such as the right to an annual paid vacation. Or a drug-company's right to suitable patent safeguards and profits can never override the priority worldwide of every sick person's right to requisite, affordable medicine. Thus, I find the Vienna concern about parity and indivisibility of rights understandable, but given the confused, inflated claims embedded in some rights legislation, not logically compelling.

After a half century, despite these and other objections to the UN catalog of civil, economic, and cultural rights, almost no one would deny that the Bill of Rights has by now achieved the practical effect of universal common law. Phrases from these documents have been transcribed into a large number of the world's national constitutions. Under charges by Amnesty International an insolent local tyrant, refusing to ratify various rights charters, can be shamed under international scrutiny to correct or disguise the charges documented. Global vindication will often win political prisoners their freedom, or at least a fresh basis for hope.

It is important to recognize that today, when many world governments are ceding more responsibility to the private sector, business leaders find themselves replacing government officials as the target of international rights codes and vigilant advocacy groups. From a business perspective, some convincing practical ways to implement the UN Bill of Rights caught my attention during conversation with a close friend, working at the Business for Social Responsibility. A non-profit organization located in San Francisco, the BSR emerged less than ten years ago as one among various mediating organizations. Corporate clients are shown how to combine moral duty with business sagacity in conforming to the UN Bill of Rights and other global regulations. The center offers training workshops, consulting services, research papers, and a weekly News Monitor that scans publications and websites for corporate responsibility trends. Its chief source of funding is foundation grants and member company dues.

As a thought-experiment I have tried to imagine myself a U.S. corporate executive at Starbucks, Levi Strauss, or some other company with global franchises or supply chains. After visiting the Business for Social Responsibility website I learned how carefully I would have to choose my overseas partners. Such a partnership, of course, must adhere to current global standards on child and forced prison labor, a living wage, working hours, environmental health and safety. Instead, if I were to blunder ahead without enlisting specialists like BSR to train my staff, I could foresee disruptive potential lawsuits abroad and pressures from the media, U.S. shareholders, and consumers, quick to pounce on any human rights violation and to discredit my company's brand name. Scanning the detailed analyses of successful programs by a few of my business rivals, I felt motivated to imitate award-winning strategies. By complying resourcefully with the UN Bill of Rights and similar global environmental and labor covenants, I saw I could advance my own business. At the same time I could give my employees pride in serving a recognized moral Cause. I could also support local regulations and reform, even in nations where graft and bribery are taken for granted.

For governments or businesses a mere show of external conformity to international rights law, imposed by external force, can only be the preliminary phase in a true human rights revolution. To internalize human rights ideals, periodic regional rights conferences would probably be wise. For instance, Native American delegates in 1996 have submitted to the Organization of American States (OAS) their own regional Inter-American Declaration on the Rights of Indigenous Peoples. Nations with similar geography, language, religious and cultural history are most likely to discern and promote a common regional moral standard. As Asian delegates asserted at the 1993 Bangkok Rights Conference, just a few months before the Vienna Declaration: "While human rights are universal in nature, they must be considered in the context of a dynamic and evolving process of international norm-setting, bearing in mind the significance of national and regional particularities and various historical, cultural, and religious backgrounds." [24]

The Neo-Confucian Perspective

At the urging of Singapore friends after my complaints there, I have been attempting since then to trace the particular influence of Neo-Confucian ethics on East Asian rights objections. Though restless throughout the last century to survive the Social Darwinian competition with Europe and America, leaders of the three so-called Confucian nations, China, Korea, and Japan today at times confess a deep regret. In the rush to import new methods of management in economy, government, and society, perhaps they surrendered essentials of their tradition   And today many want to reinstate these Asian moral values through what is often called the Confucian Revival.[25]

According to Mahbubani, the Singapore diplomat cited above, such Asian values include "attachment to the family as an institution, deference to societal interests, thrift, conservatism in social mores, respect for authority." [26] A decade ago, many social critics in the U.S. argued that East Asia's astonishing economic success stemmed precisely from these Neo-Confucian virtues. How could American businesses and schools emulate this disciplined teamwork and esprit de corps? Yet after the economic earthquake of 1997 in East Asia, similar critics pin immediate blame on the same values gone wrong. On renewed scrutiny, family attachment now turns into nepotism, a preference for personal relationships is cronyism, consensus is wheel-greasing and political corruption, conservative respect for authority is rigidity and inability to innovate, educational achievement becomes uncreative rote-learning.

To be accurate I think these Asian values cannot be identified as uniquely Neo-Confucian but are universal enough to elicit the backing of almost all traditional societies, the major religious Ways. It is important to remember the pervasive influence of Muslim ethics in Malaysia and Indonesia; the American-style rights-based Constitution imposed on Japan after the Second World War; and the common tendency in this region to interweave Taoist, Confucian, Shinto, Buddhist, and even

Christian Ways. At any rate, I intend to show in classical Neo-Confucian ethics a coherent basis for this particular combination of values.

Human rights of the first era are closely associated with the historical Euro-American milieu in which they were formulated—self-interested atomistic individuals in an arena, competing for scarce resources, yearning for protection of their liberties from invasion by others. Pushing this scenario to an extreme, people may view themselves as fiercely competitive and litigious egos, knowing just what they want and how to get it, as long as human rights abuses do not get in their way. Though the U.S. individual citizen possesses many rights by birth, some of them can be forfeited by criminal behavior. Classical Neo-Confucian ethics, on the contrary, takes a different starting point. Simply as a biological human being, an individual has no inalienable rights from birth. Genuine humanity cannot be conferred by right of birth or by law.

Defining each human being as a rational animal, Aristotle underlines the marks of continuity with the animal kingdom and the differentiating attribute of reason. The Neo-Confucian tradition, however, stresses that humanity is relational at its very core, the center of relationships radiating outward, with duties toward oneself, family and relatives, friends, neighbors, nation, world. The isolated, self-sufficient ego is not a complete human being. As the developing center of relationships within a community, an individual is expected to live compatibly, to learn empathy and civilized compromise. From the Neo-Confucian viewpoint, becoming a true human person is a potential that has to be actualized step by step. Only by proving oneself a socialized, participating member of society can an individual earn the privileges offered by that society. Despite Mao's abortive anti-Confucianism crusade, this traditional Neo-Confucian social dialectic blends readily with modern socialist and communist thought.

Classical Neo-Confucian ethics has often been called a situational ethics of relationships. We come into a social world already interrelated and construct an individual self-identity only through our relationships with other people. By "rectifying names" in the basic husband-wife, parent-child, friend-friend, elder-younger, ruler-subject relationships, we each make every effort to fulfill obligations as a true father, a true wife, a true friend. More than just performing or enacting these roles, we actually become the totality of roles we live in relation to specific other people. What each of us will be is mostly determined by those with whom we now interact, just as our response determines in part who and what those people will be. Personhood is conferred on us, just as we confer it on others.[27]

This perspective proves reluctant to back a minimum level of rights for alienated individuals uncooperative in building a humane collective society. Whereas the vocabulary of rights emphasizes individual claims first, with implicit corresponding duties, classical Neo-Confucian ethics reverses this process. Rights are just the corollary to duties. Laws cannot force people to be humane but laws can spur citizens to set aside self-interest and identify their interests with those of the community. We have first a duty of piety toward our parents and thus our parents have a claim on our respect and material support. And obliged first to provide economic security for their citizens, rulers have no right to automatic respect but have to earn it.[28]

At best, Neo-Confucian ethics relies on informal compromise and mediation to resolve conflicts. This is the very approach defended by Native American and African Primal cultures who cringe at court-centered, self-assertive rights advocacy. As the Chinese proverb puts it, "Win the lawsuit but lose your money." Avoiding the delay, cost, and bitterness of legal proceedings, both parties in an informal compromise can save face and participate in framing the solution. For example, a Jesuit colleague of mine, teaching in Tokyo, explained to me the typical way a controversial decision tends to be handled in his academic department. After a 5 to 2 majority vote the minority of two would be invited out to a friendly dinner by the department chair so that the disappointment of losing could be assuaged and departmental consensus could at last manifest itself in a unanimous vote. After this meal of reconciliation, to sustain dissent would be viewed as uncivil and divisive.

At its worst, the Neo-Confucian tradition tends to invest unlimited discretionary power in the ruler, idealized as a moral titan. Prone to overuse the rhetoric of social harmony, a government is tempted to exploit individuals vulnerable to its whims. Renowned Buddhist human rights activist Aung San Suu Kyi, long under intermittent house arrest in Myanmar for her dissent, warns of the peril in repressing or deferring individual civil rights for the sake of cultural and economic rights. When economics is regarded as the most important key to the lock of every door, then human worth will tend to be measured almost entirely by its effectiveness as an economic tool. This rationale would imply that "peace, stability, and public order are desirable only as conditions for facilitating economic transformation rather than as ends in themselves. Such an interpretation would distort the very meaning of peace and security. It could also be used to justify strong, even if unenlightened, government and any authoritarian measures that such a government may take in the name of public order." On the contrary, people must be valued for what they are, not for what they produce.[29]

In summary, objections to the UN Bill of Rights center on the jealous protection of group, regional, and national subsidiarity—one's own quasi-autonomous local moral, cultural, and religious values. In the United States, the functional equivalent to this conflict is the lively dialectic between centrifugal states rights and centripetal federal sovereignty—a painful legacy of the Civil War that still continues to animate congressional and court debates. Native Americans fear an excessive emphasis on first-era individualistic rights will undermine their collective rights as a people—their local tribal government and cultural identity. Neo-Confucian industrial powers suspect the communitarian nation-state will be eroded by divisive citizen claims based on their global individual rights. Primal and Asian Wisdom Ways emphasize moral duties rather than rights; the communal virtues of family, clan, and society, rather than the competitive claims of self-assertive egos. And both Ways prefer consensus and compromise whenever possible, rather than legal confrontation and formal contracts.

The dilemma facing the new Confucian ethics, as for any sound ethics, is how to chart a middle path between totalitarian socialism and individualistic capitalism—a socially responsive, unselfish individuality. From the U.S. perspective the image of an isolated young man stopping a line of tanks in Tienanmen Square seems a magnificent symbol of individual human rights triumphing over an oppressive society. Yet from a communist and Confucian viewpoint then and now, that man did not stand alone. Radiating from him in symbolic ripples were also his family and ancestors, his friends, neighbors, and people of the democratic counter-culture in China and everywhere else.

Robert Bellah surmises that this dialectic between social and individual values can even be located in the secret hopes of a typical American individualist. "The American dream," he says, "is often a very private dream of being the star, the uniquely successful and admirable one, the one who stands out from the crowd of ordinary folk who don't know how. And since we have believed in that dream for a long time and worked very hard to make it come true, it is hard for us to give it up, even though it contradicts another dream that we have—that of living in a society that would really be worth living in." [30]

6

HUMAN RIGHTS AND RELIGIOUS PLURALISM

T HE LAST THREE CHAPTERS HAVE SKETCHED OUT AN INCLUSIVE social ecology, a moral vision embracing humanity, the cosmos, and the Sacred. No political, religious, or environmental issue can be understood in isolation. Each issue must be sized up holistically insofar as it supports or undermines the overall context.

As Sakharov observed in the previous chapter, rights rhetoric serves as an esperanto that is neutral enough to attract socialists, capitalists, theologians, and even those tired of ideologies. I have shown that an intricate variety of arguments and passions can be uncovered to account for the endorsement of rights and also for their rejection. I traced back Native American and Neo-Confucian hesitations, for example, to their religious-moral premises most of all, but also to strong tribal and regional loyalties and an insecure hold on economic and political power. These factors hint at an even more pervasive obstacle to the moral vision I have been defending—the current atmosphere of relativity, which I will now explore. Today will be remembered as an era of postmodernism, religious pluralism, and moral relativism. A comprehensive religious ethics is challenged to search for a moral consensus among the world's divergent Ways and help it flourish. After an effort to understand this contemporary setting I will analyze one particular effort to articulate a common ground—the Global Ethic text, endorsed by the 1993 Parliament of Religions at Chicago.

I can picture a rights activist today, incited to intervene in an orgy of family abuse overheard from the apartment next door, for example, or on a larger scale, to support sending troops for rescuing defenseless civilians in Bosnia or Rwanda. Yet soon a relativist critic shows up to chip away at the activist's two certainties—first that the violence spotted represents a clear violation of rights, and second that such an intervention remains the only just and effective remedy. In any moral disagreement this sort of critic recognizes only an assortment of opinions. With no opinion intrinsically more correct than another no one can judge the violent situation right or wrong in itself. Marx might relativize the activist's moral position as just a social construct, shaped by the ideology of one's own class interests; Freud might relativize that position as just a defense mechanism to gratify personal security needs. Thus, my friend's impulse to defend human rights is sapped by the sort of reductionist critique familiar to the social sciences. The activist may be consigned to a cocoon of political and moral isolationism.

This climate of relativity even pervades my own counseling sessions with married couples, where I am expected to mediate as an agent of relativity. I coach the couple how to trim down their own rhetoric of dogmatic objectivity, often the spark beneath their mutual provocations. Perhaps neither person will complain of physical abuse by the other. However, in a quarrel erupting before my eyes he may accuse her of lying deliberately. This remark I interrupt by prompting a courteous qualification, "so it seems," or "in my opinion." I draw an imaginary circle that encloses each separate person and then persuade both individuals to bracket themselves as a single interacting unit. The task of assessing objective blame lies outside these perimeters. Each person is trained to hear the other's viewpoint with empathy, to paraphrase and act it out if asked to, and to treat one's own words as just a subjective statement. Both they and I emerge from these communication exercises reconfirmed, for better and worse, in the mind set of relativity.

The bewildering shift from modernity to postmodernity in the last half-century has left side-effects that cannot be overestimated. Showing up in so many areas of life, postmodernity triggers awareness of cultural relativity or an evolving historical consciousness—we can no longer seek *the* truth, but just *a* truth. It is important to recall that once the Copernican revolution arrived Ptolemy's earth was stunned to find itself just one among many planets in the galaxy. No longer at home in the old universe our consciousness is now roaming without a compass in what Henry Adams and William James called the multiverse or pluriverse. People often speak about reaching the limit or "end" of the Euro-American world, Christian civilization, logos-centered secularity.

In a context of geohistory *modernity* as an era and style implies a separation of the world into an authoritative center and a receptive periphery, between superior and inferior frames of reference. The center is Euro-American civilization, zealous to spread its secularity, industrial technology, economics, and democratic franchise. The ethnocentric bias in this perspective tends to lie concealed under the language of global needs and aspirations. Thus, confronting the vocabulary of global human rights, a liberation theologian today may even here suspect a newly disguised cultural imperialism, and a feminist theologian may infer a new variant of gender domination.

Postmodernity, on the contrary, suggests all the indeterminate currents remaining, once the modernist certitudes recede. Now pluralism and multiculturalism emerge, motifs suitable to an era of political and cultural decolonization. Those previously excluded or marginalized from the authoritative center can now celebrate, not just their own political liberation, but also their equal dignity, each with a unique individual and cultural history. Perceived before as fixed and monocentric, the universe now becomes a field of possibilities, its diverse components polycentric and overlapping.[1]

Voices of Moral Relativism

The switch to a postmodern point of view runs parallel to an obvious change of direction in global political history. I think decolonization is an apt analogy. The United Nations organization began with 58 nation members under Euro-American leadership. Though too exhilarated at first to recognize the ironic cost of victory, Britain and France had been left so drained by the Second World War that they had neither the might nor the will any longer to police their former colonial empires. A fresh world map was about to be drawn, registering wave after wave of emergent independent nations. Within the next two decades, power in the UN would tilt toward the Soviet bloc and nonaligned nations. Gradually the Euro-American and Soviet impasse was succeeded by a growing division between the haves of the North and the have-nots of the South. More recently, with the end of the Cold War, the voices of developing nations have dominated the General Assembly, now over 150 members. Many U.S. citizens in the last decade, complaining of disproportionate dues and managerial waste, have lost their earlier enthusiasm for the UN, whereas the average citizen of Bangladesh or Cambodia may have uncovered a new respect.

Today this decolonizing process seems to be accelerating toward an even more radical dispersal of power. Sovereign nations, once presuming they had a monopoly on organized violence within their own borders, have tried one treaty after another to extend their arms control worldwide. Yet the globe today is littered with nation-states in various stages of dismantlement, first the former Soviet empire but also the Balkans, Africa, and Afghanistan. It looks as if no single nation or regional alliance can impose a stable world peace. Pockets of anarchy seem to be emerging almost everywhere—the domain of tribal warlords, improvised terrorist networks, and religious extremists.[2]

Impact of Cultural Relativism

In 1947, a year before the pivotal UN Universal Declaration, delegates trying to draw up a global Bill of Rights uncovered an outspoken editorial in the *American Anthropologist* magazine. Signed by leaders of the American Anthropological Association, it addressed this unsettling question to the entire UN Commission on Human Rights: "How can the proposed Declaration be applicable to all human beings, and not be a statement of rights conceived only in terms of the values prevalent in the countries of Western Europe and America?"[3]

The editorial begins by outlining a chamber-of-horrors history. Mottoes about the white man's burden have been devised to justify economic exploitation, to exterminate whole populations, and to hold people in tutelage rather than let them control their own affairs. This abuse has been excused by ascribing cultural inferiority or a "primitive mentality" to these peoples. After witnessing two world wars and the economic Depression, however, Primal peoples have been revising their earlier impressions of Euro-American superiority. The civilized nations no longer seem to practice the love of democracy and freedom they profess. The so-called uncivilized are now rediscovering new values in their own religious traditions they were once taught to despise.

Reacting against Euro-American arrogance, the manifesto pounces on various excerpts circulating from the rudimentary UN Declaration. Though such a rights catalog purports to be universal, it will prove no less culturally localized than earlier rights documents. For instance, recall that the noble U.S. Declaration of Independence and Bill of Rights were written and endorsed by slave-owners who continued to remain so. Also,

France barely tried to apply the revolutionary slogan, "liberty, equality, fraternity," to its slave-owning colonies. "The eternal verities only seem so because we have been taught to regard them as such."[4]

The premise behind the editorial is a radical notion of cultural and moral relativism. Even the nature of the physical world, the colors and sounds people perceive, are conditioned by the language they speak, which is part of the culture into which they are born. "Ideas of right and wrong, good and evil, are found in all societies, though they differ in their expression among different peoples. What is held to be a human right in one society may be regarded as anti-social by another people or by the same people in a different period of their history... Standards and values are relative to the culture from which they derive, so that any attempt to formulate postulates that grow out of the beliefs or moral codes of one culture must to that extent detract from the applicability of any Declaration of Human Rights to mankind as a whole."[5]

After discovering this extraordinary text I learned it represented mostly a single school of anthropological thought, led by Franz Boas at Columbia and his famous students Ruth Benedict and Margaret Mead. Influential in the U.S. during the twenties and thirties the school waned in the anti-Communist fifties, an era conducive to self-confident moral denunciations of the enemy. Yet this movement resurfaced during the seventies in the more radical cultural relativism of Clifford Geertz. According to Geertz and his colleagues no one except those enculturated in a society could understand or interpret it completely. This type of anthropology at its most emphatic tends to view each culture as an isolated entity, its people almost incomprehensible to outsiders and thus ironically incomprehensible also to most anthropologists. Differing traditions are treated like distinct computer software programs, each with its unique virtual world, no tradition able to interact or be compared with another.[6]

More recent schools of anthropology seem to speak with less dogmatic rigidity about cultural differences. What they perceive are not reified cultures but cultural networks, flows beyond territorial boundaries, cultural penetration and overlapping. Thus, in a given social space there can be many interweaving cultural streams. I have already cited my Apache neighbor in San Francisco, a person alert to Native American treaty violations, to his universal human rights, and to every federal entitlement. He is a person immersed in the concrete multicultural San Francisco present yet trying creatively to reinterpret his particular indigenous religious and cultural past. We each reconstruct or remythologize our own social reality, which consists of several different overlapping worlds. Rights and cultural identity and moral-religious values, I believe, are distinct but inseparable facets of this inclusive construction process.[7]

The 1947 manifesto of relativism has not lost its original prophetic force. In summary, it affirms that one's own culture at the present moment offers no privileged standard of truth, and that other people's truths are mostly shaped by their own understanding and categories. It rebels against an implicit patronizing they-us armchair anthropology that once ruled the entire profession. It encourages outside observers not to impose their own a priori categories on a culture under investigation but to open themselves to values embedded in that unique world of concrete labor and everyday relationships. Its premise of relativism calls into question the pseudo-universals of modernity, a mentality fixated on Euro-American power and reason. The manifesto is rooted in a sincere aversion to crimes of imperialism and injustice, long disguised under a rationale of racial, cultural, and religious superiority. I can understand how passionate loathing can push a social anthropologist to the opposite extreme—reducing a particular ethics to the status of a culturally conditioned grammar or color-perception.

I have explained before that my own style of moral reflection embraces reasoning, feeling, thought-experiments or inner dialogues with myself, empirical research, meditation on the great moral stories. In other words, it cannot be reduced to strict deductive reasoning. I can promise only a modest confidence based on mounting probabilities— not the certainty of divine-command ethics, of course, with its guarantee of revealed absolute objectivity. For these reasons I will not attempt a thorough logical refutation of the arguments offered by anthropologists and others for cultural and moral relativism. Yet I can at least point out two different features of the manifesto above that lack the logical cogency they promise. The first is its reductivist premise. Moral judgments of right and wrong are alleged to have no legitimate existence of themselves. They are allegedly something else, such as disguised economic or cultural assertions. Because such assertions vary from civilization to civilization, then what is morally right in one place might well be considered wrong in another. I cannot imagine empirical proof for such a position, except the mere indication that many moral judgments are influenced by factors other than moral. I concede overlapping influences, of course, but not a blanket determinism or reductionism.

The second feature of this text, an appeal to diversity, strikes me as logically irrelevant. The anthropologist observer may find, say, that people judge the killing of exposed infants and elders wrong in one society but right in another. I am aware that moral judgments vary between individuals even within one's own society or between present and past in the same society. Yet what the outsider locates can only be a descriptive ethics, pointing to observed behavior and reported attitudes. A descriptive moral uniformity or diversity neither proves nor disproves the existence of a universal normative ethics. It is hard to determine in any society the extent to which each individual lives out a given moral norm as a badge of effortless conformity or as a mature inner conviction. I find any genuine moral and religious diversity something to cherish, far preferable to an imposed uniform ethics, ethnocentric in fact but disguised as a global moral consensus. A tyrannical civilization could impose its moral values on the entire world, but the resulting global uniformity would not prove such a standard inherently right. And among a number of conflicting moral judgments, one option, even if held by just a minority, might be the only right one.[8]

The evidence for cultural pluralism, I believe, offers no compelling proof for ethical relativism. Variable moral customs, recorded from all the anthropological backwaters of the world, might be explained by inferring the absence of any absolute moral standard. I think a more plausible explanation exists. What an outsider interprets as deviance may stem simply from the observer's projections—fallacious research and interpretation—or from a specific people's actual cultural isolation, temporary and reversible.

How Do You Feel about Genocide?

To committed teachers like Allan Bloom and Christina Hoff Sommers moral relativism can be identified today as the major parasite undermining the U.S. college system. Bloom's popular classic, *Closing of the American Mind*, maintains that the key virtue fostered by schools is an undisciplined openness to every imaginable viewpoint—a mind unwilling to study in depth or to argue for or against the actual values of others, so that openness itself turns narrow. The most overworked phrases among recent college students are "no problem," "You do your thing and I'll do mine," or simply "whatever." Few people seem committed enough in their beliefs or values to debate about them seriously. Exposed to all kinds of life-styles and ideologies such a mind perceives its worst enemy as someone not open to everything.[9] Bloom tries testing the limits to moral isolationism among his students. Suppose you attended a man's funeral in British colonial India and discovered his wife will be burned alive in a suttee rite. Would it be right to intervene in order to save her life? Sommers poses dilemmas just as one-sided to rattle the smug relativism of her college ethics class—scenes of someone torturing a child, starving a victim to death, humiliating an invalid. The students of both Bloom and Sommers respond, however, that whereas these scenarios may strike you and ourselves as wrong, who can say they are wrong for someone else?

One intriguing explanation for moral relativism in education keeps recurring. Sommers suspects brainwashing by earlier school drill in value-clarification, a method made fashionable by teacher training programs a few decades ago to help children discover their own likes, dislikes, and values. At its best, I think the value-clarification approach tries to liberate students from the arbitrary moralizing of an authoritarian teacher and also from the opposite extreme, a confused medley of colliding moral options. It hopes to teach, not this or that specific value, but the valuing process itself, which consists of careful listening to each person's values, prizing and comparing them, and estimating their practical consequences.[10] At its worst, the process could be parodied like this: "What is your favorite color, your flavor of ice cream? Children, how do you feel about homemade birthday presents or about hit-and-run drivers? How do you feel about abortion?" Tastes and serious moral values are juxtaposed, drawn from youngsters in the same tone of voice as if only their individual preferences mattered.

The muddle from misapplied value-formation methods in a child's earlier education can be compounded during the average college dilemma-ethics course. Now thorny issues emerge in an arena of arguments and counter-arguments. Many people leave such courses with an impression that all moral reasoning is controversial, a mere lawyer's game without serious basis. Often a paralyzing fear of moral indoctrination leads professors of ethics to remain silent about basic decency, human rights, gratuitous cruelty, political repression—the basic global consensus that should be passed along responsibly to the next generation.[11]

The evidence gathered by Sommers and Bloom indeed confirms a widespread anxiety that most U.S. schools may be hatching a population of moral stutterers or illiterates. My own perceptions about student values, however, differ widely from the conclusions of both writers. I admit a possible disparity in the identity of our three school settings, in the backgrounds of our students, and in the personality and methodology of three individual teachers. Conceding the moral anarchy or superficiality often disguised under the rationale of value-clarification, I still back the need to coach people in a disciplined perception, scrutiny, comparison, and assessment of values. This is the very process I illustrated in the case-study from childhood in my opening chapter, the complex process of detecting an authentic conscience.

I would describe most of my private counseling work as training sessions to help individuals clarify and assess their own values. Abraham Maslow often showed clients how to drop such defensive poses as the shy or tough cynical facade, then immerse themselves in an immediate experience, and at last give an honest response. When presented with a glass of wine, as Maslow advises, people should not look at the bottle label, nor search for other cues about how to respond. They must look within themselves, shut out the noise of the world, and admit how they actually like it. If they can accustom themselves to choose this way in small matters, then they are more likely to make the right life-choices— the choice of spouse, career, and their own destiny. I cannot choose wisely for a life unless I dare to listen to my own self at each moment in life and say calmly, "No, I don't like this." An emphatic "no" or "yes" can be one proof of advancement beyond an immature moral dependency.[12]

Therapy of this sort does not pretend to be value-neutral. As the counseling relationship builds over time with a particular client, the filter of social and personal censorship seems to lift and various hidden fantasies appear. What emerge at last are the values unconsciously guiding the person's past, with an added privilege now of reassessing this moral inheritance from family, church, society, and other sources. Bringing these values to consciousness might seem at first a mere prelude to ethics. But once clients become aware of their own descriptive ethics, they have already taken the first step toward release from an unconscious bondage. After that moment, each individual has yet to begin testing out and reconstructing a more mature moral vision, a normative ethics, deciding what to reaffirm, discard, or transform from before.

Such a value-scrutiny seems designed mostly for a private one-on-one counseling relationship. I cannot recommend the radical tactics of my colleague in the English Department at a nearby university. He gave failing grades repeatedly to one student's compositions for their lack of any independent assertions. In sheer exasperation, this student at last submitted a single four-letter obscenity on a sheet of paper and received an "A." Though some features of value-scrutiny can be adapted judiciously for class discussions and projects, I think sheer emphasis on the value-process can never replace forthright transmission of specific value-content—the basic moral consensus. The hieratic task of transmitting this legacy, of course, must not become an authoritarian catechism lesson, but ought to draw upon the classics of religion, philosophy, and literature, appealing to the mind and also the emotions.

Coping with Diversity

I contend that a pronounced moral consensus, at least in rudimentary detail, is actually endorsed by most people I know. My evidence for this consensus is limited, for I have limited trust in sociological value surveys, including my own findings as a teacher, counselor, and priest. Here are a few of the soundings I have attempted. In undergraduate world religions courses at the University of San Francisco I have long assigned a major reflection paper on each student's unique philosophy or religious position. The assignment is designed to elicit each individual's description of the Sacred, whether friend, ultimate value, or some other functional equivalent; then one's private or corporate forms of worship and meditation; and finally the ideal attitudes and behavior expected of oneself and others.

The value portion of this assigned essay addresses freely selected questions such as the following: In the people I admire, what values do I rate most basic, what least basic? Specifically, what are my attitudes toward the world, society, other persons, my present and future career? What particular sort of parent and citizen do I want to be, what sort of husband, wife, or friend, what sort of business person, lawyer, or other career role? Am I optimistic or pessimistic, and why? What value system would those who know me best conclude from witnessing my daily routine behavior?

Reviewing thousands of these compositions from the last three decades, I find convergence toward a recognizable consensus. Despite a measure of cultural and individual diversity, despite the gap between ideals and their implementation, almost everyone professes similar moral priorities, which I will interpret as "natural"—be grateful, hospitable, and true to your word. Of course, I question always how accurately my particular students typify the viewpoint of their elders or immediate peers or of students polled from very different religious, economic, and cultural backgrounds. It is difficult to guess the extent of their own self-knowledge or of the disparity between their values as perceived and values as actually lived out. And most important, how many of these written disclosures only mirror what students imagine I want to hear? At the same time I wonder, too, how many students of Sommers and Bloom cultivate a cool moral relativism in order to shock the professor.

At this point it may help to explain the basis for my own personal ethics, a position that is Christian but not exclusively so. My position is rooted in an inherent sense of responsibility that human beings acknowledge toward the rights of each other and toward the environment. Such inherent responsibilities have been called natural rights or natural law. I treat this norm, not as the fixed and static absolute that conventional scholastic textbooks often seem to describe, but as an evolving perception—nourished by ongoing research in the human sciences—of what it means to be genuinely human. I am convinced that every culture actually backs a set of similar basic prima facie values, mentioned above: show hospitality, tell the truth, keep your promises, and do not harm other people. In my earlier critique of divine-command ethics I have contended that these human rights and duties are not brought into existence by revealed Christian teaching but clarified and supported by it.

What the Christian perspective adds, then, is just a deeper awareness and interpretation of rights already intrinsic. According to the

Christian New Testament earth and everything on it are God's creatures, redeemed or somehow brought to completion by God incarnate. The congruence between natural rights and a specifically Christian ethics becomes the key premise for Anglican theologian John Macquarrie and the late Richard McCormick, my Jesuit seminary teacher in moral and pastoral theology. "What is distinctive in the Christian ethic is not its ultimate goals or its fundamental principles, for these are shared with all serious-minded people in whatever tradition they stand," Macquarrie concludes. Christians experience the moral life in a unique context. "This special context includes the normative place assigned to Jesus Christ and his teaching—not indeed as a paradigm for external imitation, but rather as the criterion and inspiration for a style of life." [13]

For Christians the life and teaching of Christ are accepted as the human norm because he experienced what it means to be human at the deepest level. Faith in these events, loyalty to this central figure, yields a decisive way of interpreting the world and re-valuing its values. The Christian perspective is more a value-raiser than an answer-giver. As McCormick sees it, the Gospel does not immediately yield moral norms and rules for decision-making. It tries to sharpen our gaze by underlining the genuine human factor against all cultural attempts to distort humanity. The distortions to which McCormick refers include, for example, the tendency in a technologically advanced culture to reduce elderly people to their mere functional value, and to exalt personal uniqueness into a lonely individualism or crush it under a tyrannical collectivism. [14]

Beyond Set Religious Borders

Rights activists know that sheer conformity to the minimal ethics of international law, enforced by trade and political sanctions, can only be a first step toward their final aim, a thorough moral transformation. Just as environmental scientists try to enlist every compatible theological resource, so rights advocates yearn for the support of all influential religious leaders. One priority has become obvious to almost everyone. If an interreligious moral consensus already exists, it must be disclosed more clearly, ratified and promulgated as a global ethics. Yet if this consensus does not yet exist, then every reasonable step must be taken to elicit and articulate it. I will now point out some indications of an implicit moral consensus now evolving within the current milieu of religious pluralism. Then I will study one attempt in 1993 at the Parliament of Religions to formulate an explicit moral consensus between major established religious Ways.

Hazards of Religious Labeling

I have mentioned earlier that some Euro-American rights advocates identify human rights excessively with so-called rights of the first era. Worse, they associate these individual-centered rights too closely with a specific Euro-American scenario of capitalism and democracy. Thus they tend to pin a developing nation's human rights record to its measurable exertions in adopting Euro-American economic and political institutions. As the Myanmar dissenter Aung San Suu Kyi shrewdly comments, this over-identification will tempt an authoritarian government to dismiss all local democratic reforms as conducive to an American-style plague of street violence, drug abuse, and broken marriages. Yet the United States can be defined only partly as a model democratic culture, for it is also a consumerist, mega-city, superpower, frontier, immigrant culture. Forms of democracy are not limited to "Western democracy, such as the American, British, French, or Swiss... There cannot be one form of Asian democracy. In each country the democratic system will develop a character that accords with its social, cultural, and economic needs."[15]

With a similar lack of foresight some policy makers tie down their defense of human rights to an agnostic or atheistic secularism. Functioning as an implicit religious Way, this secular ideology will tend mindlessly to creep in and distort policy. I have defined human rights as only a set of minimal moral standards for acceptable governance. Thus, UN rights are not intended to replace Christian love, for example, Islamic solidarity, or Buddhist compassion as a new alternate Way. Yet at the same time I recognize that a huge number of people expand these minimal claims into a comprehensive Way that I have called Moral Humanism. One reason for the current flood of rights manifestos is an attempt to spell out a code to govern every conceivable interaction in a humane life. This position can easily turn into a militant secular fundamentalism which dismisses various traditional religious worldviews as rival ideologies, extremist and authoritarian. According to sociologist Daniel Bell, by disdaining progressive religious traditions, secular fundamentalists play into the hands of those religious fundamentalists who reject wholesale the values and practices of the Euro-American progressive tradition.[16]

By reason of this implied secular assault and for other motives, too, official religious responses to the UN Bill of Rights have split along traditionalist and progressive lines, most obviously in the Jewish, Christian, and Muslim Ways. During ratification of the UN Universal Declaration in 1948 the Saudi Arabian ambassador abstained because the document did not acknowledge human rights to be a gift from God. He again abstained regarding freedom of conscience to change from one religious Way to another because the Quran forbids a Muslim to convert from the Muslim Way. Yet interpreting the Quran more broadly, the Muslim foreign minister of Pakistan approved the same Declaration.

The Christian responses vary as widely as those of Muslims. Some Evangelical Protestants and tradionalist Catholics have blamed the UN for trying to reduce the Gospel to the clichés of secular humanism. For instance, Evangelical theologian Carl Henry objects that the UN Declaration "says very little about human duties and nothing at all about duties to God." It "wholly ignores the subject of the ultimate source and sanction of rights." Also, the conservative editor of the official Vatican newspaper *L'Osservatore Romano* at first complained about the omission of God's name—"If God be not the builder of the house, its building will be in vain." Yet on the contrary, a large number of Liberal Protestant delegates from the World Council of Churches had been active in framing this very UN text. The UN Bill of Rights has, moreover, drawn ardent Catholic endorsement from the Second Vatican Council and the last four popes, especially John Paul II.[17]

Apparently from the start the UN Bill of Rights tended to be backed, for example, by Muslim and Christian progressives. Yet the Bill tended to be rejected or accepted only conditionally by Muslim and Christian traditionalists. The voting patterns suggest how religious-moral positions often overflow conventional historical religious boundaries. This feature prompts a few generalizations about any interreligious comparison.

How does a Muslim ethics, say, differ from a Christian ethics? The tag of specific identity may both disclose and conceal. The careful observer expects an authorized religious ethicist to be grounded in the authoritative scriptures and ethical heritage of that respective tradition. Mere citations from the Quran or hadith do not prove the El Quaeda terrorist an authoritative Muslim guide, any more than quoting the Bible confirms the Christian pedigree of a Protestant televangelist or minor Vatican bureaucrat. In traditions lacking a vertical community structure someone's claim to represent an established Way remains even more tenuous than in groups geared to authorize a delegate. It should not be forgotten that Asian Ways of Wisdom seldom invest their sacred scriptures with the canonical authority attributed to the Bible by a Jew or Christian, or especially to the Quran by a Muslim. I can think of no accurate empirical test to single out an unambiguous difference between two established Ways, each represented by its own ethicist. The religious distinction thins especially when ethicists representing two differing historical Ways emphasize, not a revealed divine-command ethics, but a cross-religious natural rights consensus.

I admit a few serious qualms about people labeling themselves Christian, Muslim, conservative, liberal, or anything at all. Dedication to searching out the truth may demand that one must at times cross party lines, cheer for the opposing team, even risk being considered an untrustworthy ally. It is wise to hunt beneath every explanation or rationalization that demands to be accepted at face value. To name something is to pass judgment on it and thus affect its destiny. Names originate as imperfect historical constructs, pointers to fluid reality they can never fully grasp. Once frozen in usage, names act as implicit questions and categories of interpretation, directing attention to some issues and away from others, admitting some evidence but filtering out the rest. As a self-fulfilling prophecy, the results that a model yields will most likely conform to the grid such a model imposes.[18]

Hidden Cross Currents

The religious factor, as defined before, is a drive, credo, or value system pervading every sector of life, a factor manifested in awe, commitment, ecstasy, and moral seriousness. Genuine moral concern, then, is virtually religious already, and genuine religious maturity ought somehow to express itself in moral action. By treating the religious factor as a comprehensive adverb or adjective I have no difficulty attributing an implicit religious identity, more or less, to the morally committed ecologist, human rights activist, or advocate for the voiceless poor. As thus defined, the religious-moral phenomenon transcends the historical distinctions between official religious Ways, and the conventional distinctions between two realms, religious and secular.

To probe further into someone's actual religious identity, it is essential to distinguish the universal, individual, and cultural features of this identity. Glancing at our own talents and quirks of personality, we each with some difficulty can sift out those attributes common to all people, those unique to oneself, and those shared only with some other people. I think this threefold distinction, too, helps clarify the interwoven dimensions of someone's religious self-understanding. First, as a basic human being, each person is religious in the inclusive way I have previously defined the term. All are engaged on a spiritual journey evoked by metaphors of flight, combat, spiritual courtship, homecoming, or rebirth—symbols spun from the finite imagination belonging to everyone. Second, each human being has a unique experience of the Sacred, or what Gandhi calls an individual religion. Third, as a social being rooted in a specific history, however, we each share particular spiritual kinship, in various overlapping circles, with anyone of the same temperament and characteristic spirituality, the same gender, race, culture, era, and family religious heritage. Two or more people, each with a unique individual spirituality, agreeing now to adopt a creedal formula, now a particular moral platform, may tone down other individual and cultural differences.

The last of these three features, a person's cultural religious identity, is a challenging venn diagram of intersecting circles. Once the conventional boundaries between religious Ways are deemphasized, a number of undetected religious-moral affinities shift into focus. One strand of this multifaceted kinship may prove more vital than another. For example, some devout individuals in each of the historical religions seem to identify themselves as pacifists first, and Christians or Buddhists, say, only second. Their moral experience prompts them to reexamine their own historical Way for a cogent pattern of meaning and purpose. One Muslim friend of mine, by moral sensibility a dissenter and total pacifist, often jokes about his incongruous birth within a Way whose founding prophet was a warrior. He strains to reinterpret the Quran's support for jihad, a justified defensive religious war, as authorizing only an interior spiritual combat.

Facing a comparable dilemma of nonviolence, the Hindu total pacifist Gandhi feels impelled to perceive no more than a scenario of self-conquest in the Bhagavad Gita, where Krishna encourages Arjuna to pursue civil war and fratricide. In a number of historical religious Ways two cultural archetypes recur, often held in dialectical suspension within a single Way—the sanctioned holy war and the peaceful garden. Guiding a nation especially during times of war, religious leaders tend to over-identify with the first archetype but neglect the arts of compromise and covenant that typify the second. The first image evokes a warrior and hunting culture under a patriarchal God, and the second an agrarian matriarchal culture. In this utopian garden men and women, the old and the young, animals and nature, coexist with equal freedom.[19]

The pacifist coalition is one cross-current defying historical religious borders. My second illustration centers on an interreligious bond among activists and also a bond among fatalists in the face of human suffering. The Hindu-Buddhist notion of karma offers a complex range of religious-moral implications, depending on an individual's spiritual maturity and unique cultural and individual background. The Dalai Lama was introduced before, pondering the karmic law of cause and effect, explaining how he developed an activist concern about the causal interconnections between present and future human generations and their environment. Perhaps in reverse his developing activist experiences may actually have led him to reconceive a traditional Buddhist notion through the lens of his evolving activism. In a comparable Buddhist context, during efforts to establish a Buddhist socialist regime in Burma during the 1950's Prime Minister U Nu lashed out at a distorted grasp of karma by the wealthy. Rich Buddhists were trying to vindicate their current superiority to the poor as the rightful destiny for both rich and poor, earned by karmic merit from past lives. In rebuttal U Nu urged the affluent to become voluntary bodhisattvas, laboring in their present incarnations to heal sources of social misery.[20]

I have already rejected the facile East-West dichotomy between cultural temperaments—mutual stereotypes that depict the average

Hindu or Buddhist as more fatalistic, the Christian more proactive. Christians cannot forget their own longstanding Lutheran-Catholic, Calvinist-Arminian, Banesian-Molinist debates about the compatibility between the omnipotent Grace of God and our created human freedom. For one Buddhist the law of karma may mean we are each stuck with the cards dealt from our past lives. Yet for another Buddhist the good karma activated in our present life can drive out any bad karma inherited from a previous existence. For a Hindu inured to the culture of poverty, future rebirth may seem a curse; yet for a Hindu wallowing in a consumer wonderland, rebirth may seem a blessing. Informed Hindus know that karmic merit may lead them to be reborn, not to higher caste and wealth, but perhaps to penury or untouchability, whatever setting offers a better spur to reach salvation.

It appears that an individual's ethics of human rights has often been influenced more by the choice to be a traditionalist or a progressive than by the choice to be a Muslim progressive, say, rather than a Christian progressive. A person's first impulse may be to declare oneself a progressive rights advocate, for instance, and taking an immediate second step, to measure this certainty by the standards of one's longstanding Muslim heritage—obligations imposed by God for protecting human dignity. Because I view religious identity as irreducible to a mere rationalization or ideology I do not suggest hypocrisy or self-deception here, but a matter of honest reflex priorities. The Islam invoked by ruling elites often differs from the Islam of the masses and the Islam of revolutionaries. Each of these groups may quote an identical Quran passage, with their own conflicting interpretations, and all are tempted to label their respective cause a classical jihad. In any debate about ethics it is wise to treat the religious factor as potentially dialectical. At times it supports, even absolutizes, the unexamined verities of a particular time and place. But next moment it can turn into a Way of the oppressed, offering people in that society the ultimate basis on which to question and overturn any penultimate certainty.

A simple label indicating, say, official Jewish or Buddhist identity does not disclose much about an individual's private spirituality or value system. For this label mostly points to a single vital influence upon someone's life without gauging its intensity. Within each religious Way some followers prove more monocentric, others more polycentric. An official Christian persona can take up all one's interior space so that this Christian identity functions as the all-sufficient integrating focus. However, the Christian persona may be more polycentric within another person, perhaps the central loyalty radiating outward, but just one among many facets. I have watched many new implicit alliances formed between Hindu and Humanist feminists, Muslim and Jewish human rights advocates, Primal and Buddhist environmentalists, Christian and Moral Humanist liberation theologians. Either reinforceing or even replacing a person's commitment to an historical Way, these new emergent affiliations may inspire a particular moral decision.

Often religious ecumenists, World Health Organization members, and other international human rights delegates discover that their primary kinship with one another proves to be tighter than with their own community of origin. According to Rabbi Jonathan Magonet, by engaging with "the other" he risks losing touch with his own community. At times it seems easier to befriend those from the other Way with a similar interest in dialogue than with his own co-religionists. Often the hardest part of dialogue is the return home, trying to explain to those not sharing his experience what it means, why it is important, and reassuring them he has not simply betrayed them.[21]

Within my own life I have found extraordinary affinities across conventional religious borders. I tended for many years to reach out to friends, expecting resonance first with fellow Catholics and other Christians, then less by degrees with Jews, Muslims, Hindus, and perhaps least with the random atheist. But experience itself has jumbled this tidy chart of intimacy. Today someone in the peace movement, Amnesty International, or the International Rescue Committee, perhaps unchurched or agnostic, often shares deeper bonds with me than do many Catholics and Christians, absorbed in a quest for doctrinal or ritual purity.

Prophets of Postmodernity

The cross-religious solidarity I have been describing did prompt one major attempt to articulate an explicit moral consensus between the major historical religious Ways. This document was signed at the 1993 Parliament of Religions in Chicago. I suggested earlier that the century-long passage from modernity to postmodernity has been mirrored in the UN's fifty years of increasingly diversified membership and decentralized power. A shift toward postmodernity also shows up in the remarkable contrast between 1893 and 1993 sessions of this Parliament of Religions.

The planning committee for the First Parliament in 1893 included a few Jewish, Catholic, and Unitarian representatives alongside the fourteen-member Liberal Protestant majority. Parliament leaders hoped to devise a spiritual equivalent to exhibitions celebrating America's triumph in industry and technology at the Chicago Exposition of 1893 that commemorated the four-hundredth anniversary of America's discovery by Columbus. All the recognized global religious communities were invited to send representatives, speaking not as official delegates but as private individuals. For various reasons, however, no Mormon, Native American, African American, Sikh, or Tibetan Buddhist representatives showed up. Major addresses referred often to the harmony and brotherhood of all religions. Yet the archives suggest that the committee Protestant majority hoped in this atmosphere of international optimism to vindicate Christianity as the answer to all the unresolved questions raised by non-Christians.[22]

At that Parliament a public that had seldom ventured beyond the Christian perimeter were initiated into Hindu and Buddhist Ways of Wisdom by two compelling advocates. One was Anagarika Dharmapala, a young Buddhist from Sri Lanka, who during a question-period asked his audience how many had ever read the life of Buddha. Only five raised their hands. How many had read the Quran? Only four. "And you call yourself a nation—and a great nation!" he scolded them. "And only four or five have ever read of the faith that 475 million people follow. How dare you judge us!"[23]

The second distinguished advocate was Swami Vivekananda, apostle of the Hindu Vedanta Movement. In this Age of U.S. Robber Barons, on the verge of large-scale American imperialism in the Caribbean and Pacific, the swami preached religious tolerance: "Your way is very good for you, but not for me. My way is good for me, but not for you. How can people preach of love who cannot bear another person to follow a different path from their own?" However, to promote religious pluralism, he was eager to speed up the very process that most other religious leaders deplore—a self-destructive splitting into countless sects, until each individual becomes a sect unto oneself. All world religions in their present form are just the kindergartens of true religion. Free to choose their own guru and religious style, people must realize every individual is actually just an aspect of Brahman the Absolute.[24]

According to many critics of the Second Parliament a century later, these historical religious boundaries, in fulfillment of Vivekananda's prediction, had now vanished, leaving a polyreligious chaos. The five-hundredth Columbus celebration a year before had been undercut by a debate over whether Columbus brought the New World progress or devastation. This 1993 Parliament centennial, launched by a loose coalition of non-mainline religious and ethnic groups, was attended by 7000 people who could choose from 750 major lectures, workshops, performances, and prayer services. Whereas the First Parliament favored a lyceum lecture style, with one assigned speaker following another, the Second Parliament would resemble a decentered convention or world's fair. Members of the First Parliament were urged to avoid criticism of any other religious tradition. In plenary sessions of the Second Parliament, on the contrary, Hindus and Sikhs and Muslims clashed loudly over Kashmir and the Punjab; four Jewish groups boycotted the Parliament when the reputed anti-semitic Louis Farrakhan, Nation of Islam leader, was permitted a formal address; and some Christian Orthodox groups quit the Parliament to protest its acceptance of various neopagans and nontheists.

Composed mostly of U.S. Protestants the Parliament's audience in 1893 for the first time met persuasive representatives of the Asian Ways. Yet a century later, a more diversified gathering encountered the Fellowship of Isis, the Covenant of the Goddess, the Lyceum of Venus of Healing—Ways of witchcraft and the Earth Mother; voodoo, santeria, and other African Ways; and various Native American Ways. Daily voluntary worship sessions at the First Parliament consisted of the Our Father, promoted by Liberal Protestant leaders as the "universal prayer." In the Second Parliament, various yoga, dance, meditation, and liturgy options competed for attention, rites that climaxed in a witch covenant casting a circle in Chicago's Grant Park to honor the full moon.

Media reactions to this Second Parliament split along partisan lines of traditionalist and progressive. They offered verbal cartoons describing some confused spectator unable to distinguish between the margins and the cutting edge, or depicting grotesque lounge lizards in a religious version of the bar scene from Star Wars. Between sessions of the Parliament a neat-suited Protestant Fundamentalist, confronting a Jewish Hindu dressed in an exotic sari, asked if she knew Jesus. And she answered, "Know him? I'm his mother!" In an editorial from *Christianity Today* Timothy George, dean of Beeson, an Evangelical divinity school, relished all this incongruity: delegates from Buddhist to Bahai, Unitarian to Zoroastrian, though convened to foster world peace and religious harmony, could descend to raucous name-calling, excoriating one another for bigotry, intolerance, and crimes against humanity. Referring to the boycott groups of Orthodox Christians, and adding an unconscious irony of his own, George remarked, "Thank God for the Orthodox, who still sense a holy disturbance in the face of modern neopagan idolatry and refuse to connive at it."[25]

New Age psychologist Jean Houston, on the contrary, thought this Parliament "really scared the day and night lights out of the fundamentalists. We saw the sun set on the current age, and darkness emerge as a gestation of a new story." In *Cross Currents* Peter Gardella, chair of religious studies at Manhattanville College, concluded: "After the solemn optimism of the last parliament came great imperialist wars, totalitarian revolutions, and the Holocaust. Is it too much to hope that the melodrama and farce of this parliament might offer a better omen?... Elite thinkers labored over tortured and pretentious statements, but the pagans came, the nontheists made their case, and the people danced."[26]

Costs of Consensus

The elite group of religious leaders whom Gardella disparages were no doubt the so-called Assembly of Religious and Spiritual Leaders, selected by trustees of the Second Parliament. They met separately from the plenary sessions and were handed a text prepared by Catholic theologian Hans Küng, *Declaration toward a Global Ethic*. Originally commissioning this statement from Küng, the "Council" of trustees intended to issue it in their own name but also signed by the presidents of the Parliament. Their obvious concern was to counterbalance the Parliament's display of polyreligious diversity by an assertion of some global common ground. However, prodded to turn such an endorsement into a wider Parliament legacy—and also a media event—they ventured reluctantly to entrust the Global Ethic to the Assembly of Leaders committee for their approval. The committee rules of discussion sound like a parody of Euro-American Modernity, with its domineering initiatives yet outward posturing about democratic process and universal rights. Pressured by media hype and restricted discussion time, these hand-picked delegates of world religions would be permitted only a week to discuss the text but not to edit or amend it!

As Küng himself and others would complain afterwards, this procedure undermined the original draft's limited purpose and raised a red flag against suspected Catholic and Euro-American imperialism from the start. Farid Esack, a Muslim scholar-activist specializing on South Africa, chosen for the Assembly of Leaders, questioned why Küng had been selected as author and whom Küng had consulted in piecing together this particular text. By what process had Esack and others been chosen for the committee? Those asked to sign were mostly different people from those who had contributed to the draft. His two major objections to the text itself were its lofty pacifism, implying a blanket rejection of self-defence, an indispensable right for all oppressed people. He disliked a recurring emphasis on "privatized reformation," as if all change must take place in individuals first, rather than a simultaneous change in both individual and socio-economic structures. I find Esack's objections to both content and process convincing. He preferred delay until trustees could find a more representative way of consultation and drafting.[27]

When I first introduced the Global Ethic text for analysis in graduate and undergraduate classes of world religions, some students faulted it for trying to assert too much, some faulted it for too little. They thought the text pretends to distill the moral essentials of all major Ways into a few paragraphs, mere generic platitudes to court the signatures of so many conflicting delegates. At times it just rehashes the UN Bill of Rights. A few Catholic students complained that it homogenizes genuine ethical diversity, precisely the tough radical particulars. Urging the protection of human life, for instance, the text avoids controversy by not mentioning unborn human life. Or seeking equity for women, it evades the specific issue of women's right to church ordination.

In a comparable situation the eighteenth-century Jewish theologian Moses Mendelssohn refused to back an easy ecumenism that strained to achieve one fold and one shepherd by enlisting everyone under a single formula. "The unifiers of faith would simply be collaborating in pinching off a bit from some concept here and there, in enlarging the texture of words elsewhere, until the words become so vague and loose that any ideas, regardless of their inner differences, could if necessary be squeezed in." Mendelssohn wonders why we should "use masks to make ourselves unrecognizable to each other in the most important concerns of life, when God has given all of us our own faces for some good reason."[28]

Global Moral Minimum

The original author of the Global Ethic has published a useful array of commentaries, rebuttals, and a textual history, all useful for spotting what the text attempts or evades and why. Küng claims that the intent of this Global Ethic is not to replicate the UN Bill of Rights, which addresses rights alone. He comes close to echoing my distinction between human dignity as the moral goal, and human rights as only one means toward this goal. "An ethic is more than rights," he says, for an ethic also includes moral duties and ideals. Whereas the UN Bill of Rights is addressed to sovereign nation-states and their citizens, the Global Ethic is addressed to the religious and ethical leaders of the world and their adherents. The UN Bill of Rights, so often ignored and violated in the political arena, needs the support of an underlying ethical will, which the religious traditions must take responsibility for shaping.[29]

I find at least three features of the Global Ethic admirable. First, I think it offers a clear, accurate summary of the moral common denominator already present in various world traditions. These essentials seem to be uncovered within the traditions, not introjected by the outsider. Yet this ethical core is spelled out in a graphic context of present drug peddling, political torture, sexual abuse, destruction of the environment, and the debt crisis of developing nations. I agree with one critic's assessment that the Global Ethic identifies an ethical agenda for the future, even while declaring an ethical consensus rooted in the past.[30]

What are the contents of this moral common ground? The text centers on the Golden Rule, rephrased in the assertion, "Treat every human being humanely." The universal imperatives not to kill, steal, lie, or sexually exploit are turned into positive obligations—commitment to a culture of nonviolence and respect for life, of solidarity and a just economic order, of tolerance and a life of truthfulness, and of equal rights and partnership between men and women. The common ideal is a just use of natural resources and a socially beneficial global economy. Every human being without distinction of age, sex, race, skin color, physical or mental ability, language, religion, political view, or national or social origin possesses an inalienable dignity. A human being must always be the subject of rights, an end and never just a means, never the object of commercialization and industrialization in economics, politics, the media, research institutes, and business corporations.

A second merit of the Global Ethic is its forthright distinction between a minimal and a maximal ethics. I have called attention earlier to the way some zealous moral humanists tend to inflate the UN Bill of rights into a comprehensive secular ethics, a functional religious Way superseding the historical religious ethical traditions. This text wants to rule out such a tendency: "By a global ethic we do not mean a global ideology or a single unified religion beyond all existing religions, and certainly not the domination of one religion over all others... We mean a fundamental consensus on binding values."[31] Küng in his commentary explains that "even in the future the global ethic cannot replace, say, the Torah of the Jews, the Christian Sermon on the Mount, the Muslim Quran, the Hindu Bhagavad Gita, the Discourses of Buddha, or the Sayings of Confucius... These sacred scriptures offer as it were a maximal ethic, compared with which the Declaration Toward a Global Ethic can offer only a minimal ethic."[32] By setting a modest limit on the Declaration's basic ethical core, the text encourages every religious Way to use this shared minimal standard in confirming, perhaps even reforming, their own distinctive maximal teachings.

Küng also gives plausible reasons for the text's shrewd avoidance of quotations from specific world Scriptures, for he surmises that one tradition would always complain about being left out. His governing principle was that "things quite incapable of commanding a consensus had to be avoided, but at the same time the consequences of particular ethical maxims had to be expressed clearly and made concrete, even if this was inconvenient for certain religious communities."[33]

A third contribution of the Global Ethic has been its ability in various passages to spark self-criticism within the religious traditions themselves. It is my experience that a sound life of faith needs exposure to free inquiry and self-questioning, even an experience of constructive doubt. George Carey, Anglican Archbishop of Canterbury, believes the common fundamentalist distortion in all Ways is an incapacity for secure self-criticism. "To counter such tendencies, which are present, even if only in embryonic forms, in most of us, we need to be honest about our own shortcomings, and not pretend we have an exclusive right to hold the moral high ground. Within the Christian tradition this means acknowledging much that has shamed our high ideals down the centuries, whether in the Crusades, or in the failure to stand up to the evils of Nazi power, or, most recently, in the tragedies of Bosnia and Rwanda."[34]

I recall a long meal to which I was treated by a former student of mine, a militant African Muslim traditionalist. During our conversation he proceeded to unload almost every grievance he had stored up against the Christian Way—historical outrages against Muslims, everyday disparities between Christian words and actions, and apparent self-contradictions in Christian theology. Though at first overwhelmed by his muscular polemics, I soon relaxed, sensing that this free meal could be expected to cost me something. With somewhat calm urbanity I decided to join in his criticisms. Reaffirming many of his objections, adding some of my own, I introduced even more forceful historical anecdotes to support a number of his arguments. If I recall correctly, our contest never lost a touch of warmth and respect. At a sudden reversal in the conversation he invited me to match his offensive against the Christian Way with a counter-offensive against the Muslim Way. However, I had picked up several indications that he did not want to criticize his own Muslim Way in my presence, and that he could not stomach a critique from religious outsiders, especially from me. We at last agreed that no genuine mutual dialogue was possible until both of us were ready to transcend the debating mode. He must be able and open as a Muslim to criticize his own Way, just as I had begun to criticize my own Way.

As the document aknowledges, the most harmful failing of religious leaders is "to dismiss another religion as of little value…When they stir up prejudice, hatred, and enmity toward those of different belief, or even incite or legitimate religious wars, they deserve the condemnation of humankind and the loss of their adherents." By targeting defective religious authorities, then, the text gains more credibility when it proceeds to denounce the lies and cynical self-interest of parallel leaders in business, government, and the media. The world needs "social and ecological reforms, but it needs spiritual renewal just as urgently." For spiritual renewal, the text expects religious Ways to offer the world "a fundamental sense of trust, a ground of meaning, ultimate standards, and a spiritual home." To be more specific, "religions are credible only when they eliminate those conflicts which spring from the religions themselves, dismantling mutual arrogance, mistrust, prejudice, and even hostile images, and thus demonstrate respect for the traditions, holy places, feasts, and rituals of people who believe differently." [35]

The Global Ethic text, despite its inflated aims and bungled entrustment to the Leaders committee, won a surprising endorsement at the Second Parliament of Religions. The document has been praised for counteracting the demons of relativism without replacing them by a distorted absolutism. Perhaps the Global Ethic's primary usefulness comes from its ability to moderate both of these extremist rebuttals to pluralism. To relativists the text affirms that absolute values exist. To absolutists it affirms that the truth they prize is not their exclusive possession but can also be found elsewhere.[36]

It would be a mistake, however, to extol the Global Ethic as a latter-day Ten Commandments. If the Parliament's huge assembly seems to represent the new postmodernity, then the hand-picked Leaders committee still shows traces of the old modernity—an inner circle chosen arbitrarily, an imposed text to be ratified without editing or discussion in depth, the secretive imperialist tactics of the First Parliament. I think the Global Ethic will achieve its original purpose only if treated as a working paper to spur future discussion and honest scrutiny within each religious constituency. Both positive and negative responses should then receive wide circulation, along with alternative drafts from other religious communities, so that no group could complain reasonably of being pressured into approving a document at odds with their own religious values.

After watching portions of videotaped highlights from the 1993 Parliament, most of my students have been touched by two particular scenes. In the first film clip Native American drummers, reacting to the noisy Hindu-Sikh quarrel mentioned before, took over the microphone for a rite of healing to quell the disorder. Gradually a line of dancers, linked hand in hand, formed in a Sacred Hoop, and then to the accompaniment of Crow and Hopi drums, began to weave through the audience, until everyone was caught up in the sacred dancing and singing. Discarding the First Parliament's repressed lyceum format and the grammar of political correctness, this new Parliament offered groups a forum to bring up longstanding grievances and religious disparities. Sometimes an eruption of frank debate gave way at last to a renewed experience of empathy, mutual respect, and healing.

The second prophetic moment in the Parliament was an impassioned talk on ecology by Gerald Barney, director of the Millennium Institute in Arlington, Virginia. The sustained applause drawn at the Congress auditorium by Barney suggests how often a serious environmentalist manifesto can elicit a near-universal moral consensus among leaders from divergent theological backgrounds. Perhaps the long-sought common ground begins here, and then extends step by step through mutually acknowledged human rights to a final respect for each person's unique religious Way. "Nations are not independent entities, subject to no other power on Earth," he remarked. "They are all interdependent and very much subject to the health and welfare of the entire ecosystem of Earth, of which they are but a modest part. The imaginary lines around nations, the 'border,' generally have no relationship to the boundaries of watersheds, airsheds, and other natural systems, and complicate the development of mutually enhancing Earth-human relationships." [37]

The boundaries between official religious Ways, in my opinion, like the boundaries between nations, often shaped by random history or providence, tend to petrify into later barriers to mutual knowledge and empathy. The United Nations is asked to balance the need for worldwide equity in human rights protection with the need for genuine regional and national diversity. Similarly, to establish a universal ethics, the common ground in today's polyreligious context, it is necessary at the same time to respect the distinctive charism of each individual, each culture, and each religious community. I have highlighted the necessity of integrating universal, cultural, and individual dimensions in all religious experience. Each Way is expected to stay faithful to its distinctive maximal religious-ethical tenets but also to the minimal global consensus. This moral consensus pervades not just all the classical religious traditions, but also new emergent Ways, and even the Ways that stand clear of religious labeling.

7

AN ETHICS OF VIRTUE, CHARACTER, AND STORY

EACH OF THE PRECEDING CHAPTERS HAS MARKED THE SHIFT FROM a worldview somewhat coherent and centralized to one increasingly more pluralistic. Chapters 1 and 2 introduce case-studies about the troublesome shaping of my own preadolescent conscience and about later efforts to help religious pacifists give public voice to their consciences. There I lower the conventional barriers between being and doing, between ordinary virtue-ethics and extraordinary crisis-ethics, between the religious and the moral dimensions of experience. Chapters 3 and 4 focused on an inclusive social ecology, reaching beyond a human-centered, logos-domineering worldview to a cosmos-centered or God-centered balance of mythos and logos. Chapters 5 and 6 explore human rights in the context of international law and a global religious ethics. These last chapters shift historically from modernity to postmodernity, from separate historical religious Ways to a polyreligious matrix, and from Euro-American imposed civil rights to a global consensus of combined civil, social, and economic human rights.

Both the UN Bill of Rights and the World Parliament's Global Ethic have often been dismissed as a mere ethics of aspiration. Yet this visionary function alone would be a worthy achievement. I have insisted repeatedly on the need to internalize human rights ideals. Sheer external conformity to the minimal ethic of international law, imposed by trade sanctions or the pressure of global scrutiny, is likely to remain just a momentary cosmetic change. I think a more genuine world consensus can be ignited by convoking regional rights conferences among nations with similar linguistic, religious, and cultural roots. In the search for lasting ecological reforms Pope John Paul II has reaffirmed the same need to internalize. He wants the next generations trained in aesthetic sensitivity and ecological responsibility from childhood onwards—an appreciation not just for natural beauty but also for human artifacts and wise urban planning.

Perhaps the most obvious thread of unity throughout the preceding chapters is the call for a more comprehensive viewpoint—shifting from one uniform method to a cluster of converging methods. I conjectured in my first chapter that the most common type of moral reflection is not a deductive argument drawn from moral axioms, but combined feeling and intuitive reasoning, an approach described by various bumbling labels, such as the terms in this chapter title. The way someone perceives a concrete moral problem will be influenced by one's individual temperament and culture, touched more by some issues than others, and by the current moral consensus that transcends historical religious boundaries. The values entering any moral decision lack a single source, nor can a single method measure so many complex interwoven factors. The present chapter will take soundings in these rich intractable facts of moral experience, which I have tended to neglect thus far for the sake of conceptual clarity. I will combine a number of similar perspectives into an overlapping ethics of virtue, social character, and story. To render such an ethics practical and transmittable I will test out its impact on everyday teaching and counseling, the lab scenarios I know best.

Virtues of Tomorrow

This book has centered thus far on social ethics—massive issues of peace, civil dissent and loyalty, the environment, and an international Bill of Rights. By raising concern at this point for an internalized ethic, however, I will shift attention to an appropriate individual ethics, the indispensable other half of a balanced social-individual moral life. Each individual virtue will also be sized up for its social implications. A cautionary tale recurs about a popular ethics teacher whose classes focused on corporate business corruption, women's oppression, capital punishment, DNA research, and other social policy questions. Pledged to awaken the social conscience of her students, she did not want to waste effort promoting the bourgeois individualistic virtues of honor, private decency, and personal responsibility. Yet she was pressed one day to reexamine her priorities. For contrary to explicit directives, almost half her students in their take-home finals plagiarized secondary sources.[1]

Counting on Virtue

To capture the subtle diversity of moral experience many ethicists today focus less on the moral deed itself than the virtuous dispositions that guide the person deciding. Particular acts of voter indifference or white-collar crime, for instance, seem far less important than the underlying cultural trait of self-centered individualism which perhaps generates the first two symptoms. This type of ethics raises questions about the person everyone ought to be, the life each ought to live, rather than the actions each ought to perform—often called a virtue ethics, agent-centered rather than act-centered. Its model is a reinterpreted Aristotle who in his Nicomachean Ethics explores one by one the major virtues needed to live the good life in an ideal Athenian city-state.[2]

By *virtue* I mean a permanent disposition, conducive toward doing good. A set of values gradually settles into a habitual pattern, a so-called second nature. Just as the seasoned carpenter, sculptor, or swimmer can fall back on their skill to guide them almost intuitively in each moment of action, so the genuinely compassionate person tends usually to act with almost unreflective compassion. Less innate than acquired, values or virtues are socialized within an actual or implicit community context. The individual is trained through the guidance of distant exemplars in history and literature, and exemplars nearby at home, work, and school. Some virtues help a person flourish simply as a human being, whereas other virtues are relative to a particular role or culture. I call these latter virtues the social character, and I will treat them later.

Each religious Way, culture, era, and individual comes up with a unique list of virtuous priorities and different nuances in understanding them. For example, trained for many years to admire a mature Christian humility, I do not share psychologist Heinz Kohut's enthusiasm for a certain type of Roman Stoic narcissism, marked by quiet pride, mild disdain for the rabble, a creative superiority that judges and admonishes with assurance. In a similar way Aristotle's highest moral ideal is personified in the so-called Magnanimous Man of his Nicomachean Ethics, a figure so large-hearted that he would never stoop to anything petty or unworthy. This figure's lofty self-image must never risk being tarnished. I cannot imagine befriending such a person, who sounds almost incapable of tenderness, self-doubt, or laughter. The United States today, as a pluralistic culture, at times defines itself as value-neutral, with no privileged dependence on any single moral tradition. I believe, on the contrary, that a distinctive American legacy of civil virtue can be pieced together, our own so-called *civil religion*. Yet because so many critics treat this value system as lost, jumbled, or eroded, I acknowledge that our society and others need a clear minimal protection, an ethics of international human rights. To make any imposed system of rights credible and congruent, however, each individual has to try fostering a genuine inner life of virtuous priorities.[3]

Frugality and Self-Worth

What are the major virtues in an era of postmodernity? The ethics of ecology and global human rights, developed in earlier chapters, hinted at a range of corresponding virtues. I will now render these priorities more explicit. Frugality is my first example, the pivotal environmentalist virtue. Unfortunately the word connotes Max Weber's Protestant Ethic, a capitalist asceticism of honesty, equity, industry, reliability, and thrift. When Ben Franklin designed a virtue inventory to gauge his daily moral progress, he singled out most of these anal bourgeois traits. For many early Americans, to live frugally was just the obvious practical means to accumulate investment capital for a hard uncertain future. An intrepid philanthropist like Franklin, however, found such a life distorted if it lacked a spirit of just and generous sharing. According to the Quaker William Penn, frugality is good only if accompanied by liberality.

Derived from the Latin root for fruitfulness, *frugality* at best implies a human plenitude of being rather than mere having, an enrichment that is qualitative rather than quantitative. It does not care about material things but cares for them. It is sparing in production and consumption, and the only prosperity it accepts must be redefined in less wasteful forms. Ethicist James Nash treats frugality as an affirmation of human dignity—our status as an end and not merely a means—against the onslaught of manipulative advertising. "Frugality is committed to sufficient production, the just distribution of products, and the reduction of wasteful byproducts in order to achieve full human development. It rejects indiscriminate material production, which has made the maximum accumulation of goods an end in itself, and which serves not as a sign of, but as a substitute for, human well-being." Frugality as a feature of individual character ethics, of course, requires the support of frugality as a social virtue. Through positive or negative incentives, social structures can act as a moral catalyst or deterrent for individuals to act virtuously. For example, the simple act of recycling, Nash observes, cannot be practical without recyclable products, recycling centers, public acceptance, and market potential, all enabled by public policy. Frugal persons can flourish effectively only with the institutional supports of frugal societies.[4]

Christian frugality adds a few distinctive nuances of its own. Liberation theologians demand a shared global responsibility for the needs and rights of all, especially a shift favoring the interests of those economically powerless and voiceless. In the monastic traditions both the community and its members try to live a calling to voluntary poverty by imitating the homeless and impoverished lifestyle of Christ. Stripping life to its essentials becomes a way to identify with the insecurity and dependency of the poor and to witness against economic injustice. Just as the monastic movement began as a subversive historical withdrawal, the frugal lifestyle today, flexibly adapted to any economic level, has a distinctive revolutionary potential.

John Maynard Keynes, the great economist of affluence, used to ridicule frugality as an anachronistic miserly virtue. The Keynesian system depends on stimulating the economy by encouraging increased consumption. Only one week after the World Trade Center and Pentagon sabotage this year, for instance, many U.S. economists and business leaders spurred the public immediately to resume their exuberant consumer habits. Return to business as usual, buy as a patriotic duty, they pleaded, or else the economy might languish, and the terrorist disruptions prove successful. Yet more and more people, aware of ecological limits and watching overconsumption destroy the ecosystem, feel compelled logically to restrict or renounce this Keynesian premise. If frugality ever becomes a pervasive social virtue, I must concede that the long-term benefit of a new economic paradigm might exact a harsh short-term price. For less buying and production within the present system could set up a recessionary chain-reaction of lower investments, then lower profits and wages, and then higher unemployment. Despite such dangers, however, even a modest life of frugality could at least reduce addictive and therapeutic buying. It inserts a breathing-space of freedom into the frantic cycle of overproduction and overconsumption.[5]

In the service of frugality a few other virtues have evident environmental implications. Pragmatic wisdom, based on competent technological knowledge, may prove the most important endowment to accomplish direct environmental reform in industry and in government. Yet geared to catalyze change less in structures than in people themselves, an ethics of virtue will focus on holistic and ecologically responsible habits of thought and feeling. The requisite virtues would surely include a cosmic humility and gratitude and also a self-acceptance that radiates out to accept other human beings and the rest of creation. A balanced sense of self-importance ought to keep people from treating animal and plant life with brutality or indifference.[6] I suspect that those perverse bug-massacres during my childhood, recounted in an earlier chapter, must have been rooted in a compensation for my own powerlessness.

The mature habit of wonder stands equidistant from extremes of nature-idolatry and self-idolatry. Both these excesses involve mismanaged projections, distortions of nature and of oneself. As the classical Hebrew prophets understood it, idolatry means treating something less than God as God, treating the proximate as the ultimate. Even the Hindu pantheist, awed by natural beauty, can mistake maya appearances for the Brahman reality. In moral and psychological terms idolatry involves worshiping sexuality, fame, intellectual or even spiritual ability, to the extent that we subordinate our entire humanity to some diminished shadow-image of ourselves. In a comparable distortion some nature documentaries and Earth First advocates indulge in arcadian nostalgia, a sappy Disneyism or "Bambi syndrome," reducing the full reality of nature to a few interludes shielded from predation and decay.

The vice of sentimentality deserves more careful scrutiny, for critics tend to pin this harmful stereotype on the serious ecologist. In fantasies recounted to me during counseling sessions and in scenarios from my favorite Victorian novels I am often introduced to a suffering moppet character, a loving subservient child with no mind of her own. She seems contrived to elicit a combination of pity and mastery. Such fantasies have the power to warp our perception of real women and can prove so absorbing that we lose contact with what is actually pitiful in the world next door. I find a comparable peril in romanticizing the nonhuman world, what literary critics label the pathetic fallacy. People viewing the threatened ecosphere through a magenta-tinted lens can become too enraptured to engage in practical environmental reform. Excessive love for animal pets can also distort awareness. In my experience this fondness, at best capable of guaranteeing pet-lovers an oasis of unconditional acceptance and sensitizing them toward human misery nearby, often seems instead to drain off all their compassion.[7]

Besides frugality, then, the virtues of technological mastery and wonder seem an indispensable basis for sound environmental activism. My second major illustration of a virtue suitable for our times has been implied in the human rights and global ethics discussions of the two previous chapters. This is a sense of human dignity, rooted in an appropriate self-respect and self-love that overflows beyond the self. I distinguished earlier between human dignity as an end in itself, and human rights as just one legal means for minimal protection of this dignity. By *human dignity* I mean human worth—worthiness or self-worth rooted in our capacity to act as responsible moral agents, a capacity that deserves respect from ourselves and others. The context for emphasizing this endowment is historical, a radical passage from an era of hierarchical social dignity to an era of human rights that attributes dignity to every person, regardless of race, gender, nationality, or especially social status.[8]

True, the common Neo-Confucian estimate is that a new-born child has no human rights simply by fact of biological birth. The child, still an incomplete person, lacks human worth until it becomes a socialized, participating member of society. Throughout most of the world today, including Confucian societies, a consensus is gradually evolving about how far standards of human worth ought to extend—to include women and children, minority populations, those mentally impaired, the seriously disabled and dying, perhaps someday even the human fetus in its earliest stages.

In a context of contemporary global rights, simply because people have been born as human persons, they possess human worth. Thus, they deserve respect for this worth, even if their sense of self-worth has been impaired. People should never be humiliated or dehumanized as workers or sexual slaves because they lack the physical or moral strength to defend themselves, even if they consent to their own degradation. I pointed out earlier that the Global Ethic text insists a person never be reduced to an object of commercialization, economics, politics, research institutes, or the media. A person must be treated as "an end and not a means," as Kant stated with admirable sensitivity. "Even if all the amenities of life are sacrificed, maintenance of human worth makes up for the loss of them all, and sustains approval. And if all else is lost, someone still has an inner worth."[9] Humanity in each of us must be respected, for otherwise we are worthless, not only in the eyes of others but in our own.

To have a balanced sense of self-worth means basically to possess a certain moral nerve, a toughness of character, the ability to love and discern. From the perspective of novelist Joan Didion, lack of respect for ourselves prompts us to despise anyone else blind enough to consort with us despite our fatal weaknesses. Since our own self-image is so untenable, we are enslaved, driven to live out other people's false notions of us. "At the mercy of those we cannot but hold in contempt, we play roles doomed to failure before they are begun, each defeat generating fresh despair at the urgency of divining and meeting the next demand made upon us."[10]

The virtue of dignity or moral worth is associated today especially with the process of dying. On some lips, the motto "death with dignity" conjures up a suicide by lethal injection. Yet for me the words suggest the right to avoid extraordinary medical interventions which try to prolong bodily life beyond one's actual human death as a self-possessed moral person. The Roman moral philosopher Seneca used to remark that though born unequal, we each die equal. The attributes of extrinsic social dignity are indeed stripped from everyone at death. As a hospital chaplain summoned to a number of death beds, I have been saddened by the futile attempts of some dying people to cling at the last minute to titles, roles, awards, or property they think identified with the best part of themselves. With a heightened sense of human dignity, however, almost everyone yearns to integrate the dying process with the sort of moral character each person has gradually been shaping throughout life. If possible, living and dying ought to cohere in a single human affirmation.

A Social Character Legacy

Frugality and human dignity are two crucial virtues, desirable for every human being. I will now treat a more limited range of human values, relative to a particular role or culture, called the *social character*. Coined by Erich Fromm this term refers to the traits shared by most members of a group, resulting from a similar mode of life. I have suggested earlier that, glancing at our own value system, each individual with some difficulty can sift out those values common to all people, those unique to oneself, and those shared only with some other people—the universal, individual, and cultural dimensions. The cultural dimension will now be brought into focus. As a social or cultural being rooted in a specific history, we each share particular spiritual kinship, in various overlapping circles, with anyone of our family, temperament, gender, race, culture, era, characteristic spirituality, or historical religious roots.

Relay of Roles

The origin and outcome of a particular social character is a two-way dialectical process. Sociologist Peter Berger offers a theory of world-construction that I think explains this dialectic clearly. An inventor may construct the first plough or computer. The invention itself then proceeds to take on a Sorcerer's Apprentice existence of its own, so that everyone must eventually conform to the tool's own logic, which perhaps had never been planned or foreseen by its original inventor. Or we create a language which by its grammar then monitors our speaking and even our thinking. In other words, through the construction process we shape communal myths and a social character, and in turn are shaped by them.

The three phases of this process can be called externalizing or projecting, then objectifying or reifying, and finally internalizing or socializing. It takes only a moment's reflection to realize the countless third-phase socializing influences, almost reified by the culture, and stamped today on the individual initiated into society. We find ourselves each socialized in a particular community by being assigned a name, legal status, or occupation, as an official interpretation of our existence. For example, in the overlapping communities to which I personally belong I may weigh my responsibilities in part as a son and brother, a priest, a male, a professor and counselor, and a U.S. citizen. In dialectical terms I can objectify a part of myself within my own consciousness, so that my real self can carry on an imaginary dialogue with myself, say, as an environmentalist or rights advocate.[11]

To ponder the implications of a distinctive social character I often turn back to the following model. A close friend, my classmate from the same grammar and high school class, often used to share stories about his widespread family, many of whom I met over the years. Retired from the U.S. Foreign Service and unmarried, he flourished at the center of a large exfoliating network of nieces, nephews, and their children. He maintained steady touch with them for many years, offering advice and financial assistance, remembering birthdays and anniversaries, sharing family news by e-mail. Last year a few weeks before Christmas he died of cancer in a hospital unit, surrounded by three generations of nieces and nephews, their many voices singing carols to him as his consciousness faded.

I try to imagine myself as this sort of uncle in Caroline Island society especially, a role my Chuuk student friends tell me about, where the social character of aunt or uncle has been established as a vital institution. A man is expected to become habitually avuncular in his attitudes toward the extended family, especially when they need personal counseling, sanctuary, or financial help. He tends to conceive of his whole past, present, and future as the biography of an uncle. He may even sacrifice himself for his nieces and nephews, and find comfort in the hope that his own life will continue in them. [12]

In a traditional small-scale society the uncle role or any other conventional social character is a predetermined script and often contains in germ an implicit life-story, chapter by chapter. Many Primal cultures, for instance, map out a fixed biography for anyone chosen to embody the role of shaman or warrior. I have often studied the imaginative African masks in glass cases at the de Young Museum in San Francisco. Though a mask looks lifeless, it is usually a long-established script to be interpreted by the dancer in a trancelike performance before a chanting audience. Balinese actors and actresses have been known to take home a sacred mask from their Hindu dance-dramas to meditate on its traits and story and pray before the mask, now propped on the family altar. They may even sleep next to it, hoping to evoke dreams associated with its image. The role or mask might contain forces within itself greater than the forces at a performer's conscious disposal, and sometimes almost by magic may transform the good performer into an inspired one.

Parallel to these mask-roles, as I interpret them, are the social roles described by Neo-Confucian ethics as a rectification of names, which I discussed earlier. Drawing upon basic husband-wife, parent-child, friend-friend, elder-younger, ruler-subject relationships, people are urged to transform their conventional role into a genuine guide. Depending on the way they treat each other in these roles, each endows the other with true personhood. What is morally right for a particular individual at this moment? The Confucian answer is that a mother should try to be an authentic mother, and any mother worthy of the name would talk and behave just so. Recall that my own moral decision to inform on a childhood friend, recounted earlier, culminated in an inner quarrel between trying to be a true friend and trying to be a true son. In a comparable way, the most commonplace duty or role in Japanese Shinto can be cultivated into a genuine art, an individual's own rigorous spiritual Way. Choosing to structure their daily schedule around self-defense, fencing, flower arrangement, or calligraphy people obey an ethics respectively of judo, kendo, kado, or shodo, which extends to every facet of life.

No tradition of social character has been spelled out with more intricacy than the Hindu caste and ashrama system. To ascertain your unique moral responsibilities it is necessary first to determine your particular caste identity, your current stage in the ashrama sequence from youth to old age, your marga or style of spirituality, your chosen individual or family God-image, and the teachings of your personal guru. Though the average outsider is repelled by the Hindu caste system for its fixed inequalities that become hereditary, I once discovered a few of its more benign facets in a small Nepali town. A scholar in the Tantric Buddhist Way offered to guide me through the town's puzzling geographical divisions. He interpreted each sector as a different sub-caste community, housing its respective allotted profession, such as barbers, tailors, or jitney-drivers. Much like the medieval European guilds with their separate apprenticeship programs, the caste system inaugurates each person at birth into a community of articulated roles and values, including a specialized profession.

This fixed legacy of character in traditional Primal, Hindu, Chinese and Japanese Ways can only seem alien to today's Euro-American individual—still the isolate enduring hero or heroine of classical American fiction—in a modern and postmodern society. Few urban Euro-Americans seem likely to attain moral validation in the ordained patterns familiar to these other Ways and civilizations. People in my own society face a jumble of fragmented, competing social roles and moral exemplars—from a far less uniform family past, from the variable fashions and icons of peer culture, from the omnipresent media. They have been taught to imagine themselves detachable from their heritage. Caught between their own anarchic individualism and a smorgasbord of so many roles and stories, people often despair of attaining a coherent sense of self or of clear moral guidelines.

In Character

I have noticed that for conservatives a fixed traditional social role is usually an indispensable context for human freedom. They tend to believe that a community will prosper insofar as its consensus grows more uniform and stable. For progressives, on the contrary, the abandonment of this established heritage, and the resulting chaos, might be just a therapeutic prelude to an even deeper freedom. They tend to prize diversity in community members' values and their flexibility of response to changing circumstances. At any rate I am convinced that within the most rootless society even the nameless individual must emerge as a particular person, and therefore still the bearer of a specific tradition. Here is someone's son or daughter, a cousin or uncle, a citizen of this city, a member of that profession or religious group. What is good for this unique individual has to correlate somehow with the good for someone embodying these roles. Given a particular mixture of inherited roles, each person takes on a variety of debts, rightful expectations, and models. [13]

I appreciate any chance to observe people exploring their unique social character legacy. The handful of overlapping role expectations affecting their life will first surface in their awareness as a superego edict from the past. At this point each individual has the chance to revise it as a genuine conscience, to reinterpret and personalize it creatively. For example, an African-American woman in her early twenties told me recently of efforts to redraft a cherished custom in her family that women always prepare the food and serve their men. For many years the ardent feminist within her resented this male prerogative to be served. She has now determined to reinterpret this value legacy as a woman's chance to serve with mature hospitality and kindness. I hope her gracious initiative will elicit from those she serves a grateful sensitivity in turn. Her new ethics owes something to the example of Martin Luther King. In the final sermon before his assassination he urged his Ebenezer Baptist congregation to achieve loving service, like Christ, transforming their enforced legacy as slaves into a free vocation to be of service.

This woman's older sister, another student of mine, has been exploring the role of elder cousin, a model college adult, the first in her family to earn and survive a higher education. Various younger women cousins find their way to her room in a student residence hall and feel pleased to discover their own crayon drawings or photos posted on her walls. When she goes home she often takes them out for ice cream, bike riding, or shopping at the mall. It makes her feel better to know someone loves and looks up to her. She hopes she will never let them down nor hint she has no time for them. Most of the girls are eager to confide about high school life, boys, and future plans. They show a huge curiosity about all the details of her courses, books, hobbies, and relationships. A few even imitate her in the way she dresses and fixes her hair. Though she finds this a cute tribute, she has to remind them always to remember who they are and be proud of who they are. She had never suspected that the role of cousin could be such a combined privilege and moral responsibility.

The moral priorities of yet another student can be explained by her early role as dependable niece and care-giver but also by her later college experience as a biology research assistant. At the age of nine she learned her uncle had contracted AIDS. Confronted by that era's drastic alarm over contagion, her family's daily contact with him required that they all be tested for infection every two months. Scared neighborhood friends refused to visit her home whenever the patient dropped by. During one discussion about the virus in her eighth grade science class, students reacted by shoving back their chairs surrounding her when the teacher happened to explain this uncle's sickness. She felt an indelible shame. Throughout her uncle's progressive decline and death the strain of caring for him left her Italian-American family members depressed, angry, and secretive about his illness. After watching AIDS destroy a person and test a family she was eager to read about infectious diseases and their cure. Later signing up for every college course on virology and immunology she hoped to find her vocation in meaningful research.

Today she calls her character ethics a code of patience and team work. Working in her university biology lab, testing the reactions of various insect specimens to the effects of an enzyme, she confronts frequent obstacles to the project's success. After dissecting hundreds of flies she is expected to run tests on the extracts. The freezer keeping the extracts broke and defrosted three times in the last year, ruining her samples and thrusting her back to the project's initial stages. Lost months of work at a time, with no one to blame and nothing to salvage, frustrated her to the extreme. Yet she had to resign herself to learn from setbacks and stay calm. In life it is essential to advance slowly, work for hidden and deferred rewards, and trust that the wider scientific community will continue her work if she cannot complete it.

I have realized that parents of my students are often divorced, too worn down by overwork, or too alienated from their own immediate past. And thus grandparents at times become the most reliable guardians of a family's value heritage. The elders are now called upon by their grandchildren hopeful to recover fading historical roots—stories, photo albums, perennial wisdom. Since childhood a Mexican-American student of mine showed enough fascination with her grandmother's embroidering that the elderly woman passed along her own unique methods. This pastime, which her grandchild still cherishes today, has remained an intimate secret just between her grandmother and her because apparently no one else in the family showed the talent or interest. Another student, hoping to test out his American youth culture in comparison with the Way of his Czech ancestors, stayed one summer at his grandparents' farm in the Czech Republic. There he picked berries for a neighbor, but was troubled when his own grandfather urged him to refuse payment offered by the neighbor for this labor. Selflessness and mutual sharing were such highly admired traits in this rural culture that a generous berry-picker could anticipate some return later on a more profound level. Admiring the Way of his grandparents, today he often measures his value system from the viewpoint of a potential grandfather himself, wondering what value heritage he will pass along.

When I exemplify a character ethics tradition within particular families I notice a tendency to single out various groups of hyphenated Americans—African, Italian, Mexican, Czech. U.S. history seems to endure periodic shifts between "pure" American patriotic revivals to emphasize our common ground, and particular ethnic revivals to emphasize our differences. Many social critics claim that as a German-American, say, an individual is culturally German but politically U.S. American. For no matter what our respective individual ethnic roots, it takes only a certificate of American citizenship to make us all U.S. Americans. More accurately this person is German-American, both politically and culturally. [14] If a uniform American value consensus is allegedly thinning out today, I think it crucial to focus on the respective hyphenated factor, with its relatively distinctive ethnic roots and a more pronounced family social character.

Many of my ethnically-aware students recount nightmares about trying to balance the value heritages of two cultures, often at odds. I recall an Indonesian-Chinese friend who kept referring to himself playfully by three personal names, each indicating a different face of his complex identity. His family was Chinese in origin, his initial citizenship had been Indonesian, but his dominant language was English-American from his formal education. Designating each of these strands in himself with a personal name, even to this day he seems unable to integrate them. A young Chicana-Comanche student of mine teeters daily between her Mexican-American Catholic devotion to the Virgin of Guadalupe and her recent investigations into the family's indigenous Comanche Way. Her mentor, a Comanche medicine woman, has initiated her into meditation and sweat lodge self-purification rituals. One Chinese-American woman was trained rigorously by her grandmother to be a suitable Confucian marriage-partner, submissive and endearing. She was not allowed anything allegedly unladylike, such as playing basketball. Yet almost all the music, TV exposure, and school-life in her San Francisco childhood eroded this strict conventional upbringing. Another woman, a Korean-American, even today sways back and forth on both sides of the hyphen. Taught by her grandparents to conform out of respect, she prefers on successive days to be one side of the hyphen, then the other, both, neither. She claims paradoxically to be energized by the hyphenated combination itself.

Some people have had to improvise their character ethics, painfully extricating themselves from one false lead after another. A high school Filipino-American couple, faced with the woman's unexpected pregnancy, decided to marry before their child arrived. The parents on both sides refused to back this marriage and the couple's former friends dropped away. The young man's own father had always been absent, his mother overly strict, and he knew only the TV soap and talk show clichés about how to be a father and husband. Thus, both husband and wife decided to create their shared values by talking them out. Another young man, an Irish-American, coaching a midget-league baseball team, found himself challenged to stay in shape, clean up his obscene jokes, act polite and forgiving—to become just the sort of person he was training his team to become. Having cultivated a reputation for cold meanness, at first he had to scare up these new values just out of consistency, to be a credible coach. Gradually the moral veneer deepened to become his genuine adult character.

This young man's growth suggests how the social character, though often acquired as a form of immature conformity, may gradually develop into a sound interdependent conscience. Transmitted from outside, his value tradition may have tamed or even rubbed him raw at first, making demands that he was not yet prepared to handle. Ironically I often find myself trapped in a priest's gatekeeper role of shielding the Catholic ritual tradition from hypocritical misuse, often by well-meaning people. A couple may ask to be united in a sacramental marriage or have a child baptized, not because they now believe or practice this Way themselves, but mostly because their grandparents or others have pressured them to follow the traditional forms. I am ready to concede that people's inner life may need time to become more congruent with the moral and creedal formulas pronounced in an external rite. Yet I must help each person to reach a free authentic religious choice.

Stories at the Heart of Things

In the ethical heritage of all communities "the telling of stories has a key part in educating us into the virtues," Alasdair MacIntyre explains. "We enter human society with one or more imputed characters—roles into which we have been drafted—and we have to learn what they are in order to be able to understand how others respond to us and how our responses to them are apt to be construed." Children are told stories about good but misguided kings, lost children, wicked stepmothers, and elder sons who waste their inheritance but return home. "Deprive children of stories and you leave them unscripted anxious stutterers in their actions as in their words. Hence there is no way to give us an understanding of any society, including our own, except through the stock of stories which constitute its initial dramatic resources. Mythology, in its original sense, is at the heart of things." 15

Sacred Rites of Story-Telling

I did not appreciate the moral impact of everyday story-telling until I lived in a society very different from my own, with its distinctive myths and vital oral tradition. A few decades ago during a research trip of four months to Nepal I came across an English translation of some touching eulogies in a Katmandu newspaper at the death of a local Jesuit priest, an American-born Nepali citizen. Teaching grammar school children for many years at St. Xavier's, Godavari, this priest was appreciated now especially for the dramas he used to stage in class. He would train the boys to act out folk tales from various cultures, including stories from the brothers Grimm and the Hindu Ramayana epic. Important Hindu business people, lawyers, and government officials testified in their eulogies that by witnessing and more so by acting in these productions during childhood, they met their first vibrant experiences of right and wrong, moral tenets which had lasted into the present.

I am convinced a sound religious ethics has much to learn from the rites of serious story-telling—retelling the great moral stories, reenacting them, and hearing or reading them attentively. It should be obvious why our most durable insights usually take narrative shape. People seek out the traditional sacred Ways in order to find a coherent sense of worth or purpose. This vital meaning is needed to steer both the individual and community confidently when faced with daily discouragement. Such a purposive design may take the shape of merely an abstract ideal or a logical argument. Yet more commonly it functions as a plan for action unfolding through time, with false starts, comic relief, foreshadowing, sudden reversals, and a plot moving from beginning, middle, to end. To give the central figures in this outline plausibility, their traits must come across as truly characteristic, and thus require some story line tracing the persistence and flexibility of these attributes over time. In my own Christian tradition I retell the salvation history about God leading his people out of Egypt through desert ordeals to the Promised Land, or about God becoming God-Man to preach and heal on earth, then to suffer, die, and triumph over death. To retell or hear such stories with genuine engagement, but especially to reenact them, means to translate the original story into the small details of my own everyday life.

Martin Buber recounts a persuasive Hasidic tale about an elderly paralyzed man who was once asked to tell about his teacher. What was the teacher like? So he began to recount stories how the holy Baal Shem Tov used to jump and dance when at prayer. In the very act of story-telling, this paralyzed man got so carried away that he had to jump and dance to show how the master had done it. From that moment he was healed. I think this is how stories ought to be told The story itself and its retelling are a sacred event. The wonder that is retold becomes powerful once more.[16]

In a Nepali classroom Hindu schoolboys were enacting moral fables that managed to transcend Hindu-Christian sectarian differences. An immigrant priest had stepped into a crucial role in that society, the vocation of sacred story teller, hoping to impart a heritage of moral wisdom. Nepali Hindu society is relatively homogeneous and small-scale, of course, far more rooted in a living tradition than the young multi-cultural United States. Yet pondering my colleague's achievement stirred me there to imagine comparable projects of role-playing and psychodrama for my classes at the University of San Francisco. In the tradition of eminent story tellers I wanted to pass along the basic moral consensus about rights, decency, cruelty, political repression. The minimal legal ethics of human rights had to be internalized— supplemented by a maximal ethics of virtue, social character, and story.

My boldest experiment in story-telling has been to host Meeting of Minds projects, borrowing some features of the original Steve Allen TV series by that name. During my course in nineteenth-century European Romanticism, for instance, students piece together their chosen character from a few select biographies and act out this first-person role for a single three-hour group performance. Trying to locate evidence for the convictions and behavior of their adopted persona, often they must conjecture in-character about behavior and motives left tacit in the actual biographical sources. They devise costumes, make-up, and whatever props they choose. Boots and a riding whip can be expected for Napoleon, a shawl and lace cap for Charlotte Bronte, a surplice for Pope

The life of each one of us is, as it were, woven of those two threads: the thread of inward development, through which our ideas and affections and our human and mystical attitudes are gradually formed; and the thread of outward success by which we always find ourselves at the exact point at which the totality of the forces of the universe converge to produce upon us the effect which God desires.

O God, that at all times You may find me as You desire me and where You would have me be, that You may lay hold on me fully, both by the Within and the Without of myself, grant that I may never break this double thread of my life.

(Teilhard De Chardin)

David L. Koesterer, S.J.

Ordained a priest
June 16, 1964

First Solemn Mass
June 21, 1964

...ar-bandage for Van Gogh. It is instructive to ...ze up their chosen persona's limitations and ...ersonality. What did each character love, hate, ...at attitudes were adopted toward the Sacred, ...nmediate political and artistic-literary scene? ...ent itself features a panel discussion among ...impromptu questions to one another and ...ues of their era.

...most vital context for moral discovery, ...ation materializes less often in my teaching ...ling and spiritual direction. I sense the ...nentors hovering nearby as I act on a hunch ...rategy of intervention. Journals of eminent ...iography of Carl Jung, have left their mark

...nacting some of the moments in therapy ...s warm empathy for the stories told by his ...moment in *Memories, Dreams, Reflections* ...d he sensed his own creativity had reached ...impasse. He knew how thoroughly his own era had alienated itself from the Christian myth pervading its European past. Jung himself had long ceased believing in this corporate vision. Also, many of his clients had regressed by settling for too narrow a spiritual horizon and for shallow or wrong answers to the massive existential questions of life. If most people lacked a corporate myth, then did Jung at least have his own private myth? Repeating these questions to himself, at first he had no answer. Shortly after, he felt an impulse to build a miniature village out of stones. And gradually through play-therapy he started to reclaim lost childhood memories and gradually rediscover his own myth.[17]

Like Jung I have been listening to vital stories in what many call a time of post-Christian secularity, an era that strikes me increasingly as more polyreligious than nonreligious. The soundings Jung took into his own story ignited his fascination for comparable stories in the lives of clients. An individual would often dredge up a wholly personal narrative that had never yet been told. Jung believed genuine therapy could only begin after the disclosure of this story, which often became a key to the particular treatment to be adopted. He cites the baffling gestures of an elderly schizophrenic woman and his discovery only after she died that she had never recovered from the brutal rejection by her shoemaker lover. The mind of this abandoned woman had so identified with the man's work that she continued to sew or trim imaginary shoe leather. If Jung had detected this hidden meaning earlier, he might have been able to help her come to terms with her loss more directly.[18]

In the spirit of Jung's quest I have also met clients apparently directionless, whose secret story neither they nor I will probably ever fathom. My attempts to elicit value-scrutiny seem at first to yield scattered impulses or just a void. One young woman, for instance, after learning from results on the Strong-Campbell Interest Test that the medical profession might suit her, froze in uncertainty, unable to take a further step in her search. Then I encouraged her to pick out a few biographies of renowned physicians, offered to discuss these books with her, and suggested a few interviews with local alumnae in the medical profession. In comparable situations I tend to recommend accessible biographies, spiritual classics, or provocative fiction, with follow-up discussions or training in meditation, for people confused about their moral values, yet yearning for some persuasive exemplar.

Tracking Down the Whole Story

Many of Jung's clients showed up with apparently no identifiable myth of their own. He would guide them to explore their family history for abandoned myths or else try to erect a myth from private symbols and stories revealed in their current dreams. "In such cases we have to observe whether the unconscious will not spontaneously bring up symbols to replace what is lacking," he explains. "I never try to convert a patient to anything and never exercise any compulsion. What matters most to me is that a patient should reach his own view of things. Under my treatment a Pagan becomes a Pagan and a Christian a Christian, a Jew a Jew, according to what his destiny prescribes for him." [19]

Despite Jung's many personal failings I can imagine myself imitating him in various ways, especially his genuine respect for religious diversity. Yet I think it preposterous to claim a privileged certainty about someone else's unique destiny. I, too, aim not to convert others into mere Catholic clones but to help them deepen and articulate their own distinctive Way. My hope is to offer those freely approaching me a temporary oasis for searching at their own pace. Like Jung I urge them to explore their unique narrative, social character background, and implicit religious Way, which perhaps both of us can then try to interpret. Two vivid examples of my attempt to recover this value legacy come to mind.

In 1965 on a train ride from Chester to London I got swept into a festive group of shop stewards headed for a labor union convention. One of the men in his early thirties initiated a conversation with me that grew suddenly serious, and resumed later by phone calls, letters, and a further meeting. Whereas his wife and daughter were fervent Methodists he had abandoned this faith during his childhood for reasons he could no longer recall. And now, feeling an impulse to return to Christ, the man wanted to hear as much as I could share with him about my own Catholic story.

About three months later this new friend of mine asked if I would help prepare him to be received into the Catholic Church. But my reaction seemed to stun him. I persuaded him instead to reexamine first of all the Methodist Way he had once abandoned. Take a hard second look at it, I said, and see if you can reclaim it in a fresh way. After all, the man could not even explain why he had rejected his family's spiritual roots. And should he decide to become an active Methodist again, he would be more fully supported within the same religious tradition lived by his wife and daughter. I urged him to befriend their minister, and beginning Bible study there, gradually to join his family at Sunday services. Only if he still felt attracted to the Catholic Church after these efforts, would I assist him in converting. A few years later he wrote me that he now felt at peace, restored to the Methodist Church of his childhood and present family.

My second memory of a reclaimed value heritage dates again to 1965. During that year's pastoral apprenticeship in Britain I worked for one month as a priest and orderly in Manchester at the Alexian Brothers' Hospital for muscular dystrophy. There on a large TV screen mounted in the men's principal ward an epic drama was developing most of each day. The undaunted Winston Churchill was near death. Before his funeral in Westminster Cathedral and the final seismic organ anthem most of the patients were following each stage in this prolonged dying process. Accompanying the death-watch were countless film retrospects of highlights from his life, his many speeches, and various World War II scenarios. At first the moderate pacifist in me felt a huge emotional separation from this tough old warrior, whose charism throughout a long political career seemed to fade at each outbreak of peace.

Unveiling a heroic moral narrative, the films began to trigger reminiscences in many of the elderly patients about their earlier lives, especially during the war years. At various bedsides I had listened earlier to weeks of installments from their most hidden stories. Yet now with an emerging gestalt shift these lives seemed to be reconfiguring in my presence. From the men's perspective Churchill now stood for what seemed best in Britain's past—brave defiance against fascism, the power of fluent classical rhetoric, the ambiguous glory of the empire, and especially, survival from mental depression and political defeat in his personal life.

For some patients Churchill turned into a sort of Christ figure, symbolizing the death and resurrection of the nation and their own lives. His noble story served as a grid through which many patients might recover lost patterns in their own private narratives. They now began to recall the most terrifying days of the rocket bombs, mutual sacrifices exchanged between neighbors, their dying war buddies, a sense of national solidarity, and so many values they wanted now to reaffirm. The men had so many heartfelt revised stories to tell me during the final week of my work there.

Whenever I have listened closely to a story recounted by someone ill or dying I cannot forget an elderly African woman's remark that "in the old days, folks didn't know what illness was. They went to bed and they died. It's only nowadays that we've learned words like liver, lung, stomach, and I don't know what!"[20] Her imagination tries to evoke the fault-line between premodern and modern medicine. By the phrase "I don't know what," she sums up the new imported Euro-American medical culture, the specialist who reinterprets her pain as symptoms, the medical charts she is neither able nor allowed to read, the hospital billing categories. Surrendering her body to the physician, she also implicitly agrees to surrender her personal story and feelings, and to translate her story into alien medical terms. She has lost her personal voice. The physician's question "How are you?" must now be answered in a secondhand medical language, the imposed categories of modernity.

Perhaps the postmodern experience of illness begins at the instant patients suspect more is involved than the professional medical story can identify. They discover at last how to tell their own authentic story. Prone to fall back, not only on abstract medical categories but on worn personal memories, most people will replay them almost by rote to any available listener. Thus, a celebrity tends to coast on the same few prepackaged anecdotes unless an interviewer is shrewd enough to disrupt the fixed patterns and launch a fresh revisiting of past experience. Sometimes a powerful catalyst like the Churchill drama can mobilize people to shake their vital Way free of its overfamiliar packaging and to reclaim it in depth.

Values, virtues, social character, and moral stories—all have a new feel in a time of postmodernity. The present book has weighed carefully the postmodern challenges of moral relativity, uncertainty, and religious pluralism. I have celebrated the easing of barriers between sovereign nations, between established religious Ways, between humanity and the natural world, between the moral and the religious dimensions of life. My aim has been to chart a middle course between an ethics of deductive absolutes and an ethics of subjectivity and relativity. Despite the differing verdicts among individuals, cultures, and religious Ways about specific moral issues, I have sought out the broadest common ground for their collaboration—a social ethics of human rights and the environment. Beneath this public legal consensus there is need to locate its spiritual counterpart, an individual ethics based on each person's unique story and moral vision. The minimal ethics of international law, imposed by trade sanctions or the force of world scrutiny, must be grounded on a maximal ethics from the world's religious Ways.

Surely this legal minimum of global rights will be remembered as the most cherished legacy from an era of secular modernity. Yet like the "more" that surfaces in postmodern illness narratives, the further reaches of moral experience will prove inaccessible without a revitalized ethics of virtue, social character, and story. Some critics of the 1993 World Parliament's Global Ethic are hoping against a quick ratification of that particular text. They want it treated as a working paper to elicit alternative drafts from inside each religious community, so that every historical Way will be prodded to locate within its unique heritage a distinctive, comparable ethics of its own. More important, for most people all these abundant rights manifestos, loyalty oaths, and precise legal codes are far less compelling than songs, proverbs, relaxed conversation, and a good story. I described earlier how Hopi and Crow drummers at the Second World's Parliament of Religions intervened in a fiery dispute over the Punjab and Kashmir. They led the audience in a Sacred Hoop dance of reconciliation that may have healed religious animosities more effectively than hours of theological debate.[21]

My opening chapter centered on two significant stories – my first efforts in childhood to dig through layers of conventional do's and don'ts and uncover a fledgling conscience, and Huck Finn's similar struggle to replace Miss Watson's unexamined version of rectitude by his own profound impulse to be fair. These decisions mark a gradual advance from the conventional superego to a post-conventional conscience. Reflecting on these two stories I underlined the need for continuity between doing and being, between a single decision of conscience and the pervading conscientious life of someone deciding. This ethics of agency or virtue-ethics has been developed more fully in the present chapter, notably by a study of frugality, disciplined wonder, self-worth, and other virtues of tomorrow.

The first chapter concluded with guidelines for making a sound moral decision. For anyone committed to this demanding search I promised no secure certitude, only the confidence of mounting probabilities. There I argued for a deeper link with model narratives in one's own religious legacy, with accessible heroes and heroines of history and fiction, and the example of friends and mentors who continue to inspire the person each of us hopes to become. We must each shape our own creative mix, a unique conscience and a unique religious Way, from the superego legacy of character roles handed along to us by family, profession, and religious tradition. I point out in the present chapter how various student friends have been piecing together an implicit ethics of their own, centered on being a model uncle or daughter, for example, a lab technician or midget-league coach. The world's established religious Ways play a crucial part in this process, of course, for they offer various well-tested visions of meaning, a sense of worth or purpose which empowers both the individual and community whenever facing daily discouragement.

I have insisted often in this chapter that we are each expected to identify and interpret our own unique story. At the risk of oversimplifying I will select a single final close-up from my sprawling cast of characters, this book's earliest image of Mark Twain's Huckleberry Finn at the pivotal moment of conscience aboard his raft.

I imagine the reader and myself trying to reenact Huck Finn's discovery of his own unique conscience, struggling to reach beyond the unquestioned verities of Huck's own culture and religious institutions. I know of no better first step toward opening oneself to the ever widening human implications in human rights, or the full global impact of global rights. The ideal global consensus tomorrow, as I understand it, will turn out to be a jury packed with idealized Huck Finns, encouraging each of us to keep sounding the depths of our own moral center. A uniform international code of ethics, articulated by the UN Bill of Rights and the Parliament's Global Ethic, is truly an important beginning. It provides a sound milieu where a person of genuine conscience can flourish. Yet it will only prove itself one more conventional façade unless it gives birth to a world of more Huck Finns.

ENDNOTES

Chapter 1: The Anatomy of a Sound Moral Choice
(PP. 1-15)

1. To review the sequence of Huck's attitudes, see chapter 31 of the novel.

2. For further illustrations of the distinction between conscience and superego see John Glaser, S.J., "Conscience and Superego: A Key Distinction," *Theological Studies* 32 (March, 1971), 36-49; and Vernon Ruland, S.J., *Sacred Lies and Silences: A Psychology of Religious Disguise* (Liturgical Press, 1994), 76-79.

3. Albert Camus, *The Rebel: An Essay on Man in Revolt*, 2nd ed., trans. Anthony Bower (Knopf, 1961, 1951), 15, 22.

4. See bibliography and the paradigm charting a more gradual type of moral development in Elizabeth McGrath, *The Art of Ethics: A Psychology of Ethical Beliefs* (Loyola University Press, 1994), 18-49.

5. For insights on an ethics of narrative, virtue, character, role, and feeling see Alasdair MacIntyre, *After Virtue: A Study in Moral Theory*, 2nd ed., (University of Notre Dame Press, 1984), especially 204-26; and Martha Nussbaum, *Love's Knowledge: Essays on Philosophy and Literature* (Oxford University Press, 1990).

6. Stanley Hauerwas, "Casuistry as a Narrative Art," *Interpretation* 37 (October, 1983), 377, 386.

7. See Thomas Kuhn, *The Structure of Scientific Revolutions*, 2nd ed., (University of Chicago Press, 1970, 1962), 24; and Tristram Engelhardt, Jr., "Introduction," in Tristram Engelhardt, Jr., and Daniel Callahan, eds., *Knowledge, Value, and Belief* (Hastings Center, 1977), 22.

Chapter 2. Religious and Moral Faultlines
(PP. 16-43)

1. For sources of all legal texts cited hereafter, with commentary and background, see the unsigned editorial "U.S. versus Seeger," in *United States Reports* 380 (1965), 163-93; (editors); and "Conscientious Objectors," *Vanderbilt*

Law Review (June, 1965), 1564-73. See also Robert Rabin, "When Is a Religious Belief Religious? United States vs. Seeger and the Scope of Free Exercise," *Cornell Law Review* 51 (1965-6), 231-49.

2.   See the following selected passages in context: "Declaration on Religious Freedom," pars. 1-8; "Declaration on the Relationship of the Church to Non-Christian Religions," pars. 1-2, 5; "Dogmatic Constitution on the Church," par. 16; and "Pastoral Constitution on the Church in the Modern World," par. 79, in *Documents of Vatican II*, eds. Walter Abbott, S.J , and Joseph Gallagher (Guild Press, 1966).

3.   Notice one recent effort to revive the military draft, the Smith-Weldon Bill entitled *Universal Military Training and Service Act of 2001*, introduced in the U.S. House of Representatives on December 20, 2001. On the Internet see *http.//thomas.loc.gov/*. Section 10 refers specifically to religious Conscientious Objectors. The document insists they must "when inducted, participate in basic military training and education that does not include any combatant training component. The person may be transferred to a national service program…"

4.   See the sources and implications for my definition of the religious factor within a context of psychological maturity in my *Sacred Lies*, 2-7; and within a context of social anthropology in Vernon Ruland, S.J. *Imagining the Sacred: Soundings in World Religions* (Orbis, 1998), 10-11.

5.   Cited in Daniel Liechy, ed. and tr., *Early Anabaptist Spirituality: Selected Writings* (Paulist Press, 1994), xxi.

6.   See the overview and bibliography in Franklin Littell, *The Origins of Sectarian Protestantism: A Study of the Anabaptist View of the Church* (Macmillan, 1964, 1952), especially 101-108 on the non-violence motif. For a study of separatist and non-separatist Anabaptist-Calvinist movements in England and America, see Vernon Ruland, S.J., "Theology of New England Puritanism," *Heythrop Journal* (April, 1964), 165-9.

7.   Cf. the two helpful editorials entitled "The Dialectic of Romans 13:1-7 and Revelation 13," in *Journal of Church and State* 18-19 (1976-77): 5-20, 433-43; see also Alan Richardson, *The Political Christ* (Westminster, 1973).

8.   Cited in Austin Warren, *The New England Conscience* (U. of Michigan Press, 1966), 55; see also John Garrett, *Roger Williams: Witness Beyond Christendom*, 1603-1683 (Macmillan, 1970). For the Puritan theology context see Vernon Ruland, S.J., "Covenant Theology," in *New Catholic Encyclopedia* (1967) 4: 405.

9.   Cardinal Alfredo Ottaviani, "Church and State: Some Present Problems in the Light of the Teaching of Pope Pius XII," *American Ecclesiastical Review* 128 (May, 1953), 321-34. See further sources and discussion in my *Imagining*, 165-67.

10. See the *Euthyphro*, trans. G.M.A. Grube, in John Cooper, ed., *Plato: Complete Works* (Hackett, 1997), 8b, 10a: pp. 7, 9. See further conjectures about Euthyphro's values in Michel Despland, *The Education of Desire: Plato and the Philosophy of Religion* (University of Toronto Press, 1985), 1-14.

11. Benjamin Franklin, *The Autobiography* (Vintage, 1990, 1986),78, 92.

12. "Letter to Joseph Huey (1753), in *Benjamin Franklin: Writings* (Library of America, 1987), 475-77.

13. Ibid.

14. "A Parable against Persecution" (1755), in *Writings*, 420-21.

15. For Kierkegaard sources and commentary see discussion in my *Imagining*, 171-72, 236-37; Alastair Hannay and Gordon Marino, eds., *The Cambridge Companion to Kierkegaard* (Cambridge University Press, 1998); and Robert Perkins, ed. *International Kierkegaard Commentary: Fear and Trembling and Repetition* (Mercer University Press, 1993).

16. Kant cited in Seung-Goo Lee, "The Antithesis between the Religious View of Ethics and the Rationalistic View of Ethics in Fear and Trembling," in Perkins, 105.

17. Immanuel Kant, *Lectures on Ethics*, ed. Peter Heath and J.B. Schneewind, trans. Peter Heath (Cambridge University Press, 1997) 27:343, p. 124.

18. Franklin, *Autobiography*, 88, 55-56.

19. Sigmund Freud, F*uture of an Illusion, in Standard Edition of the Complete Psychological Works*, ed. and trans. James Strachey (Hogarth Press, 1953-74), 11:39.

20. Ignatius Loyola, "Rules for Thinking, Judging, and Feeling with the Church", #13, in *The Spiritual Exercises*, trans. George Ganss, S.J. (Institute of Jesuit Sources, 1992), 133-37. For an attempt to revise and reinterpret these Rules in the context of a more recent Catholic ecclesiology see Gerald Fagin, S.J., "Fidelity in the Church—Then and Now," *Studies in the Spirituality of Jesuits* 31:3 (May, 1999).

21. See the discussion in Philip Quinn, "Religious Obedience and Moral Autonomy," in Paul Helm, ed., *Divine Commands and Morality* (Oxford University Press, 1981), 49-66. Calvin is cited in Janine Idziak, "In Search of 'Good Positive Reasons' for an Ethics of Divine Commands: A Catalogue of Arguments," *Faith and Philosophy* 6 (January, 1989), 50. Idziak gives persuasive excerpts to trace this ethical style in figures like Hugh of St. Victor, Ockham's disciple Gabriel Biel, Luther, and the Puritan theologians John Preston and William Perkins.

22. *Midrash Rabbah*, Genesis (Vayera), 49: 8-10, cited in Belden Lane, "Hutzpa K'Lapei Shamaya: A Christian Response to the Jewish Tradition of Arguing with God," *Journal of Ecumenical Studies* 23:4 (Fall, 1986), 577.

See also James Crenshaw, *A Whirlpool of Torment: Israelite Traditions of God as an Oppressive Presence* (Fortress Press, 1984).

23. Hugh Nissenson, "The Blessing," *The Elephant and My Jewish Problem* (Harper and Row, 1988), 110.

24. See the sources and commentary in Lane, 582-83.

25. Cited in Lane, 581.

26. *Babylon Talmud*, Tract Baba Metzia 4:59b, cited in Lane, 578.

27. See the sources and discussion in Ruland, *Imagining*, 84-87, 69.

28. Aldous Huxley, *Brave New World* (Buccaneer Books, 1932, 1946, 1991), vii-ix.

Chapter 3. An Earth-Centered Ethics
(PP. 44-67)

1. Cited in Howard Eves, *Mathematical Circles Adieu: A Fourth Collection of Mathematical Stories and Anecdotes* (Prindle, Weber, Schmidt, 1977), 60.

2. Carl Jung, *Modern Man in Search of a Soul*, trans. W.S. Dell and Cary Baynes (Harcourt, Brace, 1933), 209, 206, 209.

3. Cited in Andrew Dobson, ed., *The Green Reader: Essays toward a Sustainable Society* (Mercury House, 1991), 14.

4. Karl Jaspers, *The Origin and Goal of History*, trans. Michael Bullock (Yale University Press, 1949, 1959), 4.

5. Ibid., 3-4. For the Hegel citation see 76. See further discussion of the changes associated with the Axial Period in H. and H.A. Frankfort et al., *Before Philosophy: The Intellectual Adventure of Ancient Man* (Penguin Books, 1946, 1971); and Ewert Cousins, *Christ of the 21st Century* (Element, 1992), 1-14.

6. John Updike, *Roger's Version* (Knopf, 1987), 32.

7. Mary Shelley, *Frankenstein: Complete Text, Critical History, and Essays*, ed. Johanna Smith (St. Martin's Press, 1992), 114, 54-55, 181.

8. Cited in Connie Barlow, *Green Space, Green Time: The Way of Science* (Copernicus, 1997), 11.

9. See Ernst Schumacher, *Small Is Beautiful: Economics as if People Mattered—25 Years Later, with Commentaries* (Hartley and Marks [1973], 1999)

10. See the Massasoit source in Jace Weaver, ed., *Defending Mother Earth: Native American Perspectives on Environmental Justice* (Orbis Books, 1996), 10. Weaver gives other evidence to rebut claims that the earth-mother concept is

only a recent innovation in Native American spirituality. For the Wintu quote, see Dobson, 248-49.

11. For data on the uranium menace to Native Americans, see Donald Fixico, "The Struggle for Our Homes," and Grace Thorpe, "Our Homes Are Not Dumps," in Weaver, 29-46, 47-48.

12. Cited in Weaver, 11.

13. Vine Deloria, Jr., *For This Land: Writings on Religion in America*, ed. James Treat (Routledge, 1999). 257-59.

14. See Ernest Becker, "The Primitive World: Economics as Expiation and Power," in *Escape from Evil* (Free Press, 1975), 26-37. See also the sources for John Grim, "Native North American Worldviews and Ecology," in Mary Evelyn Tucker and John Grim, eds., *Worldviews and Ecology: Religion, Philosophy, and the Environment* (Orbis, 1994), 41-54; and Thomas Daffern, "Native American Cultures," in *Encyclopedia of Applied Ethics*, ed. Ruth Chadwick, (Academic Press, 1998), 3: 295-321.

15. Leslie Silko, *Man to Send Rain Clouds* (Viking, 1974).

16. See Tu Wei-ming, "Beyond the Enlightenment Mentality," in Tucker and Grimm, 27.

17. See Daniel Guthrie, "Primitive Man's Relationship to Nature," *BioScience* 21:13 (July 1, 1971), 721-23.

18. See Campo case details and comparable examples in Fergus Bodewich, "Revolution in Indian Country," *American Heritage* (July/August, 1996), 34-46.

19. David Lodge, *Thinks* (Viking, 2001), 26-7.

20. Deloria, 250, 254.

21. Ibid., 250, 281, 264. See also Deloria, *God Is Red: A Native View of Religion*, 2nd ed. (North American Press, 1992, 1972), 40ff.

22. Wendy Rose, *Lost Copper* (Malki Museum Press, 1980), 23.

23. D.T. Suzuki, "Lectures on Zen Buddhism," in Erich Fromm, D.T. Suzuki, Richard De Martino, *Zen Buddhism and Psychoanalysis* (Harper and Row, 1960, 1970), 1-4.

24. To find these same two painting styles contrasted, with more subtlety than I have attempted, see Francis Cook, "The Jewel Net of Indra," in Baird Callicott and Roger Ames, eds., *Nature in Asian Traditions of Thought: Essays in Environmental Philosophy* (State University of New York Press, 1989), 217-19.

25. Ramachandra Guha, "Radical Environmentalism and Wilderness Preservation: A Third World Critique," in Louis Pojman, ed., *Environmental Ethics: Readings in Theory and Application*, 2nd ed. (Wadsworth, 1998), 273.

26. See Alexander Stille, "In the 'Greened' World, It Isn't Easy to Be Human," *New York Times* (July 15, 2000), A17-19.

27. Yi-Fu Tuan, "Our Treatment of the Environment in Ideal and Actuality," *American Scientist* 58 (May-June, 1970), 244-49, especially 244.

28. Ibid., 244, 248.

29. See Nancy Wilson Ross, *Buddhism: A Way of Life and Thought* (Vintage, 1980), 54.

30. See sources and discussion of this Buddhist concept in Ruland *Imagining*, 112, 115, 116.

31. Dalai Lama (Nganang Tenzin Gyatso), *Freedom in Exile: The Autobiography of the Dalai Lama* (Harper Collins, 1990), 269-70.

32. See the statistics, with further illustrations of renewal, in the series of articles by Eugenia Yun, James Hwang, and Winnie Chang in *Free China Review* 44:12 (December, 1994), 4-35. See also Duncan Ryuken Williams, "Bibliography on Buddhism and Ecology," in Mary Evelyn Tucker and Duncan Ryuken Williams, eds., *Buddhism and Ecology: The Interconnection of Dharma and Deeds* (Harvard University Press, 1997), 403-25.

33. See Ruland, *Imagining*, 46-47.

34. Feng, Chi-tsai, *Chrysanthemums and Other Stories*, trans. Susan Wilf Chen (Harcourt Brace, 1985).

35. Masao Abe, "The Buddhist View of Human Rights," in Abdullahi An-Na'im et al., eds., *Human Rights and Religious Values: An Uneasy Relationship?* (William Eerdmans, 1995), 145, 152.

36. Ramakrishna, *The Gospel of Shri Ramakrishna*, trans. and ed. Nikhilananda (Ramakrishna-Vivekananda Center, 1942), 779, 66.

37. Satapatha Brahmana 13:1; 6:1,2,12-13, cited in Ruland, *Sacred Lies*, 88-89.

38. Swami Vivekananda, *Complete Works*, 9th ed. (Advaita Ashrama, 1963-66), 3:425.

39. Cited in Anuradha Roma Choudhury, "Hinduism," in Jean Holm, ed., *Attitudes to Nature* (Pinter, 1994), 77.

40. Cited in Buddhadasa, *Me and Mine: Selected Essays*, ed. Donald Swearer (State University of New York Press, 1989), 112.

Chapter 4: A God-Centered Ecology
(PP. 68-91)

1.   Mark Twain, "Bible Teaching and Religious Practice," in *What Is Man? And Other Philosophical Writings*, ed. Paul Baender (University of California Press, 1973), 71-75.

2.   Cited in Walter Kaufman, "Nietzsche and Rilke," in *The Owl and the Nightingale* (Faber and Faber, 1959), 209.

3.   Connie Barlow, *Green Space, Green Time: The Way of Science* (Copernicus, 1997), 3, 10-16.

4.   Ibid., 10-11.

5.   I am indebted to the discussion of religious meaning and history in Langdon Gilkey, *On Niebuhr: A Theological Study* (University of Chicago Press, 2001), 53-56.

6.   Cited in Frank Burch Brown, *Religious Aesthetics: A Theological Study of Making and Meaning* (Princeton University Press, 1989), 128-29.

7.   See Sufi and Kabbalist sources cited in Ruland, *Imagining*, 139-40, 223-26.

8.   T. Coraghessan Boyle, "Top of the Food Chain," *Stories* (Viking, 1998).

9.   Ray Bradbury, "A Sound of Thunder," *Stories* (Knopf, 1980).

10. For example, see the critique of the Alaska Energy Bill by William Cronon, "Neither Barren Nor Remote," *New York Times* (February 28, 2001), A25. The Internet currently offers various websites on the Alaska Energy Bill itself (s.1683), Frank Murkowski, the Gwich'in nation, and even the Caribou.

11. See Stephen Clark, "Global Religion," in Robin Attfield and Andrew Belsey, eds. *Philosophy and the Natural Environment* (Cambridge University Press, 1994), 114-15.

12. See citations in Ronald Wolf, "God, James Watt, and the Public's Land," *Audubon* 83:3 (May, 1981), 58-65; and Susan Power Bratton, "The Ecotheology of James Watt," *Environmental Ethics* 5 (Fall, 1983), 225-36.

13. See the Murray Bookchin excerpt cited in Dobson, 59-60. For the eco-feminist perspective described, see especially Rosemary Reuther, "Symbolic and Social Connections of the Oppression of Women and the Domination of Nature," in Carol Adams, ed., *Ecofeminism and the Sacred* (Continuum, 1993), 13-23.

14. Muhammad Talbi, "A Charter of Duties and tasks for All Human Beings," in Hans Kung, ed., *Yes to a Global Ethic* (Continuum, 1996), 199.

15. Cited in Maeil Izzi Deen, "Islamic Environmental Ethics, Law, and Society," in Pojman, 261, 260.

16. Kohelet Rabbah 1, on 7-13, cited in Bradley Artson, *It's a Mitzvah: Step-by-Step to Jewish Living* (Behrman House: Rabbinical Assembly, 1995), 50.

17. Norman Solomon, "Judaism," in Jean Holm, ed., *Attitudes to Nature* (Pinter, 1994), 106.

18. Cited in Samuel Belkin, "Man as Temporary Tenant," in Milton Konvitz, ed., *Judaism and Human Rights* (W.W.Norton, 1972), 252, 258. [251-58]

19. Notice that in God's renewed covenant with Noah God says, "Fear and dread will fall upon all the wild beasts and all the birds of heaven... They are handed over to you." (Genesis 9:2) This passage, in my reading, marks the transition from a vegetarian to a carnivorous culture. By losing paradise, or harmony with the natural world, the human race will now experience competition and hostility in dealing not only with the serpent but also the other beasts.

20. See the Gregory of Nyssa citation in Pierre Teilhard de Chardin, *The Divine Milieu: An Essay on the Interior Life* (Harper and Row, 1957), 110. See the quotations from "Le Christique" and "Le Coeur de la Matiere," in Claude Tresmontant, *Pierre Teilhard de Chardin: His Thought* (Helicon Press, 1959), 351.

21. Fyodor Dostoyevsky, *The Brothers Karamazov*, trans. Constance Garnett (Modern Library, 1950), 351.

22. Tayeb Salih, "A Handful of Dates," trans. Denys Johnson-Davies, in Nadezda Obradovic, ed., *African Rhapsody: Short Stories of the Contemporary African Experience* (Anchor Books, 1994), 2-7.

23. I will use the N.J. Dawood translation-interpretation, *The Koran* (Penguin, 1974).

24. S. Nomanul Haq, "Islam and Ecology: Toward Retrieval and Reconstruction," *Daedalus* 30:4 (Fall, 2001), 146-55.

25. John Paul II, "The Ecological Crisis: A Common Responsibility (January 1, 1990)," in Drew Christiansen, S.J., and Walter Grazer, eds., *And God Saw That It Was Good: Catholic Theology and the Environment* (United States Catholic Conference, 1996), 215-22, especially par. 13. Hereafter the latter papal document will be cited as "Ecological Crisis," and just by paragraph numbers.

26. John Paul II, "Saving Tropical Forests," in *The Pope Speaks* 35 (September, 1990), 371-73; and "Ecological Crisis," par. 5.

27. See excerpts cited in Dobson, 225-32.

28. See Editors, "Ecoterrorism: Brutal Elves in the Woods," *The Economist* (April 14, 2001), 28-29; and Sam Howe Verhovek, "Fires Believed Set as Protest against Genetic Engineering," *New York Times* (May 23, 2001), A1, A12.

29. Cited in Guy Beney, "Gaia: The Globalitarian Temptation," in Wolfgang Sachs, ed., *Global Ecology: A New Arena of Political Conflict* (Fernwood, 1993), 189-91.

30. Charles Darwin, *Descent of Man, and Selection in Relation to Sex* (Princeton University Press, 1981, 1871), 168-69.

31. See the Internet website for sources and debates: "Sierra Club and overpopulation," and the splinter group of dissenters, "Sierrans for U.S. Population Stabilization (SUSPS)."

32. See Ian Barbour, "Attitudes toward Nature and Technology," in Ian Barbour, ed., *Earth Might Be Fair: Reflections on Religion, Ethics, and Ecology* (Prentice-Hall, 1972), 151.

33. See Dwight Hopkins, "The Religion of Globalization," in Dwight Hopkins, Lois Ann Lorentzen, et al, eds., *Religions/Globalizations: Theories and Cases* (Duke University Press, 2001), 7-32.

34. For an analysis of ambivalent attitudes toward Free Trade by the Mohawk Nation at the U.S.-Canadian border, see Rick Hornung, "On Native Land, a Fear of Free Trade," *New York Times* (April 21, 2001), A25.

35. Cited in Robert McCorquodale and Richard Fairbrother, "Globalization and Human Right," *Human Rights Quarterly* 21:3 (1999), 744.

36. John Paul II, "Ecological Crisis," par. 7.

37. Ibid., pars. 8, 9.

38. Leonardo Boff, "Liberation Theology and Ecology: Alternative, Confrontation or Complementarity?" in Leonardo Boff and Virgil Elizondo, eds., *Ecology and Poverty: Cry of the Earth, Cry of the Poor* (Orbis Books, 1995), 75.

Chapter 5: Human Rights — The Human Minimum
(PP. 92-115)

1. See Warren Smith, "Are You a Humanist? Some Authors Answer," *Humanist* 41 (1981), 15-26, a reprint of the 1951 article. Endless qualifications about the label emerge as people like Russell, Santayana, Mann, and Koestler apply it to their situations.

2. See the insightful application of these principles to Brazilian indigenous issues in James Nickel and Eduardo Viola, "Integrating Environmentalism and Human Rights," *Environmental Ethics* 16 (Fall, 1994), 265-73.

3. Hans Küng and Leonard Swidler, "Editorial: Toward a Universal Declaration of Global Ethos", *Journal of Ecumenical Studies* 28:1 (Winter, 1991), 124.

4. See Stephen Scharper, "Singapore Squeeze: Church-State Friction," *Commonweal* 115:9 (May 6, 1988), 262-64. Scharper provides factual information here that compensates for lapses in my own recollections.

5. Cited in Robert Traer, *Faith in Human Rights: Support in Religious Traditions for a Global Struggle* (Georgetown University Press, 1991), 210.

6. The distinction between human dignity and human rights is developed in Jack Donnelly, "Human Rights and Human Dignity: An Analytic Critique of Non-Western Conceptions of Human Rights," *American Political Science Review* 76 (1982), 303-316.

7. Karl Marx and Frederick Engels, *The Communist Manifesto*, in Marx and Engels, *Collected Works*, trans. Richard Dixon et al. (International Publishers, 1975), 6:501, 503.

8. See sources on human rights history in Winfried Brugger, "The Image of the Person in the Human Rights Concept," *Human Rights Quarterly* 18:3 (1996), 595-98. See also Robert Drinan, S.J., *Cry of the Oppressed: The History and Hope of the Human Rights Revolution* (Harper and Row, 1987); and *The Mobilization of Shame: A World View of Human Rights* (Yale University Press, 2001).

9. Heiner Bielefeldt, "Muslim Voices in the Human Rights Debate," *Human Rights Quarterly* 17 (1995), 588.

10. See John Quigley, "Human Rights Defenses in U.S. Courts," *Human Rights Quarterly* 21:3 (1998), 555-91.

11. Cited in James Zion, "North American Indian Perspectives on Human Rights," in Abdullahi Ahmed An-Na'im, ed., *Human Rights in Cross-Cultural Perspectives: A Quest for Consensus* (University of Pennsylvania Press, 1992), 196.

12. See Traer, 152.

13. Cited in Zion, 195. Further reasons for distrust of rights commissions are suggested in Allen McChesney, "Aboriginal Communities, Aboriginal Rights, and the Human Rights System in Canada," in An-Na'im, *Human Rights in Cross-Cultural Perspectives*, 225-27.

14. For background to the Declaration Draft, see Marvine Howe, "UN Panel Backs Indigenous Peoples' Rights," *New York Times* (October 15, 1992) A12; Russell Barsh, "Indigenous Peoples and the UN Commission on Human Rights: A Case of the Immovable Object and the Irresistible Force," *Human Rights Quarterly* 18:4 (1996) 782-813; Robert Coulter, "Commentary on the UN Draft Declaration on the Rights of Indigenous Peoples," *Cultural Survival Quarterly*

18:1 (Spring, 1994), 37-41; and Don Wilkinson, "The Meaning of Self-Determination," *Quadrant* 43 (March, 1999) 23-6.

15. The text can be found on the current internet and also in "UN Draft Declaration on the Rights of Indigenous Peoples," *Cultural Survival Quarterly* 18:1 (Spring, 1994), 65-8. I will cite the article numbers given in this version.

16. See especially #10, 17, 26.

17. See #28, 11, 13, 12.

18. Cited in Barsh, 792.

19. Note the sources cited in Wilkinson.

20. Bilahari Kausikan, "Asia's Different Standard," *Foreign Policy* 92 (1993), 38.

21. Cited in Christina Cerna, "Universality of Human Rights and Cultural Diversity: Implementation of Human Rights in Different Socio-Cultural Contexts," *Human Rights Quarterly* 16 (1994), 745. [740-52]

22. Cited in Ibid., 741.

23. See the discussion in Peter Berger, "Are Human Rights Universal?" *Commentary* (September, 1977), 60-63.

24. Cited in Ibid., 743.

25. For a history of this movement see Tu Wei-ming, "The Search for Roots in Industrial East Asia: The Case of the Confucian Revival," in Martin Marty and R.Scott Appleby, eds., *Fundamentalisms Observed* (University of Chicago Press, 1991), 740-81.

26. Cited in (editors) "Asian Values Revisited: What Would Confucius Say Now?" *Economist* (July 2, 1998), 23-25.

27. See Henry Rosemont, Jr., "Why Take Rights Seriously? A Confucian Critique," in Leroy Rouner, ed., *Human Rights and The World's Religions* (University of Notre Dame Press, 1988), 177.

28. For further treatment of Confucian ethics, see my *Imagining*, 34-40. My summary draws from R.P. Peerenboom, "What's Wrong with Chinese Rights?: Toward a Theory of Rights with Chinese Characteristics," *Harvard Human Rights Journal* 6 (1993), 29-57.

29. Aung San Suu Kyi, "Towards a Culture of Peace and Development," in Hans Küng, ed., *Yes to a Global Ethic* (Continuum, 1996), 225, 231, 233.

30. Robert Bellah, et al., *Habits of the Heart: Individualism and Commitment in American Life* (University of California Press, 1985), 285.

Chapter 6: Human Rights and Religious Pluralism
(PP. 116-144)

1. For a discussion of this transition to postmodernity, see Richard Seager, "The Two Parliaments, the 1893 Original and the Centennial of 1993: A Historian's View," in Wayne Teasdale and George Cairns, eds., *The Community of Religions: Voices and Images of the Parliament of the World's Religions* (Continuum, 1996), 31. See also Richard Ruland and Malcolm Bradbury, *From Puritanism to Postmodernism: A History of American Literature* (Viking, 1991), 370-73.

2. See John Gray, "Where There Is No Common Power," *Harper's Magazine* (December, 2001), 15-19.

3. Editors, "Statement on Human Rights," *American Anthropologist* 49:4 (October-December, 1947), 539.

4. Ibid., 542.

5. Ibid., 542.

6. See the survey "From Relativism to Evaluation" in Robert Edgerton, *Sick Societies: Challenging the Myth of Primitive Harmony* (Free Press, 1992), 16-45.

7. See Ann-Belinda Preis, "Human Rights as Cultural Practice: An Anthropological Critique," *Human Rights Quarterly* 18:2 (1996), 286-315.

8. See the discussion in Paul Taylor, "Social Science and Ethical Relativism," and John Ladd, "The Issue of Relativism," in John Ladd, ed., *Ethical Relativism* (Wadsworth, 1973), 95-107, 107-29. For a typology of relativisms and a spirited defense of her own non-objectivist position, see Barbara Herrnstein Smith, *Contingencies of Value: Alternative Perspectives for Critical Theory* (Harvard University Press, 1988), 150-84.

9. Allen Bloom, *The Closing of the American Mind* (Simon and Schuster, 1987), 26-27.

10. Standard value-clarification theory and teaching applications can be sampled in Louis Raths, et al., *Values and Teaching: Working with Values in the Classroom* (Merrill Publishing, 1966); and Sidney Simon, et al., *Values Clarification: A Handbook of Practical Strategies for Teachers and Students* (Hart Publishing, 1972).

11. Christina Hoff Sommers, "Teaching the Virtues," *Public Interest* 111 (Spring, 1993), 3-13. and also "Ethics without Virtue: Moral Education in America," *American Scholar* 53:3 (Summer, 1984), 381-89.

12. Abraham Maslow, *The Farther Reaches of Human Nature* (Penguin Books, 1978, 1971), 44-46.

13. John Macquarrie, "Rethinking Natural Law," in Charles Curran and Richard McCormick, S.J., eds., *Readings in Moral Theology #2: The Distinctiveness of Christian Ethics* (Paulist Press, 1980), 126.

14. Richard McCormick, S.J., "Does Religious Faith Add to Ethical Perception?" in Ibid., 168-70. Notice McCormick distinguishes between essential ethical demands, stemming from the Christian's dignity as a human person, and essential Christian ethical demands, stemming from a Christian's specific membership in a worshiping community. Membership may require particular duties of church observance, for instance, the Christian education of one's children, and other responsibilities. See 157-59. [156-73].

15. Aung San Suu Kyi, 228, 232.

16. Daniel Bell, "The East Asian Challenge to Human Rights: Reflections on an East-West Dialogue," *Human Rights Quarterly* 18 (1996), 652, N.32. [641-67]

17. Cited in Traer, 56, 176. To sample in more detail the range of Protestant, Catholic, and Muslim responses see 19-84, 111-28.

18. This insight is developed in John O'Malley, S.J., *Trent and All That: Renaming Catholicism in the Early Modern Era* (Harvard University Press, 2000), 1-3, 138.

19. For example, see Elise Boulding, "Two Cultures of Religion as Obstacles to Peace," *Zygon* 21:4 (December, 1986), 501-18.

20. See discussion of Buddhist socialism in Ruland, *Imagining*, 106-108.

21. Jonathan Magonet, "Judaism and a Global Ethic," in Hans Küng, ed., *Yes to a Global Ethic* (Continuum, 1996), 96.

22. For background on the two Parliaments, see Seager, 22-36; Leo Lefebure, "Global Encounter," *Christian Century* 110 (September 22, 1993), 886-89; Peter Gardella, "Two Parliaments, One Century," *Cross Currents* 44 (Spring, 1994), 97-104; and Karl-Josef Kuschel, "The Parliament of the World's Religions, 1893-1993," in Hans Küng and Karl-Josef Kuschel, eds., *A Global Ethic: The Declaration of the Parliament of the World's Religions*, trans. John Bowden (Continuum, 1995), 77-106.

23. See the editor's summary of Dharmapala's exchange with his audience in Ananda Guruge, ed., *Return to Righteousness: A Collection of Speeches, Essays, and Letters of the Anagarika Dharmapala* (Sri Lanka Government Press, 1965), 44-45.

24. Swami Vivekananda, *Complete Works*, 9th ed. (Advaita Ashrama, 1966), 3:425.

25. Timothy George, "A Holy Disturbance," *Christianity Today* 37 (October 25, 1993), 17.

26. Huston is cited in the interview, "Epilogue: Continuing the Dance," in Teasdale and Cairns, 233-34. See Gardella, 104.

27. Cited in June O'Connor, "Does a Global Village Warrant a Global Ethic?" *Religion* 24 (1994), 162. [155-64]

28. Moses Mendelssohn, *Jerusalem and Other Jewish Writings*, trans. and ed. Alfred Jospe (Schocken, 1969), 109.

29. Hans Küng, "The History, Significance, and Method of the Declaration Toward a Global Ethic," in Küng and Kuschel, *A Global Ethic*, 55-56.

30. O'Connor, 163.

31. Küng and Kuschel, A Global Ethic, 21.

32. Ibid., 73.

33. Ibid., 70-71.

34. George Carey, "Tolerance and the Integrity of One's Own Faith Are Not Mutually Exclusive," in Küng, ed., *Yes to a Global Ethic*, 135.

35. Küng and Kuschel, *A Global Ethic*, 30-31, 22.

36. This insight is developed notably by Sallie King, "A Global Ethic in the Light of Comparative Religious Ethics," in Sumner Twiss and Bruce Grelle, eds., *Explorations in Global Ethics: Comparative Religious Ethics and Interreligious Dialogue* (Westview Press, 1998), 138-39, 135.

37. Cited by Kuschel in *A Global Ethic*, 99.

Chapter 7: An Ethics of Virtue, Character, and Story
(PP. 145-169)

1. Cited in Sommers, "Teaching the Virtues," 3-5.

2. See William Galston, "Introduction," in John Chapman and William Galston, eds. *Virtue* (New York University Press, 1992), 1-22; and Roy Perrett and John Patterson, "Virtue Ethics and Maori Ethics," *Philosophy East and West* 41 (1991), 225-26.

3. This argument is developed in Robert Louden, "On Some Vices of Virtue Ethics," *American Philosophical Quarterly* 21 (1984), 227-36.

4. My frugality apologia follows closely the defense by James Nash, "Toward the Revival and Reform of the Subversive Virtue: Frugality," *Annual of the Society of Christian Ethics* (1995), 153, 145. [137-60]

5. Nash traces this potential economic subversion in Ibid., 157-59.

6. See Geoffrey Frasz, "Environmental Virtue Ethics: A New Direction for Environmental Ethics," *Environmental Ethics* 15 (Fall, 1993), 259-74.

7. See Mary Midgley, "Brutality and Sentimentality," *Philosophy* 54 (1979), 385-89. Midgley singles out Dickens' Little Nell as the sentimental nadir. For a

discussion of the bambi syndrome see Frans de Waal, *The Ape and the Sushi Master: Cultural Reflections of a Primatologist* (Basic Books, 2001), 71-74.

8. My insights into human dignity draw especially from Michael Meyer, "Dignity, Death, and Modern Virtue," *American Philosophical Quarterly* 32 (January, 1995), 45-55.

9. Kant, *Lectures on Ethics*, 27:344, p. 125.

10. Joan Didion, "On Self-Respect," in *Slouching Towards Bethlehem.* (Farrar, Straus and Giroux, 1968), 147-48.

11. Peter Berger, *The Sacred Canopy: Elements of a Sociological Theory of Religion* (Doubleday, 1967), 14. This theory stems from a combination of Hegel, Feuerbach, and G.H. Mead.

12. For Berger's analysis of the uncle role see Ibid., 17-18.

13. This concept of a role legacy is developed and illustrated in MacIntyre, 220-21. For a deft critique of what she calls MacIntyre's nostalgic traditionalism see Barbara Smith, 85-94. See also John Horton and Susan Mandus, eds., *After MacIntyre: Critical Perspectives on the Work of Alasdair MacIntyre* (University of Notre Dame Press, 1994).

14. See the discussion by Michael Walzer, "What Does It Mean to be an American?" *Social Research* 57 (1990), 591-614.

15. MacIntyre, 216.

16. Cited in Johann Baptist Metz, "A Short Apology of Narrative," in Stanley Hauerwas and L. Gregory Jones, eds., *Why Narrative? Readings in Narrative Theology* (William Eerdmans, 1989), 253.

17. Carl Jung, *Memories, Dreams, Reflections*, ed. Aniela Jaffe, trans. Richard and Clara Winston (Vintage Books, 1965), 171, 175.

18. Ibid., 117, 124-25.

19. Ibid., 140, 138.

20. Cited in Arthur Frank, *The Wounded Storyteller: Body, Illness, and Ethics* (University of Chicago Press, 1995), 4-5. See also 7 and 196, n.34.

21. See O'Connor, 163.

BIBLIOGRAPHY

Abbott, Walter, S.J., and Joseph Gallagher, eds. *Documents of Vatican II.* Guild Press, 1966.

Adams, Carol, ed. *Ecofeminism and the Sacred.* Continuum, 1993.

An-Na'im, Abdullahi, ed. *Human Rights and Religious Values: An Uneasy Relationship?* William Eerdmans, 1995.

————, ed. *Human Rights in Cross-Cultural Perspectives: A Quest for Consensus.* University of Pennsylvania Press, 1992.

Artson, Bradley. *It's a Mitzvah: Step-by-Step to Jewish Living.* Behrman House: Rabbinical Assembly, 1995.

"Asian Values Revisited: What Would Confucius Say Now?" *Economist* (July 2, 1998): 23-5.

Attfield, Robin, and Andrew Belsey, eds., *Philosophy and the Natural Environment.* Cambridge University Press, 1994.

Barbour, Ian, ed. *Earth Might Be Fair: Reflections on Religion, Ethics, and Ecology.* Prentice-Hall, 1972.

Barlow, Connie. *Green Space, Green Time: The Way of Science.* Copernicus, 1997.

Barsh, Russell. "Indigenous Peoples and the UN Commission on Human Rights: A Case of the Immovable Object and the Irresistible Force." *Human Rights Quarterly* 18:4 (1996): 782-813.

Becker, Ernest. *Escape from Evil.* Free Press, 1975.

Bell, Daniel. "The East Asian Challenge to Human Rights: Reflections on an East-West Dialogue." *Human Rights Quarterly* 18 (1996): 641-67.

Bellah, Robert, et al. *Habits of the Heart: Individualism and Commitment in American Life.* University of California Press, 1985.

Berger, Peter. "Are Human Rights Universal?" *Commentary* (September, 1977): 60-63.

———— *The Sacred Canopy: Elements of a Sociological Theory of Religion.* Doubleday, 1967.

Bielefeldt, Heiner. "Muslim Voices in the Human Rights Debate." *Human Rights Quarterly* 17 (1995): 588-617.

Bloom, Allen. *The Closing of the American Mind.* Simon and Schuster, 1987.

Bodewich, Fergus. "Revolution in Indian Country." *American Heritage*
(July/August, 1996): 34-36.

Boff, Leonardo, and Virgil Elizondo, eds. *Ecology and Poverty: Cry of the Earth,
Cry of the Poor.* Orbis, 1995.

Boulding, Elise. "Two Cultures of Religion as Obstacles to Peace." *Zygon* 21:4
(December, 1986): 501-18.

Boyle, T. Coraghessan. *Stories.* Viking, 1998.

Bradbury, Ray. *Stories.* Knopf, 1980.

Bratton, Susan Power. "The Ecotheology of James Watt." *Environmental Ethics*
5 (Fall, 1983): 225-36.

Brown, Frank Burch. *Religious Aesthetics: A Theological Study of Making and
Meaning.* Princeton University Press, 1989.

Brugger, Winfried. "The Image of the Person in the Human Rights Concept."
Human Right Quarterly 18:3 (1996): 595-8.

Buddhadasa, Bhikku. *Me and Mine: Selected Essays.* Ed. Donald Searer. State
University of New York Press, 1989.

Callicott, Baird, and Roger Ames, eds. *Nature in Asian Traditions of Thought:
Essays in Environmental Philosophy.* State University of New York Press, 1989.

Camus, Albert. *The Rebel: An Essay on Man in Revolt.* Trans. Anthony Bower.
Knopf, 1961.

Cerna, Christina. "Universality of Human Rights and Cultural Diversity:
Implementation of Human Rights in Socio-Cultural Contexts." *Human
Rights Quarterly* 16 (1994): 740-52.

Chapman, John, and William Galston, eds. *Virtue.* New York University Press,
1992.

Christiansen, Drew, S.J., and Walter Grazer, eds. *And God Saw That It Was
Good: Catholic Theology and the Environment.* United States Catholic
Conference, 1996.

"Conscientious Objectors." *Vanderbilt Law Review* (June, 1965), 1564-73.

Coulter, Robert. "Commentary on the UN Draft Declaration on the Rights of
Indigenous Peoples." *Cultural Survival Quarterly* 18:1 (Spring, 1994):37-41.

Cousins, Ewert. *Christ of the 21st Century.* Element Press, 1992.

Crenshaw, James. *A Whirlpool of Torment: Israelite Traditions of God as an
Oppressive Presence.* Fortress Press, 1984.

Cronon, William. "Neither Barren Nor Remote." *New York Times* (February 28,
2001): A25.

Curran, Charles, and Richard McCormick, S.J., eds. *Readings in Moral Theology
#2: The Distinctiveness of Christian Ethics.* Paulist Press, 1980.

Daffern, Thomas. "Native American Cultures." *Encyclopedia of Applied Ethics.*
Ed. Ruth Chadwick. Academic Press, 1998.

Dalai Lama (Nganang Tenzin Gyatso). *Freedom in Exile: The Autobiography of the Dalai Lama.* Harper Collins, 1990.

Darwin, Charles. *Descent of Man, and Selection in Relation to Sex.* Princeton University Press, 1981, 1871.

De Waal, Frans. *The Ape and the Sushi Master: Cultural Reflections of a Primatologist.* Basic Books, 2001.

Deloria, Vine, Jr. *For This Land: Writings on Religion in America.* Ed. James Treat. Routledge, 1999.

——— *God Is Red: A Native View of Religion.* North American Press, 1992, 1972.

Despland, Michel. *The Education of Desire: Plato and the Philosophy of Religion.* University of Toronto Press, 1985.

"Dialectic of Romans 13:1-7 and Revelation 13." *Journal of Church and State* 18 (1976): 433-43, and 19 (1977): 5-20.

Didion, Joan. *Slouching Towards Bethlehem.* Farrar, Straus and Giroux, 1968.

Dobson, Andrew, ed. *The Green Reader: Essays toward a Sustainable Society.* Mercury House, 1991.

Donnelly, Jack. "Human Rights and Human Dignity: An Analytic Critique of Non-Western Conceptions of Human Rights." *American Political Science Review* 76 (1982): 303-16.

Dostoyevsky, Fyodor. *The Brothers Karamazov.* Trans. Constance Garnett. Modern Library, 1950.

Drinan, Robert, S.J. *Cry of the Oppressed: The History and Hope of the Human Rights Revolution.* Harper and Row, 1987.

——— *The Mobilization of Shame: A World View of Human Rights.* Yale University Press, 2001.

"Ecoterrorism: Brutal Elves in the Woods." *Economist* (April 14, 2001): 28-29.

Edgerton, Robert. *Sick Societies: Challenging the Myth of Primitive Harmony.* Free Press, 1992.

Engelhardt, Tristram, and Daniel Callahan, eds. *Knowledge, Value, and Belief.* Hastings Center, 1977.

Eves, Howard. *Mathematical Circles Adieu: A Fourth Collection of Mathematical Stories and Anecdotes.* Princle, Weber, Schmidt, 1977.

Fagin, Gerald, S.J. "Fidelity in the Church—Then and Now." *Studies in the Spirituality of Jesuits* 31:3 (May, 1999).

Feng, Chi-tsai. *Chrysanthemums and Other Stories.* Trans. Susan Wilf Chen. Harcourt Brace, 1985.

Frank, Arthur. *The Wounded Storyteller: Body, Illness, and Ethics.* University of Chicago Press, 1995.

Frankfort, H. and H.A. *Before Philosophy: The Intellectual Adventure of Ancient Man.* Penguin Books, 1971, 1946.

Franklin, Benjamin. *The Autobiography*. Vintage, 1990.

———— *Writings*. Library of America, 1987.

Frasz, Geoffrey. "Environmental Virtue Ethics: A New Direction for Environmental Ethics." *Environmental Ethics* 15 (Fall, 1993): 259-74.

Freud, Sigmund. *Standard Edition of the Complete Psychological Works*. Ed. and trans. James Strachey. Hogarth Press, 1953-74.

Fromm, Erich, D.T. Suzuki, and Richard De Martino. *Zen Buddhism and Psychoanalysis*. Harper and Row, 1970.

Gardella, Peter. "Two Parliaments, One Century." *Cross Currents* 44 (Spring, 1994): 97-104.

Garrett, John. *Roger Williams: Witness Beyond Christendom, 1603-1683*. Macmillan, 1970.

George, Timothy. "A Holy Disturbance." *Christianity Today* 37 (October 25, 1993): 17.

Gilkey, Langdon. *On Niebuhr: A Theological Study*. University of Chicago Press, 2001.

Glaser, John, S.J. "Conscience and Superego: A Key Distinction." *Theological Studies* 32 (March, 1971): 36-49.

Gray, John. "Where There Is No Common Power." *Harper's Magazine* (December, 2001): 15-19.

Greenberg, Joanne. *Rites of Passage*. Holt, Rinehart, Winston, 1972.

Guruge, Ananda, ed. *Return to Righteousness: A Collection of Speeches, Essays, and Letters of the Anagarika Dharmapala*. Sri Lanka Government Press, 1965.

Guthrie, Daniel. "Primitive Man's Relationship to Nature." *BioScience* 21:13 (July 1, 1971): 721-23.

Hannay, Alastair, and Gordon Marino, eds. *The Cambridge Companion to Kierkegaard*. Cambridge University Press, 1998.

Haq, S. Nomanul. "Islam and Ecology: Toward Retrieval and Reconstruction." *Daedalus* 30:4 (Fall, 2001): 141-77.

Hauerwas, Stanley, and L. Gregory Jones, eds. *Why Narrative? Readings in Narrative Theology*. William Eerdmans, 1989.

———— "Casuistry as a Narrative Art." *Interpretation* 37 (October, 1983): 377-88.

Helm, Paul, ed. *Divine Commands and Morality*. Oxford University Press, 1981.

Holm, Jean, ed. *Attitudes to Nature*. Pinter, 1994.

Hopkins, Dwight, Lois Ann Lorentzen, et al., eds. *Religions/Globalizations: Theories and Cases*. Duke University Press, 2001.

Hornung, Rick. "On Native Land, a Fear of Free Trade." *New York Times* (April 21, 2001): A25.

Horton, John, and Susan Mandus, eds. *After MacIntyre: Critical Perspectives on the Work of Alasdair MacIntyre*. University of Notre Dame Press, 1994.

Howard, Rhoda. "Cultural Absolutism and the Nostalgia for Community."
    Human Rights Quarterly 15 (1993): 315-38.
Howe, Marvine. "UN Panel Backs Indigenous Peoples' Rights." *New York Times*
    (October 15, 1992): A12.
Huxley, Aldous. *Brave New World.* Buccaneer Books, 1991, 1932, 1946.
Idziak, Janine "In Search of 'Good Positive Reasons' for an Ethics of Divine
    Commands: A Catalogue of Arguments." *Faith and Philosophy* 6 (January,
    1989): 47-64.
Ignatius Loyola. *The Spiritual Exercises.* Trans. George Ganss, S.J. Institute of
    Jesuit Sources, 1992.
Jaspers, Karl. *The Origin and Goal of History.* Trans. Michael Bullock. Yale
    University Press, 1949.
John Paul II. "Saving Tropical Forests." *The Pope Speaks* 35 (September, 1990):
    371-73.
Jung, Carl. *Memories, Dreams, Reflections.* Ed. Aniela Jaffe. Trans. Richard and
    Clara Winston. Vintage Books, 1965.
———— *Modern Man in Search of a Soul.* Trans. W.S. Dell and Cary Baynes.
    Harcourt, Brace, 1933.
Kant, Immanuel. *Lectures on Ethics.* Ed. and trans. Peter Heath and J.B.
    Schneewind. Cambridge University Press, 1997.
Kaufman, Walter. *The Owl and the Nightingale.* Faber and Faber, 1959.
Kausikan, Bilahari. "Asia's Different Standard." *Foreign Policy* 92 (1993): 24-41.
Konvitz, Milton, ed. *Judaism and Human Rights.* W.W. Norton, 1972.
The Koran. Trans. N.J. Dawood. Penguin, 1974.
Kuhn, Thomas. *The Structure of Scientific Revolutions.* University of Chicago
    Press, 1970.
Küng, Hans, ed. *Yes to a Global Ethic.* Continuum, 1996.
———— and Karl-Josef Kuschel, eds. *A Global Ethic: The Declaration of the
    Parliament of the World's Religions.* Trans. John Bowden. Continuum, 1995.
———— and Leonard Swidler. "Editorial: Toward a Universal Declaration of
    Global Ethos." *Journal of Ecumenical Studies* 28:1 (Winter, 1991): 123-25.
Ladd, John, ed. *Ethical Relativism.* Wadsworth, 1973.
Lane, Belden. "Hutzpa K'Lapei Shamaya: A Christian Response to the Jewish
    Tradition of Arguing with God." *Journal of Ecumenical Studies* 23:4 (Fall,
    1986): 567-86.
Lefebure, Leo. "Global Encounter." *Christian Century* 110 (September 22, 1993):
    886-9.
Liechy, Daniel, ed. and trans. *Early Anabaptist Spirituality: Selected Writings.*
    Paulist Press, 1994.
Littell, Franklin. *The Origins of Sectarian Protestantism: A Study of the
    Anabaptist View of the Church.* Macmillan, 1964.

Lodge, David. *Thinks*. Viking, 2001.

Louden, Robert. "On Some Vices of Virtue Ethics." *American Philosophical Quarterly* 21 (1984): 227-36.

MacIntyre, Alasdair. *After Virtue: A Study in Moral Theory*. University of Notre Dame Press, 1984.

Marty, Martin, and R. Scott Appleby, eds. *Fundamentalisms Observed*. University of Chicago Press, 1991.

Marx, Karl, and Frederic Engels. *Collected Works*. Trans. Richard Dixon et al. International Publishers, 1975.

Maslow, Abraham. *The Farther Reaches of Human Nature*. Penguin, 1978.

McGrath, Elizabeth. *The Art of Ethics: A Psychology of Ethical Beliefs*. Loyola University Press, 1994.

Mendelssohn, Moses. *Jerusalem and Other Jewish Writings*. Trans. and ed. Alfred Jospe. Schocken, 1969.

Meyer, Michael. "Dignity, Death, and Modern Virtue." *American Philosophical Quarterly* 32 (January, 1995): 45-55.

Midgley, Mary. "Brutality and Sentimentality." *Philosophy* 54 (1979): 385-9.

Nash, James. "Toward the Revival and Reform of the Subversive Virtue: Frugality." *Annual of the Society of Christian Ethics* (1995): 137-60.

Nickel, James, and Eduardo Viola. "Integrating Environmentalism and Human Rights." *Environmental Ethics* 16 (Fall, 1994): 265-73.

Nissenson, Hugh. *The Elephant and My Jewish Problem*. Harper and Row, 1988.

Nussbaum, Martha. *Love's Knowledge: Essays on Philosophy and Literature*. Oxford University Press, 1990.

O'Connor, June. "Does a Global Village Warrant a Global Ethic?" *Religion* 24 (1994): 155-64.

O'Malley, John, S.J. *Trent and All That: Renaming Catholicism in the Early Modern Era*. Harvard University Press, 2000.

Obradovic, Nadezda, ed. *African Rhapsody: Short Stories of the Contemporary African Experience*. Anchor Books, 1994.

Ottaviani, Cardinal Alfredo. "Church and State: Some Present Problems in the Light of the Teaching of Pope Pius XII." *American Ecclesiastical Review* 128 (May, 1953): 321-34.

Peerenboom, R.P. "What's Wrong with Chinese Rights? Toward a Theory of Rights with Chinese Characteristics." *Harvard Human Rights Journal* 6 (1993): 29-57.

Perkins, Robert, ed. *International Kierkegaard Commentary: Fear and Trembling and Repetition*. Mercer University Press, 1993.

Perrett, Roy, and John Patterson. "Virtue Ethics and Maori Ethics." *Philosophy East and West* 41 (1991): 225-36.

Plato. *Complete Works*. Trans. John Cooper. Hackett, 1997.

Pojman, Louis, ed. *Environmental Ethics: Readings in Theory and Application.* Wadsworth, 1998.

Preis, Ann Belinda. "Human Rights as Cultural Practice: An Anthropological Critique." *Human Rights Quarterly* 18:2 (1996): 286-315.

Quigley, John. "Human Rights Defenses in U.S. Courts." *Human Rights Quarterly* 21:3 (1998): 555-91.

Rabin, Robert. "When Is a Religious Belief Religious? United States vs. Seeger and the Scope of Free Exercise." *Cornell Law Review* 51 (1965-66), 231-49.

Ramakrishna, Shri. *The Gospel of Shri Ramakrishna.* Trans. and ed. Nikhilananda. Ramakrishna-Vivekananda Center, 1942.

Raths, Louis, et al. *Values and Teaching: Working with Values in the Classroom.* Merrill Publishing, 1966.

Robert McCorquodale and Richard Fairbrother. "Globalization and Human Right." *Human Rights Quarterly* 21:3 (1999): 733-66.

Rose, Wendy. *Lost Copper.* Malki Museum Press, *1980.*

Ross, Nancy Wilson. *Buddhism: A Way of Life and Thought.* Vintage, 1980.

Rouner, Leroy, ed. *Human Rights and the World's Religions.* University of Notre Dame Press, 1988.

Ruland, Richard, and Malcolm Bradbury. *From Puritanism to Postmodernism: A History of American Literature.* Viking, 1991.

Ruland, Vernon, S.J. "Covenant Theology." *New Catholic Encyclopedia* 4:405. McGraw-Hill, 1967.

——— *Imagining the Sacred: Soundings in World Religions.* Orbis, 1998.

——— *Sacred Lies and Silences: A Psychology of Religious Disguise.* Liturgical Press, 1994.

——— "Theology of New England Puritanism." *Heythrop Journal.* April, 1964: 165-9.

Sachs, Wolfgang, ed. *Global Ecology: A New Arena of Political Conflict.* Fernwood, 1993.

Scharper, Stephen. "Singapore Squeeze: Church-State Friction." *Commonweal* 115:9 (May 6, 1988): 262-64.

Schumacher, Ernst. *Small Is Beautiful: Economics as if People Mattered—25 Years Later, with Commentaries.* Hartley and Marks, 1999, 1973.

Shelley, Mary. *Frankenstein: Complete Text, Critical History, and Essays.* Ed. Johanna Smith. St. Martin's Press, 1992.

Silko, Leslie. *Man to Send Rain Clouds.* Viking, 1974.

Simon, Sidney, et al. *Values Clarification: A Handbook of Practical Strategies for Teachers and Students.* Hart Publishing, 1972.

Smith, Barbara Herrnstein. *Contingencies of Value: Alternative Perspectives for Critical Theory.* Harvard University Press, 1988.

Smith, Warren. "Are You a Humanist? Some Authors Answer." *Humanist* 41 (1981).

Sommers, Christina Hoff. "Ethics Without Virtue: Moral Education in America." *American Scholar* 53:3 (Summer, 1984): 381-9.

——— "Teaching the Virtues." *Public Interest* 111 (Spring, 1993): 3-13.

"Statement on Human Rights." *American Anthropologist* 49:4 (October-December, 1947): 53-43.

Stille, Alexander. "In the 'Greened' World, It Isn't Easy to Be Human." *New York Times* (July 15, 2000): A17-19.

Teasdale, Wayne, and George Cairns, eds. *The Community of Religions: Voices and Images of the Parliament of the World's Religions.* Continuum, 1996.

Teihard de Chardin, Pierre. *The Divine Milieu: An Essay on the Interior Life.* Harper and Row, 1957.

Traer, Robert. *Faith in Human Rights: Support in Religious Traditions for a Global Struggle.* Georgetown University Press, 1991.

Tresmontant, Claude. *Pierre Teilhard de Chardin: His Thought.* Helicon Press, 1959.

Tucker, Mary Evelyn, and John Grim, eds. *Worldviews and Ecology: Religion, Philosophy, and the Environment.* Orbis, 1994.

——— and Duncan Williams, eds. *Buddhism and Ecology: The Interconnection of Dharma and Deeds.* Harvard University Press, 1997.

Twain, Mark. *What Is Man? And Other Philosophical Writings.* Ed. Paul Baender. University of California Press, 1973.

Twiss, Sumner, and Bruce Grelle, eds. *Explorations in Global Ethics: Comparative Religious Ethics and Interreligious Dialogue.* Westview Press, 1998.

Updike, John. *Roger's Version.* Knopf, 1987.

"UN Draft Declaration on the Rights of Indigenous Peoples." *Cultural Survival Quarterly* 18:1 (Spring, 1994): 65-8.

"U.S. versus Seeger." *United States Reports* 380 (1965): 163-93.

Verhovek, Sam. "Fires Believed Set as Protest against Genetic Engineering." *New York Times* (May 23, 2001): A1, 12.

Vivekananda, Swami. *Complete Works.* Advaita Ashrama, 1963-66.

Walzer, Michael. "What Does It Mean to be an American?" *Social Research* 57 (1990): 591-614.

Warren, Austen. *The New England Conscience.* University of Michigan Press, 1966.

Weaver, Jace, ed. *Defending Mother Earth: Native American Perspectives on Environmental Justice.* Orbis Books, 1996.

Wilkinson, Don. "The Meaning of Self-Determination." *Quadrant* 43 (March, 1999): 23-6.

Wolf, Ronald. "God, James Watt, and the Public's Land." *Audubon* 83:3 (May, 1981): 58-65.

Tuan, Yi-fu. "Our Treatment of the Environment in Ideal and Actuality." *American Scientist* (May-June, 1970): 244-49.

Yun, Eugenia, et al. *Buddhist Revival in Taiwan.* Special issue of *Free China Review* 44:12 (December, 1994): 4-35.

INDEX